I felt like Dorothy in Frank Baum's
fantasy about *The Wizard of Oz.*
I wanted to get back to my
equivalent of Dorothy's Kansas,
back to where I was whole
and focused
and myself again.

But, unlike Dorothy,
my yellow brick road
has never just stretched out before me,
each yellow brick gleaming in sunlight.
Oh no! My yellow brick road
was (and still is) very elusive.
It only appears in front of me
at what seems to be one brick
at a time.

I am amazed that somehow, in some way,
my own crazy, unorthodox, often elusive
but ever-beckoning-onward
Yellow Brick Road
has given me some power
to change the world.

To Marie,

    We have walked along the beaches of our lives together!

    Thank you for your friendship through these many years.

        Much love,

        Liz

ELIZABETH DODSON GRAY

—*A Memoir*—

WALKING MY YELLOW BRICK ROAD

ROUNDTABLE PRESS
WELLESLEY, MASSACHUSETTS

ALSO BY ELIZABETH DODSON GRAY

Green Paradise Lost (1979)

Patriarchy As a Conceptual Trap (1982)

Sunday School Manifesto (1994)

— editor —

Sacred Dimensions of Women's Experience
(1998)

WALKING MY YELLOW BRICK ROAD: *A Memoir*

*Table of Contents**

Introduction

Friendship stays forever green

Chapter 1—Prologue

Life is luminous with meaning

Chapter 2— "When I with Autumn Had a Talk"

Chapter 3—Growing Up

This day is given to us

Chapter 4—Split-Apart Heart: Growing Up in Segregation

Chapter 5—Becoming Myself

Chapter 6—Poems at the Turning of a Life:
A Poem Cycle at the Time of Engagement

Each moment is a gift

Chapter 7—Intimacy Means Risking Vulnerability

Chapter 8—Non-Hierarchical Partnering

Chapter 9—A New Balance of Power:
Dependence, Independence, Interdependence

Love yourself

Chapter 10—Walking My Yellow Brick Road, Part 1.

Celebrate your existence

Chapter 11—Painting the Seasons Sacred

Chapter 12—Color: A Meditation on Our Daughter Lisa

Chapter 13—Motion: A Meditation on Our Son Hunter

Chapter 14—Raising a Non-Sexist Son

Chapter 15—Grieving My Mothering Self

Chapter 16—A Feminist Meditation on Motherhood

Mothers Day Prayers

* Italicized lines are Dodson Gray valentines.

Chapter 17—Choosing the Family You Want
Mothers' Day cards

Chapter 18—Walking My Yellow Brick Road, Part 2.

Chapter 19—Reflections on a Double Twenty-fifth Reunion
Do not resent growing old

Chapter 20—Ministry by Inadvertence: "Nudged" by God
There are many more possibilities

Chapter 21—Come Inside the Circle of Creation:
The Ethic of Attunement

Chapter 22—Seeing and Hearing the Living Earth
Pledge: A commitment to walk lightly on the earth
To be religious today is to act on behalf of the planet

Chapter 23—Power—That Hot Potato!

Chapter 24—Looking for God

Chapter 25—Interpreting the Furor over
the RE-imagining Conference

Chapter 26—The Ancient Call to Newness:
Venturing Forth from an Old Land

Chapter 27—Toward a Theology of Diversity:
A Way Out of the Cultural War over Homosexuality

Chapter 28—"Beauty and the Beast": A Feminist Parable
One must care about a world one will never see

Chapter 29—Hidden Life-Metaphors

Chapter 30—Breast Cancer:
Choosing Aesthetics, Identity, Survival?
Every day is a renewal. This joy you feel is life.

Chapter 31—Glimmer: Meditation on Death and Living

Chapter 32—Sometimes the Mystery Speaks
Mystery reveals itself

Chapter 33—Why Do the Birds Sing?: Healing after Trauma

Chapter 34—Scattered Families: Maintaining Intimacy &
        Connection in the Long-Distance Relationship
              May the love we share
        What is the Theological Opportunity at TOP?
Chapter 35—What TOP Has Meant to Me
              Life is short and we never have enough time
Chapter 36—Surfing at the TOP Planning Process
Chapter 37—Lifelines and Miracles
Chapter 38—TOP Retirement Garden Party
Chapter 39—Looking Back: Who Am I As a Woman?
              I breathe in the universe and say yes to the now
Chapter 40—A Memorial Meditation
              We are enveloped in the generosity of time
Chapter 41—The Season Is Turning
              Ten thousand flowers in the spring

Introduction

Imagine this book as being like a quilt

—with many colors
and many patterns,
written at different times
for different occasions,
but each with a unique glimpse
into the journey of my life.

You will find interspersed throughout the quilt
a selection of Dodson Gray Valentines.

In the early years of our marriage,
David and I began
the custom of sending hand-made customized
Valentines of affirmation
to good friends we appreciated in our lives.

In my mid-fifties,
complications after my cancer surgeries
interfered with my arm movements.

We accommodated.
The hand-made Valentines
of our earlier times
we could no longer make,
so we shifted to printed
"mantra-for-the-year" Valentines.
Now we could send Valentines
to a wider list of good friends,
who have much-appreciated our Valentine custom.

Those Valentines which seem relevant
to particular patches of the quilt
are what you will find here.
Enjoy!

time goes so fast
life asks so much
no wonder friends
get out of touch
but in our hearts
deep, true, unseen
friendship stays
forever green

liz/David Dodson Gray

1.

Prologue

•

Elizabeth Dodson Gray

From *Green Paradise Lost,* p.vii

1.

Prologue

From *Green Paradise Lost,* p.vii

A journey always has a beginning. It is possible the journey recorded in this book began in my earliest memory—a memory of golden sunshine and of being a child small enough to play sheltered among the massive white and blue hydrangea bushes planted by my grandfather in my back yard. The sun is warm, and I feel connected and companioned by all that is around me. I think this is where my religious feelings first joined my feelings for nature. I have always felt connected in some profound way with the ultimate transcendent dimensions of my life whenever I have allowed myself to experience the mystery and majesty of the created world.

I am grateful to my strong Southern Baptist religious heritage which fostered my connection to the transcendent dimension of life and also my perception of nature as the foundational communication of the Creator God. I am also grateful to my experience of motherhood which has powerfully motivated me to anticipate and care deeply about the time of my children and grandchildren on this planet.

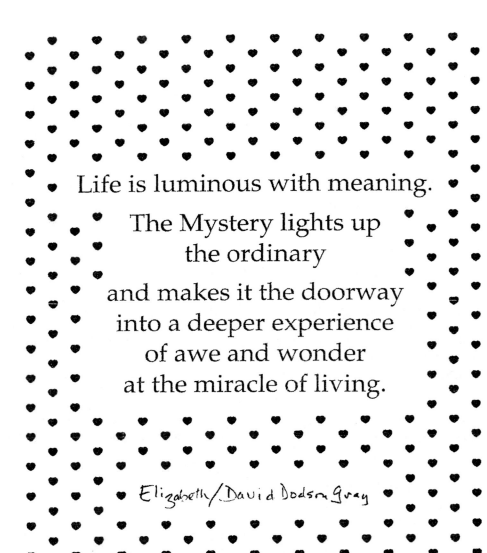

Life is luminous with meaning.

The Mystery lights up
the ordinary

and makes it the doorway
into a deeper experience
of awe and wonder
at the miracle of living.

— Elizabeth/David Dodson Gray

EDG 2010

2.

"When I with Autumn Had a Talk"

Elizabeth E. Dodson

—age 15, 1944—

"When I with Autumn Had A Talk"

by Elizabeth E. Dodson, age 15—1944

I love to walk down country lane
and view the wondrous streakéd skein
that Autumn weaves on leaves of trees,
as if by gifts She might appease
the winds that seek to strip them bare
and leave them there to Winter's air.

I love to lean on ancient stiles
and see the drying hay in piles,
as from the pungent earth I get
the smell of moldy leaves still wet
from rain that washed the country scene
and left the air all fresh and clean . . .

I love to stride against the wind
and struggle with what has me pinned
to earth as I, with hair awry,
am reaching for the twilight sky
to seize a memory of this walk,
when I with Autumn had a talk.

3.

Growing Up

—July 2008—

3.

Growing Up

July 2008

A Beloved Child

I was a much-beloved daughter. My mother was forty and my father was forty-six when I was born, which was very old in that day. They must have had difficulty conceiving both my six-years-older brother and me. They said they were so pleased to have a girl, so they could stop trying! I am told my brother rode a bicycle down a flight of steps on the day I was born. He clearly was not too thrilled!

For many years he told with irritation how on a long car trip I was allowed at age two-and-a-half to sing "Donga dinga banner" (my version of the "Star Spangled Banner") over and over again and I was not stopped.

On another occasion during the Terrible Twos we were vacationing in a hotel at Atlantic City. It seems I had several times "raided" the paper drinking-cup holder on the wall in the hotel lobby. I came home one day from a walk with a parent and found the hotel had moved the cup-holder *up* the wall to escape my "raiding" fingers. I was furious and screamed and kicked and beat on the wall. I do not remember being spanked, so I don't think I was. I think I was just led sadly away.

I was much loved, and clearly parented with amazing tolerance for my behavior. I was told that in second grade when my teacher told my mother that "talking" broke out wherever I was moved in the classroom, my mother (who had been a teacher) said, "My daughter is wonderful. You deal with the problem!" So I spent the rest of the year at a single desk on the back wall between the doors to the cloakroom, more than ten feet away from anyone to talk to.

An Accident Makes a Big Change

That summer we were visiting relatives in rural Virginia when a pony ran away with me in a farmyard, and I fell off. The fall scraped a large oozing wound in my lower left thigh. My parents, desperately afraid of an infection, knew only to pour raw alcohol onto my wound. This was my first experience with intense pain.

To heal that wound would take several months at home in bed. During those months my mother tutored me and also she administered daily doses of pain and alcohol on the wound. I expected her to hold my hand, tell me a story, and pour the dreaded stuff, all at the same time. I realize now that, because these were the days before penicillin, I could easily have gotten an infection and perhaps lost my leg! How changed my life would have been.

I arrived back in school and found that, thanks to my mother's tutoring, I was academically six-months ahead of my class. But I was six-months behind the half-year class ahead of me, to which I had been promoted. They clearly didn't know what to do with me. I remember sitting in the principal's office for several hours with nothing to do except watch the big clock "inch" incredibly slowly from moment to moment. It was an experience of the slowness of time which I shall never forget.

The principal and my teachers finally decided to put me in a mid-year class. As someone born in July I had started school in September in a regular graduating-in-June class. But now I found myself in a class that would start a new grade always in January and not in June.

I also found myself in a classroom situation which would traumatize me. The class was doing subtraction and had daily small tests. The teacher, thinking she was helping me, asked before the whole class the boy next to me, "How did our new pupil do today on the test?" Scornfully he replied, "Aw, she added!" I was humiliated, big time. So the next day I subtracted. But they were either back to adding or on to multiplying.

I never seemed to pay attention to the symbols which told you which process to use. I only tried to "catch up" today to what I had not done properly yesterday. And each day the boy reported my mistake. I think my "unease" with math probably goes back to that painful experience.

In these years I was also having my teeth straightened, and I remember difficult times talking when I had so much "stuff" in my mouth that I could hardly form the sounds.

Outings

One day when I was about eleven or twelve (fifth-grade, perhaps), my mother, the teacher, woke me up with the strangest words: "You are not going to school today. We are going to the movies." She told me that the movie *Gone with the Wind* had just begun playing at one of the theatres in downtown Baltimore, and we were going to go see it together. We got dressed and made a lunch because it was a very long movie. The lunch was to be concealed in a brown paper bag because we were not supposed to eat in the theatre (strange behavior for my very law-abiding Baptist mother!) and off we went.

The movie was long and intense—with the childbirth and a leg amputation and the burning of Atlanta! We ate our sandwich very surreptitiously so we would not be discovered. I felt pleased to be on a special outing with my mother. I don't remember what I "made" of the movie or if we talked about it.

Then another day, sometime later, the same thing happened. This time it was *Pride and Prejudice.* We did the same thing, packed our lunch of sandwiches, and we were off by street car (Mother didn't drive). *Pride and Prejudice* was not nearly as intense as *Gone with the Wind,* but it was fascinating with all of its reflections of the mother-and-daughter life of courting and marriage in that era.

Again, I don't remember if we discussed *Pride and Prejudice,* or whatever we said. It was just a very different experience for me—a "time out" from ordinary days of school and the expectation upon me to live by the rules. This was my school-teacher mother waving all the rules aside and leading me off to a day of "playing hooky," seeing very adult films, taking forbidden food into a theatre, and having a very special "outing' with only the two of us.

As I look back on that now, I raise questions I never thought to ask at the time. Why didn't we go as a family? Did my father know? Had he refused to go? How about my older brother who was still at home? Why wasn't he included?

I also remember that my mother took me to the New York World's Fair in 1939. I must have been ten years old. Once again, why me and why not the entire family? David's mother also took him! We both remember the General Motor's exhibit, Futurama, with its vision of our future with cars not just on local streets but also speeding down marvelous superhighways with curving cloverleafs.

My mother was a pretty woman. She was only about 5 feet 2 or 3 inches tall, plump, and beautiful blue eyes and a "peaches and cream" Irish complexion which I always envied because I had drab brown hair and brown eyes and what I felt was a sallow complexion. My father was a good-looking, charming Southern raconteur. After his "nervous breakdown" he had waited eight years to marry her. My mother had wanted to be sure he was "put together" again.

For a reason I never discovered he always called her "Bill," even though her name was Lillian Mabel! Somehow I always knew that in any *real* crisis, my charming father would be "brittle" and my mother would be "solid like a rock." Perhaps the name "Bill" was an acknowledgment of that!

The Unwanted Shadow

By fifth grade I was clear that I was bright. I learned to dread report-card time because everyone else would talk about their fear of taking home their report card. I felt like hiding because I knew that my card would have all A's, and I would bask in parental approval. My older brother was also bright, and I enjoyed knowing that "I could play that game too!"

But for many years the social disability of making good grades dogged my life like an unwanted shadow. It was a little like the problem of arguing race with my parents' guests. If I argued, I hurt my parents. If I didn't argue, I hated myself. The same grades which alienated my friends reflected the emerging vitality of my mental processes. One of my close friends in college, walking with me to an exam, turned and said, "Liz, I have to work really hard not to hate you!"

First an Enemy, Then a Mentor

My older brother Fitz, he who the day I was born rode his bicycle down the front steps, probably looms large in my early consciousness. My mother said that we fought "like cats and dogs" in my young years, and then suddenly, peace was declared when he became my mentor.

Fitz aspired to be my Pygmalion, my Dr. Henry Higgins. I was to be his Eliza Doolittle. He taught me to dance, and by that I mean he taught me "close" dancing, in which the male leads and the female follows. (What a training in patriarchy!) In my junior-high years he gave me the college courses he had been getting at Johns Hopkins University. My brother was attending college while living at home in Baltimore. One course I remember was Ancient History. He assigned me weekly readings taken from his own courses, and then he quizzed me on the material. I think I also wrote final exams.

In high school he arranged a few dates for me with his college friends from Johns Hopkins, and he advised me on my appropriate dress and dating behavior.

My father was an enormously conservative Southern Democrat. He called FDR a "murderer." When I asked who he had murdered, he told me FDR had murdered the law of supply and demand. So I know it had to have been my brother who saw to it that I read good Quaker literature about the union movement and about anti-racism. I am sure my brother widened my thought world of possible perspectives, and I am grateful to him for that.

A Life Rich with Friendship

My parents in those years modeled for me an adult life rich with friendships. My father had a good friend, Uncle Jimmy, who married late a Miss Lula, and in that era before television they often spent the evening with us. But it was my mother who had a wide and cherished circle of friends. There were five of them who had gone to high school with her, and she saw them frequently and talked by phone with them several times a week. One of these friends, Martha Traeger, lived an hour north of the city, and my parents (with us children in tow) often traveled up to see Martha and her husband on a Sunday afternoon.

In her early years as a young mother, our University Baptist Church had put my mother in a church women's "circle" with eleven other young mothers. They enjoyed each other enormously. They named themselves the Ann Judsons, after the woman missionary of that name. When the church decided to "reshuffle" the women's circles, fearing they were turning into tight cliques, the Ann Judsons refused to disband. In addition to talking to each other three times a week at church (Sunday morning, Sunday evening and Wednesday evening prayer meeting), they talked almost daily by phone. For many years they met together once a month as a group at a different member's home. The three who had "shore places" took the summer months.

The Ann Judsons were a force in our family's life. They companioned each other in good times and bad. They were always there as a resource and support. When my mother died at 72 she was the first of the circle to die. I will always remember the circle of twelve white roses on her casket, with one rose missing.

My parents did not do concerts and museums or sports— they did friends. I am sure that I expected my life ahead of me also to be "rich in friends." This is probably the backdrop for my own experience of a life rich in friends in the Theological Opportunities Program from age 45 to the present.

My Secret Garden

During these years I was enthralled by what I called "my secret garden." In walking around with my little red wagon gathering stuff for the war effort, I walked beyond my usual terrain and discovered "my secret garden." It was in a more fancy part of my middle-class suburb of Roland Park and was adjacent to a country club. A large part of an entire block had been encircled by a high stone wall, and of course I climbed that wall to peek in and see what was inside.

What I saw enchanted me. They must have had a gardener because the deep green lawn was always mowed, and the shrubs and trees were always trimmed. And the flowers in spring and summer and fall were glorious in color and there were creatures—rabbits and squirrels and birds—that seemed to romp and play and sing as though humans did not exist.

I brought friends to look and, finally, we dared to climb over the stone wall and actually go into the beautiful garden and walk on the lawn.

No matter how often I came by to look, there never seemed to be anybody living in that little stone Swiss chalet. There was only a caretaker or gardener who very occasionally spied us when we were inside the garden. Of course, we ran away. But once he almost caught us and I was terrified. My parents would have had a fit; trespassing on private property was not in my Baptist play book!

But despite my fears, the garden would attract me back again. It felt to me like a glimpse into the original biblical Garden of Eden—so quiet, so beautiful, so full of the glory of God-given nature. The animals and birds seemed so free and unafraid, romping in *their* garden of delights. It was indeed a "peaceable kingdom."

It seemed like a garden out of time, out of space, and speaking to me in beauty and in quiet of the marvelous wonders of creation, wonders which the God of all creation has given to us with our birth into this world. It was magical for me, another place and time like my early "under the hydrangeas" experience, a plumb-line of God's blessing once again into my life.

Two Thousand Girls

I had attended from first grade through ninth grade a neighborhood school five blocks from my home. But in tenth grade I took a succession of four trolleys and buses to get to Eastern High School, a large all-white two-thousand-girl high school.

I didn't realize until I got to college how well that school had educated me. One English teacher (who later became Faculty Advisor to the yearbook when I was editor-in-chief) really taught me how to write. She spent months helping *each* student in our English class write their one essay. She did this sentence by sentence, one sentence a week—which she would critique and return for us *to re-write.* We wrote a humorous essay one semester and a serious essay the next semester. We wrote topic sentences, and shaped every paragraph to her approval. We actually learned to write, because she cared enough to spend enormous amounts of her own time critiquing our efforts, and insisting that we *re-write* and thus really learn *how* to write better.

We had good sports possibilities at Eastern. I was number two on the tennis varsity, although I actually played tennis badly. But I was low on the totem pole on the badminton varsity because we had some stars who played in all-city tournaments and won!

I remember many winter late-afternoons coming home alone after dark on the trolleys and buses. I stayed late because of badminton-varsity practice. I can only marvel now that such an experience of coming home alone after dark was considered normal and safe for an adolescent girl.

I also remember as a teenager going out *alone* before dawn to board a neighborhood trolley and take another bus to the large municipal stadium to experience the rising sun in a huge outdoor Easter sunrise service. Once again, I can only marvel that as a teenage girl I was allowed to travel alone "in the dark." Was it really safer then? Or did the adults only *think* it was safer?

The Legacy of My Church

That Divine Presence which permeated my life was *not* created by my church. But the church gave me language to talk about it.

When I was age three under those hydrangea bushes I had no words for what I was experiencing. I just knew I felt loved and connected to all of life. But at age seven when I was walking home from school alone in a snow storm and in awe of the world of glistening white which I saw, this time I said to myself with childish innocence, "*God* has *painted* the world white, for *me!*" Now I had some words.

The church helped nurture and shape my *understanding* of that Divine Presence in my life, and I will always be grateful for that.

And the Bible which this church taught and interpreted to me *joined together* the God who created the universe with the God of justice who spoke to Moses from the burning bush to free the Israelites from slavery (Exodus 3), and who in Amos says "Let justice roll down like waters, and righteousness like an ever-flowing stream" (Amos 5:24). And the Jesus in the gospels who says, *"If* you have done it unto the least of these my brethren, you have done it unto me" (Matthew 25).

So that sense of the Divine Presence in my life was helped to grow into a deep sense of Mystery and a passionate concern for justice.

There is promise and there is peril in a church that teaches the Bible. The children will read there, in the Bible, and I did, of the God who wants—demands—justice. And they will look around and discover how the adults in their lives are dealing with the justice issues in their day. If children are nurtured on the Bible, the adults are not believable unless they perceive and care about the justice issues of the day.

Today, as in my childhood, race is a justice issue. Gender is a justice issue. Poverty is an overwhelming justice issue. What happens to gays and lesbians is a justice issue. War and peace is always a justice issue, as is caring for and protecting our earth and planet. This is the promise and the peril of a biblical church, and I have experienced both.

Lottie Moon and Ann Judson As Role Models

I remember when as a small child my mother would take me to church for the whole day, while she and many of the other women of the church would cook all day.

I and the other kids would run around in the big hall while the janitors were setting up the saw horses and putting the planks on them creating the tables, and rolling out the long white paper tablecloths. As we got bigger we children would set the tableware along the endless tables and we would all prepare for a big missionary dinner and ingathering honoring Lottie Moon or Ann Judson, dinners which happened every fall and spring, year-in and year-out.

What did those particular occasions *mean* to me?

I saw all the husbands and fathers attending. I saw all the male speakers including my senior minister, all of them gathered to eulogize and pay homage to these two *women*—Lottie Moon and Ann Judson, one unmarried and one married—who had heard the call of God and *responded* to go forth.

I concluded that if *I* heard God's call and responded, my entire home church would rise up and call me blessed! Did I notice that I had never seen a woman in our pulpit?—no! But I did understand that the biblical call of God was always gender-free—and it came to Miriam, to Deborah, to Hannah, to Esther, to Mary, to all the women who in his lifetime responded to Jesus and followed him, and to the women described (in the Book of Acts and Paul's letters) as heading the house-churches where the early Christians met for worship.

This calling spirit of God *cannot* be boxed into our cultural categories—and *that* is something I learned at those Lottie Moon and Ann Judson dinners.

Glimpsing a Vision

My constant friend in high school was Jeannette Griffin, who lived down the street from me. Jeannette and I met every morning to do our trolley-and-bus hegira together, to run for the first trolley, because we were always late. We belonged to different cliques in school, but it was Jeannette who took me into her lunch-table group when I was thrown out over our discussion about race. Jeannette was a great Red Sox fan.

I had involved Jeannette in my Young People's group at my University Baptist Church, and we were both enthusiastic participants in weekly Sunday-night meetings and occasional week-end retreats. All of this involved the leadership of Roberta Dorr, the paid Director of Christian Education at my church. After college Roberta graduated from the Louisville Baptist Seminary—which meant she had graduate professional training in ministry. She was working in Baltimore while her husband finished his medical training at Johns Hopkins Medical School. Then they both planned to begin their lives as missionaries somewhere outside the U.S.

Roberta was very charismatic, a deeply spiritual and out-going person, who attracted young people to her vision of life and religion. Jeannette and I were both hugely attracted and aspired to be like her.

This was when I glimpsed, through Roberta, a religious vocation for myself. I decided that after college I would go to Divinity School, as she had, and take up a life of ministry, perhaps working with college students.

It was because of Roberta that I could imagine a committed professional life of ministry, and also imagine myself at the same time married and having children. My Roman Catholic girlfriends felt they had to choose between the celibate life as a Roman Catholic woman religious (religious professional), and a married life with a husband and children. Thanks to Roberta, I aspired to have it all!

In due time I graduated in mid-year and I found myself a temporary job working at an insurance company, filling out forms. I looked around at a huge room of identical desks with dozens of people filling out forms. I was told some of these men and women had been doing this work for twenty years. The boredom was so strong that some began eating candy at 9:00AM.

Watching this and experiencing this made me clear about the necessity to get a higher education to get out of that room. The endless boredom reminded me of my watching the clock in the principal's office. I now realized that I needed to prepare for and find a job so absorbing that you were not even aware of the passing of time.

What Do I Believe?

Finally I quit that job and went for a month to Atlantic City with my parents. My father had had a stroke and they used Atlantic City as a rest cure by the water. We stayed in a small hotel filled with other older people, and I was the only young person in sight. So I spent hours on the beach alone, reading and watching the ocean.

I also spent time alone on my bed at night, assessing "what I believed." I was very clear that my early experience of the presence of God, when I was under my grandfather's hydrangea bushes, made it easy for me to be clear that I "believed in God."

I was influenced a lot by the way the minister in my church talked about our relationship to God. I remember being in our side pew and looking up at my pastor, Vernon Richardson, in the pulpit, resplendent in his black morning coat and striped trousers, which were his every-Sunday attire when he preached. And I heard his words echoing in my head: **"Deep calleth unto deep."**

This was Dr. Richardson's way of talking about God speaking to us. The background metaphor is of whales in the ocean communicating with sounds too deep for words. Dr. Richardson must have used that phrase a lot because it is engraved in my memory.

And in that memory I understood that what I was experiencing in the deepest part of my being, was **the call of the deepest origin of All the Being that exists in our many-galaxied universe.**

That **deep was calling to** *my* **deep.**

And in that place too deep for words, we could communicate.

So for me, God is not "high," but deep! **Deep as the origin of all life. Deep as the source of all being, all energy, all love.** And I have Dr. Richardson to thank for that understanding.

The God Who Will Not Let Us Go

Dr. Richardson also referred frequently to Francis Thompson's poem "The Hound of Heaven"—

" . . . down the nights and down the days . . .

. . . down the arches of the years . . .

. . . those strong Feet that followed, followed after . . ."

This is a poem about God's relentless pursuit of a relationship with us, never giving up on us, always opening up new possibilities, always *persisting* in offering us love.

You remember that wonderful hymn, "Oh love *that will not let me go.*"

I know that in the hard times in my life, *this sense of God* has been a lifeline which I needed to stay afloat.

What I Could Not Believe

So when I was on that hotel bed in Atlantic City, I had total clarity about my belief in God. But I was very ambivalent about the deeply-held theology of the crucifixion, which my Southern Baptist Church found central to Christianity. This theology said: "Christ died for your sins" and "Believe on the Lord Jesus Christ, and thou shalt be saved." As I reflected, I felt no resonance in my interior being with that whole crucifixion theology. God to me was Presence and Social Justice. As Jesus embodied to some degree that presence and social justice, I could consider myself a follower in the Jesus movement. But I had zero sense of being a sinner, and the many good Baptist sermons about human sin and our sinfulness had not convinced me otherwise.

I could not imagine that the God I knew as Presence was also at the same time a terrible judge who would sacrifice Jesus on the cross, and that this sacrifice to that God was *necessary* so that God could love me. This so-called "substitutionary theory of the atonement"—I thought of it as "blood on the cross"—made no sense to me. I was quite clear that what did not make sense to my inquiring mind or did not resonate with my emotional experience—this I did *not* believe!

So while I spent those nights on that hotel bed, I cleared the deck of many of my possible religious beliefs, and I was prepared to go off to college with that settled in my mind and heart.

Severing an Important Connection

I was still in Atlantic City when I received the fateful letter from Jeannette, telling me that her Hodgkin's cancer had returned. She had been sick before I had known her. But her disease had gone into remission by the power of prayer, or so her parents believed for they were active in a small faith community. I was incredulous and horrified, because I had quite accepted that her cancer had been healed and was gone!

When I returned to Baltimore and got to visit her, I was shocked and appalled. She looked like a Holocaust survivor, all skin and bones, her flesh stretched taut over her skull with no hair at all. She was being treated with mustard gas. We just looked at each other and couldn't believe what we were living.

I knew enough to know that God had not done this. I knew that the loving God I experienced wanted only the best for Jeannette. So I could pray for her healing. But I knew that death can come and that miracles don't always happen.

But we had been so close, so "joined at the hip" by our daily transportation-time together, so close in our spiritual lives at the church, that I could scarcely conceive of being separated, even though I knew that I was going off to college in the fall, and Jeannette was not. That seemed somehow natural and normal. But this separation seemed unnatural. In a terrible way DEATH had slashed down a sword between us, severing our connection, dooming her to die but allowing me to live.

When I couldn't see her because she was so ill, I tried to write her what I felt I would want to read if I were there, lying in her bed. I wrote about God's love for her, and my love for her. She never responded, which didn't surprise me. The unfairness of it all was overwhelming. Jeannette died before I went off to college. *Somehow I felt I had to live my future for the two of us, since she couldn't live her own future.*

My growing up years, begun so blissfully in gentle loving parenting, had ended in a deep experience of death. But I had received an admirable education in the public schools, been deeply shaped in my sense of God and justice, been sustained by a daily friendship, and glimpsed the promise of a life of ministry that would fulfill me in the future. It was more than enough!

This day
is given to us.
From it
we make life.

Liz /David Dodson Gray

4.

Split-Apart Heart: Growing Up in Segregation

Talk
November 6, 2003
Theological Opportunities Program
Harvard Divinity School

4.

Split-Apart Heart: Growing Up in Segregation

Talk, November 6, 2003
Theological Opportunities Program
Harvard Divinity School

INTRODUCTION

ELIZABETH DODSON GRAY was born in 1929 in Baltimore, Maryland, which was a segregated city and in a state considered in the Civil War a border state.

She grew up in a comfortable but not large frame house in Roland Park, a residential suburb within the city limits, a house which was home to her parents, her brother six years older, and to three grandparents.

Liz attended elementary and junior high school in a local public school within walking distance, five blocks away. High School was a large 2,000 girls-only public school, which she reached by riding four different trolleys and buses.

Her parents' roots were in rural tidewater Virginia, where for their vacation she and her brother and parents visited relatives every summer. The farming relatives they visited, except for one, had no modern plumbing, and Liz hated the "outhouses" she had to experience.

Her parents were staunch Southern Baptists and very active in their church, which was an imposing building modeled in appearance upon Jefferson's Monticello, his home in Virginia. It faced the major entrance to Johns Hopkins University and was called, not surprisingly, University Baptist Church.

Her father was a conservative Southern Democrat. Even though her father was a partner in the investment banking firm of Stein Brothers & Boyce, he had no formal education past high school. Her mother had gone to a so-called "normal school" for two years training to be a teacher, which she was in the years before she married.

ELIZABETH DODSON GRAY

They were good parents, pillars of the community, and they all attended church every Sunday morning, Sunday evening, and Wednesday-evening prayer meetings.

But the crucial thing to know is that Liz' childhood, from birth through high school, was spent in a segregated city. This is the story she wants to tell you.

I. SCENES FROM MY CHILDHOOD

My Mother's Eyes Told Me Everything

I was three-years-old and somehow I needed to be consoled for some hurt, and I had run to our Negro[1] cook who was in the kitchen with my mother and myself. I had run to her instead of to my mother.

I knew exactly what my mother's eyes were telling me. I had transgressed some terrible law I did not understand. I was never to do that again—run to the cook for my consolation when my mother was in the room.

At three I also knew it was because our cook was a Negro. And I knew that what my mother was forcing me to do was wrong. Deep down in my heart, at three, I knew it was wrong.

Family Life in Our Kitchen

The kitchen in the house of my childhood had a big dining table at its center where the family ate our everyday meals. The dining room was special and we ate our Sunday dinner as well as our Christmas and Easter dinners there, and whenever my parents had dinner guests they used the dining room.

But the kitchen was the everyday center of our mealtimes. It was a large room and along one wall there was a couch where my mother could lie down. There was a small table by the window with magazines and the day's newspaper, and by it a comfortable rocking chair for reading by the good light coming in the window. On the same wall there was a large bureau.

On the opposite wall there was a kitchen sink, towered over by a tall cylindrical water tank under which a gas flame could be lit and in 20 to 30 minutes there was available a quantity of hot water for washing dinner dishes or for taking a bath upstairs in a tub.

Next to the sink was a door going outside to our icebox on the back porch. Until after World War II an iceman came every day and replenished its cooling capacity with a huge new block of ice.

Opposite the icebox on the porch was the door to our Negro cook's changing room and toilet. I knew I was never to go into "her room." When she went in or came out I glimpsed that she also had in there a bureau for her things and a wooden chair, probably for her to sit on while she changed.

The point of all this is to say that I early knew there were two worlds in our kitchen which overlapped slightly, and I was to stay, with my family, in our own world.

---

[1] I am using the language of my household in that period.

So while our family was eating a meal in the kitchen, a meal which our cook had prepared, our cook ate her own meal in the small room just off the kitchen which contained the stove. There, in addition to the stove and a wall full of pantry shelves, she had the small table and stool she used when she ate her meals.

I hated our family's eating arrangements. I just knew it was wrong.

An Evening with Family Friends in Our Living Room

Family social occasions were quite frequent. These were evenings when my parents would invite over my father's friends from high school, my mother's friends from high school, and our church friends.

And as was quite common in those days, conversation swirled often into what we would today call "racist" comments. But "racist" didn't exist as a category then. They were comments and jokes about Negroes. In that era in Baltimore, in my family's circles, white adults talked and joked, among other things, about Negroes.

I couldn't seem to stop "rising to the bait." Someone would make a comment and—I am now about twelve, I think— I would say something, and I would argue with my parents' friends. It was not something you did in the South!

And in those social occasions, I was not supposed to be somewhere else playing. I was to be sitting there being quiet, being respectful of my elders. Instead I was fighting with them. And I did not seem to be able to stop doing it.

What I remember most is standing at the door as they are leaving, saying goodbye to my parents. I knew I had destroyed the evening. They would go home and know that the whole evening had been rendered horrible by this big fight about race—which I had made happen.

Every time I did it, my parents would look at me with these hurt eyes which said to me, "Why did you do this to us?" Next time I would swear to myself I wouldn't do it. And the next time I might manage to hold my tongue—and after the occasion I would go back to my room and hate *myself*. It was a choice between my conscience and hurting my parents. So the next time I would argue. And we would go on and on.

At the Railroad Station, Coming Back to My Family

I am about fifteen perhaps and I have just come back from a week away at an interracial summer camp in Pennsylvania sponsored by the Quakers. I think my older brother knew about it and I had gone despite my father's feelings. He knew there were going to be some Negroes there.

Most of the girls, Caucasian and non-Caucasian, had a deep crush on the most interesting boy there who just happened to be—we would now say—black. He was good looking, charismatic, fun; you would fall in love with him. And we all did!

My father's first question upon meeting me at the train which brought me home, was "How many Negroes?"

And I said brightly, "Oh, about half!" I think he expected me to say one or two; he could live with that.

Later that night my father came into my room and told me "You can never write to those friends, any of them, ever!" I looked at my father and thought, "You are prejudiced to the core."

That was my father, and I hated that!

Life at University Baptist Church

As a teenager I was really obsessed with race. I spent a lot of my time agitating in my Baptist Youth Fellowship at church. If they didn't know what to do for programs, I would say, Let's do one on segregation, let's do one on race. So even though "race" was never preached about at church, we did discuss and hotly debate the topic in our youth programs.

I remember my mother standing at the door in our front hall and saying, "Can you please calm it down at church? You will go away to college. I have to live in this church."

In retrospect, what is interesting to me is that my father felt he could order me not to write to those friends from summer camp. Yet my parents never ordered me not to open my mouth about race at church, and they never ordered me not to speak at our family social occasions with their friends.

I think the reason is that I began having mystical experiences when I was three, and they were clear that, even though they were pillars of University Baptist Church, I was more religious than they.

Like Joan in television's "Joan of Arcadia," God and I conversed. At some point in my childhood I forced them into prayer meetings at dawn, which even they were uncomfortable with. I really don't think they had the nerve to ask me not to do something when I was clear that God and I knew what we were doing.

At High School

I was sitting at a lunch table with the group I ate with every day. We were in a lunch room for two thousand girls, and we had just finished a debate in our English class about race. Frieda and I had taken the anti-segregation side in the debate.

You ate at your table with your friends, your clique, and someone started up the classroom debate again. It turned quickly, as it always did, to the question and challenge: "Well, could you *marry* one?" And remembering the boy I had had a crush on at Quaker camp, I said, "Yes!"

I was then told, "Well, you can't eat with us." Frieda and I were forced to leave the table. I remember picking up my brownbag lunch and searching frantically to make sure I recovered my orthodontic retainer. Frieda and I left that table, never welcome to return again to that group which had been our lunch group.

We stood there, suddenly without a group of friends, without a clique, without a "home" for lunch.

Fortunately I spied Jeannette from my Roland Park neighborhood. She and I walked up together to the trolley and navigated the trolleys and buses together every morning and evening to and from high school.

I asked Jeannette if I could eat with her group. Jeannette slid over, and I ate lunch with her group for the rest of my time in high school.

This was always the understood threat in the South. The first consequence was ostracism. The second would be violence.

Richard Wright's *Black Boy*

I was fifteen when I read *Black Boy.* I realized that I could have been born black. My being white was truly an "accident of birth."

As I read, I knew that everything which happened to him could have happened to me. What was involved in being Negro became much more vivid in my mind and imagination.

II. WHAT WAS THE EFFECT ON ME?

Segregation in Baltimore in the 1930s and '40s was like living with an elephant in the middle of the room which everyone knows is there, but chooses to ignore.

Segregation, Jim Crow, made me sick to my stomach. It was a continuing sick reality I could never get away from.

Most important of all, it alienated me from all the adults in my life. My parents and my grandparents who were living with us when I was small. My teachers. My Sunday School teachers and my pastor. I knew I could not talk sympathetically with any of them about this.

The result was that I did not believe anything that the adults in my life told me.

What did they know of justice, if they did not know that segregation was wrong?

What did they know of love, if they did not know that segregation was evil?

What did they know of God, if they didn't know that segregation was wrong?

What did they know of Jesus, if they didn't know that segregation was wrong?

I was surrounded in my Southern Baptist circles by people who could tell you the day and hour when they "met" Jesus (which is to say, when they took Jesus into their hearts and were saved).

But these same people saw nothing wrong in segregation. Their hearts didn't shrivel in horror at the thought of lynching—and I *knew* that they had *never met Jesus!* Because I knew that God hated slavery and its lingering shadow of segregation *more* than I did!

You see, I believed the Old Testament account of God rescuing the Israelites from slavery in Egypt. "The Lord said, 'I have seen the affliction of my people who are in Egypt, and have heard their cry because of their taskmasters; I know their sufferings, and I have come down to deliver them out of the hand of the Egyptians'" (Exodus 3:7–8a).

Here were all these pious Baptists identifying with the Israelites being rescued out of slavery, and not ever perceiving that in our segregated Baltimore life *they were* the Egyptians!

I asked myself, what did they know about *how to live,* if they did not know that segregation was wrong?

How could they teach me anything, if they didn't understand that segregation was wrong?

I was like a parentless child, a student without teachers I could trust, a Biblical Christian in a church that never spoke out about the evil all around us. Not once!

I was an alien in my home, in my church, in my city, forever singing a strange song of what I thought was justice, a song which no one seemed to understand. And I could not wait to leave all this to go off to college.

III. *KILLERS OF THE DREAM*

All through my childhood and teenage years I did not understand what had happened to me. I only knew that I did not believe the adults around me, because they could not seem to understand about the evil of segregation.

Then somehow, sometime, I found Lillian Smith's *Killers of the Dream.* I don't know whether I read this at Smith College or at Yale Divinity School. It was an autobiography of a Southerner and an analysis of the South.

Lillian Smith describes in her book what I had experienced. The dream which was killed was the ideals of the white children in the South. The killer was the experience of living in segregation. Listen to Lillian Smith:

[R]ace feeling in the South had reached its peak [by the end of the 1800s]. The decade before we were born, a thousand Negroes were lynched. The Klan had ridden in almost every county drawing under its hood the haters and the hotheads from many families. People were terrified not only of Negroes but of their own capacity for cruelty, and panic-stricken at the lack of wise leadership. And in church, not a word was preached about these matters. . . .[1]

Even its children knew that the South was in trouble. No one had to tell them; no words said it aloud. To them it was a vague thing weaving in and out of their play, like a ghost haunting an old grave-yard or whispers after the household sleeps—fleeting mystery, vague menace to which each responded in his own way. Some learned to screen out all except the soft and the soothing; others denied even as they saw plainly, and heard. But all knew that under quiet words and warmth and laughter, under the slow ease and tender concern about small matters, there was a heavy burden on all of us and as heavy a refusal to confess it. The children knew this "trouble" was bigger than they, bigger than their family, bigger than their church, so big that people turned away from its size. They had seen it flash out and shatter a town's peace, had felt it tear up all they believed in. They had measured its giant strength and felt weak when they remembered.

This haunted childhood belongs to every southerner of my age.[2]

The mother who taught me what I know of tenderness and love and compassion taught me also the bleak rituals of keeping Negroes in their "place."[3]

ELIZABETH DODSON GRAY

Neither the Negro nor sex was often discussed at length in our home. We were given no formal instruction in these difficult matters but we learned our lessons well. We learned the intricate system of taboos, of renunciations and compensations, of manners, voice modulations, words, feelings, along with our prayers, our toilet habits, and our games.

I do not remember how or when, but by the time I had learned that God is love, that Jesus is His Son and came to give us more abundant life, that all men are brothers with a common Father, I also knew that I was better than a Negro, that all black folks have their place and must be kept in it, that sex has its place and must be kept in it, that a terrifying disaster would befall the South if ever I treated a Negro as my social equal and as terrifying a disaster would befall my family if ever I were to have a baby outside marriage.[4]

I knew that to use the word "nigger" was unpardonable and no well-bred southerner was quite so crude as to do so; nor would a well-bred southerner call a Negro "mister" or invite him into a living room or eat with him or sit by him in public places.[5]

He [the politician] is saying these things not caring that they hear, as if they were not human! And then would come the tearing dialogue: *Well, are they? are they? of course they are! they're just like me! but are you sure? Of course! then why are they not in our church? why are they not in our school? why can't we keep playing together? what is wrong what is wrong—*[6]

I wrote [this book] because I had to find out what life in a segregated culture had done to me, one person.[7]

I knew my father and mother whom I passionately admired had betrayed something which they held dear. And they could not help doing it. And I was shamed by their failure and frightened, for I felt they were no longer as powerful as I had thought. There was something Out There that was stronger than they and I could not bear to believe it. I could not confess that my father, who always solved the family dilemmas easily and with laughter, could not solve this. I knew that my mother who was so good to children did not believe in her heart that she was being good to this child. There was not a word in my mind that said it but my body knew and my glands, and I was filled with anxiety.

But I felt compelled to believe they were right. It was the only way my world could be held together. And, slowly, it began to seep through me: *I was white. She was colored. We must not be together. It was bad to be together. Though you ate with your nurse when you were little, it was bad to eat with any colored person after that.*[8]

A student at a summer camp says: "How do you begin? I guess," she said slowly, "if you hated your family, it would be easier to fight for what is right, down here. It would be easier if you didn't care how much you hurt them."[9]

"They gave us ideals they did not practice and did not expect us to practice and which we could not have practiced had we wanted to. And yet they urged us to believe in them."[10]

I began to know that people who talked of love and children did not mean it.[11]

Something was wrong with a world that tells you that love is good and people are important and then forces you to deny love and to humiliate people.[12]

"When I have children, I am not going to give them a single ideal they can't practice. I don't want them torn up like this."[13]

Lillian Smith concludes: "However they dealt with it, nearly all men—and women—of the dominant class in the South suffered not only the usual painful experiences of growing up in America but **this special southern trauma in which segregation not only divided the races but divided the white child's heart.**"[14]

My Final Story

I return now to my own story and a later time which was for me some healing for *my* divided heart.

My mother once said to me, "Why does it bother 'them' that I don't want to eat with them?" My mother never "got it"!

Fast forward now some years. My mother is senile in Baltimore, and we are in St. Louis and our daughter Lisa is two-years-old. David has become the associate rector of a large church, and the church has just bought us a large house. I had hired a cleaning woman for one day a week, and because we are in St. Louis, she is black.

I find I cannot give Irene orders about what needs to be done. David has to say to her what needs to be done.

But what I can do is become a friend. Her son Carl is the same age as Lisa, and I invite her to bring Carl to Lisa's birthday party and she invites us to come to Carl's birthday parties. We are the only whites at Carl's party, just as they are the only blacks at Lisa's.

On Tuesdays when Irene comes, I fix lunch and we all eat together. We hold hands and sing a blessing before we eat. When Lisa was six months old, we discovered at a small conference we held in our home for soon-to-be-married college couples that Lisa was delighted when we sang a mealtime blessing, and she clapped in delight. So we started singing all our mealtime blessings. And as Irene and we held hands and sang together, I felt good that I could now eat with whom I chose in my dining room.

We had the space now so we brought my mother to St. Louis to live with us. The next Tuesday Irene comes to clean and I fix lunch as usual. I am not thinking about my mother when I call everyone to the table to eat. We hold out our hands around the table, and I suddenly realize I have placed Mother *next* to Irene.

Mother looks at me wordlessly, and even though she is senile, I can *read* her eyes, just as I could when I was three. She is saying, "You surely can't expect me to take this colored person's hand and *eat with them!*"

ELIZABETH DODSON GRAY

And I said, *out loud,* "Yes, Mother, I do expect that! Now take Irene's hand and sing the blessing!" And Irene took my mother's hand— and we sang the blessing.

NOTES

1. Lillian Smith, *Killers of the Dream: An Autobiography of a Southerner and an Analysis of the South* (Garden City, NY: Anchor Books, Doubleday, 1949, 1963), p. 53.
2. Smith, p. 15.
3. Smith, p. 17.
4. Smith, p. 17.
5. Smith, p. 18.
6. Smith, pp. 2–3.
7. Smith, p. 3.
8. Smith, pp. 26–27.
9. Smith, p. 58.
10. Smith, p. 52.
11. Smith, p. 27.
12. Smith, pp. 27–28.
13. Smith, p. 41.
14. Smith, p. 1 16. Emphasis added.

5.

Becoming Myself

—July 2008—

5.

Becoming Myself

July 2008

One thing Eastern High School did not have was a college counseling program. I had read two magazine articles about some women's colleges whose names began with "S." One article was about a college president who was from England. The other article lauded an unusual curriculum which included cosmetics and flying lessons. That appealed to me! My memory remembered the college I liked as Smith College. Smith is a rigorous women's college in Northampton, Mass., and I applied there. It was only much later that I discovered that the cosmetics and flying lessons went with Stephens College, a small liberal arts women's college in central Missouri. I sometimes wonder how my life would have been changed had I gone to Stephens.

Since my father's stroke, he had been pressuring me to go to Goucher College in Baltimore. He felt himself to be ill and perhaps dying—and he was. Not amazingly, he wanted to spend time with me. But one problem of being older when you have your children is that your declining years can coincide with their adolescent need to get away. I was eager to try my wings and fly away. My parents had a friend who had devoted her adult life to a "declining" mother, and I feared that fate for myself. My mother said, "Go," and I went!

But with no college counseling, I applied only to that one "S" college, knowing practically nothing about it. I graduated with a 92 average as second in my class but it was both perilous and foolhardy to apply only to one college. But I was lucky. I was admitted to Smith. I was not surprised at the opening orientation session to be told that everyone in the room had graduated at the top of their class. This was our introduction to our fellow students, colleagues, and competitors!

A Hint of Class

Shortly before I left Baltimore to go to Smith, I attended a dinner given by my University Baptist Church for new Johns Hopkins students. (The church is immediately adjacent to the campus.) I was seated next to a young man who when he learned I was about to begin at Smith, said to me, "My moth-ah went to Smith. My grandmoth-ah went to Smith! Did your family go to Smith?"

For the first time I glimpsed ahead of me at Smith a legacy of generations and assumptions of upper-class privilege which I had not even imagined was connected to my college of choice. I had not even known to attend a Smith alumnae tea for prospective students, which, had I done that, might have given me a clue.

Those hints of upper-class privilege were confirmed when I arrived in my Smith dorm. Everyone felt to me very "private school" and "boarding school." They came to Smith with a patina of sophistication I felt I did not share. My father had applied for a scholarship, but he refused to share his financial information so I did not receive either a scholarship or a room in one of the two scholarship dorms.

My dis-ease was compounded in those early fall days by all my clothes being delayed in a trunk caught in a labor strike in NYC. I was forced to live out of a suitcase of summer clothes I had arrived with, even as the temperatures dropped. I was forced to borrow other women's sweaters and warmer clothes. And, adding insult to injury, that fall women's hemlines fell. So even when my skirts and dresses did arrive, everything I had was suddenly "out of style." And I could not afford to buy more.

I discovered that "clothes do make the woman." Clothes embodied and presented my identity to the world, and I felt very tentative and disconnected from myself while I was wearing other people's clothes.

All of that made me behave "quietly" as I related to the other women in my dorm. I felt like a timid rabbit poking my head up through a hole in the ground, uncertain about who I was and how to behave in this strange landscape. Being subdued was quite different from the person I had been in high school—confident student, editor of the year-book, tennis and badminton varsities, and a leader in my church group. So I buried myself in studying.

I was lucky that in January someone moved out of a tiny room in one of the co-op dorms, and I was given that space. Here I looked around and I couldn't see a private school nuance in sight! I blossomed into long late-night bull sessions with my new dorm mates, whom I found diverse (though all white), interesting, and excited to share viewpoints and life-experiences in these late-night encounters. It is a mystery to me how I ever managed to study now that I was so enjoying my housemates.

Academic Rigor

I very much enjoyed the exciting teaching and rigorous standards of my chosen liberal-arts college. There were many strong and talented older women on the faculty, who served not only as inspiring teachers but also as mentors and role models of what we might become as we flexed our intellectual muscles and tried out our wings on solid scholarship, lectures, mountains of reading, exciting small-discussion "sections," and difficult essay-question final exams. It was exhilarating to see if one could measure up to the challenges, so despite the hard work, it was a race which I wanted to run. And as the four years of college passed, the academic enterprise as I had experienced it gave me great confidence in my own mind and intellectual abilities. I was asked much later when my husband and I were teaching at the MIT Sloan School of Management if I did not find intimidating all the "great minds" at MIT. I found myself saying that, after Smith, I did not find anybody's mind intimidating! That was a lovely gift to me from those college years.

Learning to Lead

Smith was a laboratory of leadership-training for me. At the end of my sophomore year I was elected president of the small Christian Association. This was possible for a sophomore because the departing seniors, in their wisdom, had changed the entire program to a silent Quaker meeting—which had eliminated the juniors and left only a few sophomores. So it fell to me to try to renew an abandoned program to the entire campus. I still remember hanging out with my cabinet in the sofa chairs in the chaplain's basement, trying to plan public evening lectures to attract the whole college. It was that year that I slowly realized that when we planned programs for "them," the lectures were only minimally attended. But when we found ourselves digging deep into our *own* issues and questions, and put that out to a speaker, we attracted lots of attenders.

We were the microcosm of that macrocosm, and when we paid attention to our own issues and questions, we found our colleagues there also. That was a lesson which I was to draw upon many years later when I dreamed up what we came to call "the process" for our Advisory Committee planning at the Theological Opportunities Program (TOP) lecture series at Harvard Divinity School. And the logic of that premise to plan from our own issues worked as well for us in Cambridge as it had worked at Smith.

The spring of my Junior Year I was elected in an all-college election to be head of the Religious Association—which comprised the three faith groups of Protestants, Roman Catholics and Jews as well as the large and wide-ranging social-service organizations Smith had on campus.

As head of the Religious Association I was given one of the five honorary telephones. That was an era of *no* private phones and no cell phones. In the kitchenette on each floor in each dorm there was one phone for everyone on that floor. My having an honorary phone all to myself was a big deal, but you needed that to phone all the women you were working with.

But those dorm phones were a big problem because it was hard to find women at home except right before or after meals. And then they were just as likely to be washing their hair, or downstairs playing bridge, or they had left early to study at the library. Having your own phone was only half the struggle, because you had to hope someone would answer the hall phone, and call down to the room, or be nice enough to write a message and put it upon her door. How different it would be today with answering devices and cell phones.

I learned to be confident leading meetings, projecting future plans, negotiating with my cabinet members, representing my organization to the college as a whole. All of that proved to be extremely helpful when after Yale Divinity School I found myself in Cambridge, Massachusetts, as associate to the Baptist minister to students at Harvard Square.

I also taught myself to preach in the Smith Little Chapel. On the first floor of the Library there was a very small chapel and we held a fifteen minute mini-service there every weekday evening at 9:45. The library closed at 10PM and we had to be signed into our dorms by 10:15. The service consisted of one five-minute hymn with opening prayer, a five-minute mini-sermon, and a five-minute closing hymn with benediction.

For one year I did the job of being responsible to "staff" the Little Chapel services with organist (the same person for one week) and preacher (for one night). That meant signing people up for particular dates, as well as filling in when either organist or preacher did not show up. My organ playing was barely credible but I did play hymns on a piano.

I aspired to learn how to preach extemporaneously and well in that five-minute sermon, either when I signed up or when I filled in. It was an amazing opportunity to rehearse speaking from my bare notes to empty Little Chapel pews, over and over again until the sentences flowed easily from my thoughts. I'm not sure why I wanted to do that—but I do know that in my later years this ability was very helpful to me on many occasions.

When I Called on God to Help, and I Got No Answer

Even when God did not heal my dear friend Jeanette, during my college years I still believed in praying for others and I practiced intercessory prayer. At some time during those years I gathered together a morning prayer group. We met every morning early, three or four of us. So when my father died in October of my senior year, we were already meeting as a prayer group.

After I returned from the funeral, I found I could not sleep. And I had a constant refrain beating in my head, telling myself that I was going to have a nervous breakdown.

My father had been ill since his stroke in my sophomore year of high school, and you will recall that he did not want me to go away to college. He wanted me to live at home and go to Goucher, a good liberal-arts women's college in Baltimore.

As a typical adolescent, I wanted to "go away." And when my mother said, "Go!" I gladly "went"! But neither of us had counted on my father saying to me bluntly every time I went back to college after vacation (Christmas, spring break, and summer recess), "You are killing me."

I surely knew I was not responsible for what was killing him. But the constant reiteration of that comment *did* take its toll on my consciousness.

So when my father died that October, something in me got "de-wired" and I couldn't sleep. And I had this refrain running constantly in my head, "You are going to have a nervous breakdown." I knew I was in trouble but my choices, I felt, were painful.

If I went to psychological services at Smith, I would lose my "psychiatric standing" which made it possible for me to do my job as president of the Religious Association. I had a deep commitment to that job. I think I probably even felt that God "wanted" me to do that job. My vice-president of the Religious Association had already lost her "grade-standing" and been forced to resign. So there was just me—and I felt that commitment.

And yet, I argued with myself, if you *don't* go get some help, suppose you really do have a nervous breakdown and end up spending the rest of your life in a mental hospital? Would that be an intelligent thing to do or risk to take? Would God be pleased with that?

So I argued with myself and I didn't sleep—and the internal refrain went on. I prayed to God to heal me and to let me sleep! And every morning that prayer group would say, "Did you sleep last night? Did God answer your prayers?" And the answer, sadly delivered by me, was always "NO!"

So November and early December passed, until I went home for Christmas vacation. My mother, of course, was grieving my father's death. (It seemed to me it had been a happy marriage.) Then when I got home she got some kind of infection and phoned the doctor to come. (Doctors in those days were still making house calls.) I decided that when the doctor came, I would tell *him* of my problem and see what help he could get for me that didn't involve Smith. Imagine my consternation when, on his way to our house, the *doctor* got sick and never arrived!

I can remember being in the drugstore, waiting for my mother's medicine and being marooned for an interminable hour with nothing to do while I waited, and my refrain pounded in my head, and I wondered if this was why people committed suicide—when consciousness became just too painful. I honestly don't think I actually was suicidal but I did wonder about painful consciousness which just wouldn't stop.

Since the doctor didn't work out, I racked my brain to think up another alternative which might bring help but would not involve Smith.

Finally, on New Year's Eve, I decided to seek out a nice lady in the house behind our house. Mrs. Weakley had been a nurse. I had baby-sat for her when I was in high school, so I knew her. When I appeared at her back door, she was giving a party and she took me into her bedroom to talk. My problem poured out from me, and she listened and then said with utmost confidence, "You are *not* having a nervous breakdown."

Looking back now, I ask myself, "How did she know that?" But I believed her. And I went back to my house, and back to college, feeling better about my internal argument, but still with the refrain going on in my mind and still not sleeping.

Soon after I returned to Smith I was in a late-night bull session in which we chanced upon some topic which evoked from me my story about my father's parting words, "You are killing me!" I cried, and my friends comforted me, and said, "Liz, you surely don't think that you *really* killed him! It was terrible of him to say that to you!"

That bull session was cathartic for me. I went to bed feeling spent and somehow cleansed. And I slept! All night I dreamt I was in the front line in a Civil-War-like battle, firing a Civil-War musket and with people dropping dead to my left and to my right. In my dream we fought all night, with people dying all around me, and when dawn came, I was still alive! When I woke up, the refrain in my head was gone!

I really didn't understand at all what had happened to me but I truly didn't care. The demons were gone, even if only temporarily, and I could only rejoice in the reprieve. But the demons did not return, and I was apparently "home free" at last.

In February I was reading a sociology text and I read about a case which so closely resembled my own story that I could now identify the inner psychic source of my refrain as my superego—that, in us, which will punish us for what the superego regards as unforgivable!

And then I remembered a dream I had once had, in which my father was falling over, and I knew he would hit his head and be hurt—*and I did not move to save him.* And I understood that my superego was punishing me for *not wanting* to save my father!

I had prayed to God for sleep—and God had been absent, and sleep had not come. But the healing I prayed for *did* happen, slowly through time, and through many different people. It was a deliverance not immediately accomplished or immediately visible. It was partial at many points, not complete, and it was made possible by the normally-flawed human beings present in my life. Reassurance from Mrs. Weakley, which enabled me to cease arguing with myself about my choices and trust myself to go on. Tears and catharsis and support from a college bull session. The highly symbolic battle dream, which allowed me to decide to let *me* live, and not die. And the blessing of sleep itself. And my awakening in the morning to find the refrain no longer with me.

Finally a month later there came the rational understanding of what had happened, and the role which my superego had played in my punishing refrain.

It was a terrible period in my life. And it raised questions for me about God's power to heal. But I knew also that I really had been delivered, although not in a manner nor at a pace which I wanted.

Was this what Leslie Weatherhead called "the ultimate will of God"[2]? He suggests that God's ultimate will is *constantly creating new possibilities* for achieving in new ways the abundant life which God from the beginning has intended for all creation.

Deliverance and healing *had* taken place, within the mysterious interconnections of the complexities of my life, and I was grateful for that.

Being Myself, Either Single or in Relationship

My life was not intersected by dating at all until I got to Yale Divinity School. There had been no boys at my two-thousand girl high school, and no men at my two-thousand woman college at Smith. Looking back now as a feminist, I realize that I escaped the socialization to female subordination which happens in teenage dating.

My non-dating made life simpler for me. Of course I wanted to date; I fantasized about dating. I dreamt of romance and marriage. But I felt myself to be plain and unattractive, and I decided I had better design for myself a happy and fulfilling life as a single woman, because it was entirely possible, if not probable, that romance and marriage might never happen for me.

One of my college professors was very helpful, though she did not know it. I took several religion courses with Virginia Corwin and she seemed like such a happy person in her life that I took heart.[3] Other single-women professors at Smith seemed very bright but somewhat "dour," which I did not find encouraging!

But the best advice came from my brother, who was by now a graduate of Yale Divinity School and a Presbyterian minister. He told me, *"Don't* just lie around wishing you were dating, reading romantic stories and eating chocolates. *Instead, become the most interesting woman you can be,* and then when you meet the most interesting man you have ever met, *he will find you to be the most interesting woman he has ever met!"*

This is, in capsule form, the story of my relationship with David!

NOTES

1. For three out of my four years at Smith College I was a Sophia Smith scholar (one of the top ten scholars in a class of 500). I graduated Phi Beta Kappa, with the history prize.

2. Leslie Weatherhead, *The Will of God* (Nashville: Abingdon Press, 1944).

3. Many years later I discovered that Miss Corwin had told a good friend of mine: "In a lifetime of teaching, you have one or two truly outstanding students, and Elizabeth Dodson is one of these."

6.

Poems at the Turning of a Life:

A Poem Cycle at the Time of Engagement

November 1956 to May 1957

6.

Poems at the Turning of a Life

A Poem Cycle at the Time of Engagement

—November 1956 to May 1957—

WHERE IS THE GLORY?

Where is the glory of those first few weeks
Now only remembered?
When our new-found love was treasure full and overflowing,
For which we had sold all our fields—our pearl of great price.
A song inside which set the very sky to singing,
A bursting radiance like Roman candles breaking high on a summer's eve.
Where has it gone, that glory?
Is it lost—ebbed out into the sea of adjustment?
Blurred away into the mingled colors of joy and pain in difficult "encounter"?
Fallen in the battleground of preserving our separate identities?

Was it only romantic illusion?
Was its joy unreal—not counting the cost of dying in the blending of two
complex selves?

Will it come again to bless the marriage even as it consecrated the engagement?
Or are these leaves of glory destined in our humanness to belong to autumn—
dropping off to leave behind only
the stark outlines of "here we are, together, forever."
And will this starkness leave us in the brittle
sherry of "The Cocktail Party,"
a man and woman, alone, tho' married?

My heart cries out
"Come back, you leaves of glory!"
Come again to this parched and thirsty land.
Give me again the gift of whole-souled love for him whom I know in weakness.
Come bring some balm of sureness to my doubting heart.
Come bring some hymns of gladness to my numbed and ice-bound spirit.
Come bring some healing to my scarred and hostile self,

That I may walk
with truly festal rejoicing
and integrity
to kneel and take my solemn vows
to him to whom I am pledged.

Dear God, do Thou give some glory back
to her who waits, and weeps, and prays
with a lively remembrance of what has been
and a hope, and a prayer
for what may yet be.

IMAGES

Thou art thou, my beloved
and that is the problem.
You are like a kaleidoscope—as the days wear on
your selfhood shatters into many images.
And I wander this endless hall of mirrors,
seeing you convex, concave, distorted, free—
but seldom integrated, whole, total.

There is the free David, whom I love most dearly,
the healthy, exuberant, male spirit which growls
at me in making love, which cave-mans me

into undreamed-of responsiveness.
This is the Biblical David—passionate, vibrant,
free to hate and love and fight and rule
and mourn and die, still free, to be.
This is the David that winks at me in that wonderful
grin of yours in that brief moment when you
are free to laugh, even at yourself.

Then there is the solid, tenacious David,
by whom I am loved both tenderly and consistently.
Here is the Rock of the shifting sands of our days
together, the sturdy rope of your tenacious
love which will not give me up, no matter what.
I spend myself and my hostility upon the absorbing
quality of your love, and find myself held
and anchored by the "solid" you, which does
not despise me when I despise myself.

But there is also the fearful you, your freedom
trapped in a child-long bondage which I
loathe, and struggle to rip from you.
The tight face, the moving or protected hands,
the inhibitions which suddenly strike to
cripple and paralyze—the fear which gnaws
each present moment with the haunting question,
"Will I measure up?"
This strange land of fear in which you live
sometimes is horrible to me; I struggle to
resist its creeping boundaries lest I too
be sucked into its tyranny.

Strong and weak,
my high tower and my gaping pit,
all these you are, and they are really you.

But yet another image dominates the hall:
my ideal man—he to whom I gave my heart—
thou must be he, else I have chosen wrong,
and I am doomed to live in life with another
fallen man.
But not me, others perhaps, but not me.

I have waited too long, chosen too precisely, to
be so cheated;
thou must be he, lest I be me,
and not the "happily ever after" female I desire to be.
Thou must be he.

But thou art not.
With your slivered mirrors of fragmented selfhood
you have broken my image,
and I resent you for it.

Mixed and many-mirrored images,
Can I know you as a whole?
Can I love you as integrity?
Or must I split you up, accepting some and rejecting others?

Strong and weak,
my high tower,
my solid rock,
that high barbed fence and gaping pit—
Thou art thou, my beloved.
I could never love another—but can I love you?
Ah, that is the problem.

I ASK OF SPRING

Many a year I have asked of Spring a gift,
a blessing, a kiss,
as the earth blooms into fruitfulness
and the rigors of winter fade like a bad dream.

Before I have asked for a love,
someone I could cherish with all of me,
a man to match the ache in my bones and the
fire of my desires,
a man to evoke all of woman there is in me, waiting
to be born and full-grown.

And now the gift has been given, the bargain made.
I have my man, as a gift from Fall—the glory of
Autumn come down from the trees to lodge
in my heart.
And yet I come to Spring, asking the greatest gift
of all, the way to love.

I thought my need was dire before, as I walked the
warm wet streets and dreamed of the lover
that might come.
But now I know my need is not for the gift,
but for the open hand which can receive
and the joyous suffering heart which can give.

YEARNING

I need you.
A pleasant evening—
steak, wine, and Bach—
all these have not filled me,
and I hurry home to phone you,
impatient to hear the sound of you,
tired, exuberant, or mad,
eager to match thoughts and feelings,
to coo and cuddle by intonation and inflection,
to ease a little the yearning
for the see and touch and feel of you.

The metallic operator connects me,
and the slender tentacles of sound unite us
briefly
and tenuously,
and I discover the miles of emotion
which lie between us.
One loving, one alienated;
one moving toward, one moving away.
And I am helpless.

I reach out tiny tentative fingers
along this unseen wire to you,
and feel the distance which I cannot bridge,
the fleeing impulses I cannot quell.
Desperately I yearn to enfold you,
to tell you of my love
in caresses that know no words,
that in touching I might bridge this ocean,
and bring the ship fleeing down the horizon
safe to port, here, in my hand.

But such oceans permit no such easy bridges,
and in my still small voice I know
we are apart tho' we were together.
No hands of mine can clutch the vessel of your freedom
and tow it into port.
My impotent yearning is not born of telephone wires,
but of horizons
built into your very soul,
and I know this—and tremble.

And so I speak of casual things,
argue a little, patter a little,
and know that soon I must lay you down
with the handle of the phone,
try to pocket my yearning in a larger trust,
write a poem,
and lay down the day
unsatisfied.

Yet lay it down I must,
and commit myself and it
to mercy and to sleep.
There is a parable here:
just as the fullness of the day eludes me,
so do you.
My overweening capturing can never be.
I must rest content
in the smallness of my trust,
and lay you down,
that I may wake, perhaps, to greet with you,
a new ship in my harbor
fragrant with spices and with myrrh
from your long voyage home.

JUST AS I AM
A gospel hymn,
an invitation down the aisle,
is symbol well for what I feel.

Without one plea,
except I'm me,
and not just what

ELIZABETH DODSON GRAY

I know your search of ideal image—and that at points I match,
else you would not have chosen me.
I know at times your rebuke—at points where I match not,
and I feel like crying out,
"Have you chosen me, or your own image?"

I know your need for love,
for reassuring hearth-fire, and tumbling kids;
and I fear to ask,
"Did you choose me, or merely wife and mother?"

Cook and clean and make a home I will,
Bear your kids, I hope I can;
Love you tender and passionate,
Live with you on the outer reaches of your mind:
All this, God willing, I shall do
But please, my dear, remember
I am just a human "I am,"
and what I fear to ask, I need to know—
That as I stretch to be what you want me to be,
you can nevertheless love me,
just as I am,
wherever I am,
please, my man.

CAN IT BE?

Can it be
that our love is not to be?

Are they right—
those who say
all is bliss,
and if not
you are not
meant to be, you and me?

They did not tell me of the pain,
of the suffering, of the tears.
They told me of the joy, of the ecstasy,
but not of the wounding of each other,
for such as we, you and me.

And when I tell them, they wonder.
With an eyebrow and "perhaps . . . ?"

ELIZABETH DODSON GRAY

They say to me
"It should not be thus,
you and he,
you must not be right,
you and he,
it should not be thus."

Yet can it be,
that two like we
can mate our passionate complexity
like gluing together two coins with equal surfaces?

And do they think that loving is all joy and bliss?
Let them try it in intimacy, I say scornfully.
Then they too shall reap the wild wind of wounding,
live with the mingled taste of love and
bitterness in your mouth.
While others stand beyond the felt necessity of this
kind of living, and mock saying,
"Let him come down, if this be love.
It is not necessary to suffer thus,
Love is easier than this."

But is it?
For God? Then, so for us?

As for me, I find dying to difference
difficult, damned difficult.
And attempt it, I would not
without my passionate conviction
that we are to be,
you and me.

That there is in us such depths of joy and pain
that can drain both wells deep and full,
and somehow be thereby fed and nourished, one with another,
even though the taste maytimes be bitter
and the salt not of savor but of wound.
Yet there is glory here, full enough for me,
and on this I bet my life
that we can be in height and depth,
for all eternity
you and me.

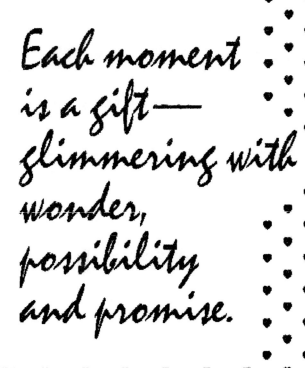

Each moment
is a gift—
glimmering with
wonder,
possibility
and promise.

Elizabeth/David Dodson Gray

7.

Intimacy Means Risking Vulnerability

Talk, April 7, 2005
Theological Opportunities Program
Harvard Divinity School

7.

Intimacy Means Risking Vulnerability

TOP Talk—April 7, 2005

I think it never occurred to me when I was a teenager that I would *not* have a wonderful, deep intimacy in my marriage relationship. But did I have a clue that being intimate meant risking vulnerability? I don't think so.

The Risk of Intimacy

As I grew older, I realized that for me the risk of intimacy—the *crucial* vulnerability—was being KNOWN, truly KNOWN—not just the surface Me, but the deep-down central Me.

I remember being appalled when a fellow student at Yale Divinity School whom I was dating (not David) said to me something about my Phi Beta Kappa key. Now I did have a Phi Beta Kappa key, which I kept carefully hidden in my jewelry box. But I knew that men didn't like women who were "too smart." So I had deliberately hidden the key, and consciously "damped down" my usual intellectual assertiveness in small classes. I was attempting to "fly under the radar" and pretend to be a non-threatening female.

So imagine my horror when he casually referred to my key. "How could you know?" I asked him. He said, "It's obvious." I was appalled!

"It is obvious"?—I felt as though he had stripped off all my clothes and left me naked. "Obvious"? *Did I have no choice about being known?* Even when I tried to be more stereotypically "feminine," even then, I couldn't pull it off? *I felt "known" when I did not wish to be known!*

It was fortunate for me that I was not now a teenager but a twenty-two-year-old in graduate school and with some maturity. Upon reflection I decided that "I was who I was," and I was too old to change. If that was a problem for relationships of intimacy, then I would have to figure out for myself a satisfying life as a single.

Being Known in All My Emotions

I remember another, different, defining moment six years later in my struggle with vulnerability and intimacy. David and I were now engaged, and my intellectual talents were never a problem in our relationship. I knew I could relax and think and confront, and in perfect freedom do and *be* whatever I wanted intellectually—and David found it wonderful. The best that my mind can produce is always a delight to David. He enjoys the many hours he has spent editing and typesetting my writing. And he always says when he finishes, "This is *good!* I enjoyed typing it."

But there were other dimensions to vulnerability for me. Being known meant being known in all my moods and all my feelings—the positive and also the negative ones. That indeed did feel risky to me. Suppose my beloved only liked me, loved me, when I was sweet and cheerful, demure and submissive? What about when I was mean and childish, critical and nasty? To be revealing to anyone about *all* the feelings inside me—to be real, to be genuine—that meant *risking rejection* big time!

My feelings about this came to a head one evening when David and I were having dinner in his apartment in Providence (I was working in Cambridge at the time), and I found his way of handling washing the dishes somewhere between weird and totally annoying. But did I tell him that? No, I consciously "bought into" the principle that "real women" or "nice girls" don't fight with their fiancé about how he did the dishes in his own apartment.

But I still had all those negative feelings, which "laid low" in me until about 10:00PM when they emerged in a theological argument. Now David, having the blessing of three-and-a-half years of psychoanalysis, could detect that something was going on.

So he enticed from me my earlier *un*expressed feelings, and we both agreed that it would be simpler to deal with our feelings "on the spot," "in the moment," "in real time," rather than deal with them hours later (or days or months later) when they would be wrapped around and embedded into different issues to which they did not belong.

The Risk of Being Transparent

Thus began what we came to call *"transparency"*—the risk of being truly open to each other not just "in sickness and in health" but in good feelings and in bad feelings.

Transparency has always felt risky to us, a little like jumping off a cliff into thin air—and hoping that the love and trust and affirmation of the other will be there to catch you, and that you will not be rejected but affirmed in all your particularity and uniqueness.

But *not* being transparent has always felt even riskier to us —because that path leads to playing roles, to pretending, to fearing rejection but never knowing, to wanting love for who you *are,* but never being sure you have it because you are not actually real and authentic moment by moment.

The risk of *that* kind of relationship has always frightened us more than the risk embodied in "transparency." It has seemed to us clear that if you are not transparent about the little things that "bug you," how can you work them through before they become the big things which can truly alienate and divide you?

Green Winter

I want to close by reading briefly something from my first book, *Green Paradise Lost*. First there is a poem from *Green Winter,* written by someone else, and then a paragraph I wrote to follow the poem. Together, they capture for me the poignancy in a relationship lived in the emotional landscape of risk, vulnerability and intimacy.

Preserve me from the occupational therapist, God,
She means well, but I'm too busy to make baskets.
I want to relive a day in July
When Sam and I went berrying.
I was eighteen,
My hair was long and thick
And I braided it and wound it round my head
So it wouldn't get caught on the briars,
But when we sat down in the shade to rest
I unpinned it and it came tumbling down,
and Sam proposed.
I suppose it wasn't fair
To use my hair to make him fall in love with me,
But it turned out to be a good marriage,
And years later when our daughter said
She thought she'd cut her hair,
I said, "Oh don't. There's something
Mystical about long hair. If after a year
You still want to cut it, do, but think it
over." A year later,
She said, "Oh Mom, I'm so glad you told me not to cut my hair,
Jeff loves it so."
Oh, here she comes, the therapist, with scissors and paste.
Would I like to try decoupage?
"No," I say, "I haven't got time."
"Nonsense," she says, "you're going to live a long, long time."
That's not what I mean,
I mean that all my life I've been doing things
For people, with people, I have to catch up
on my thinking and feeling.
About Sam's death, for one thing.
At the time there were so many things to do,

ELIZABETH DODSON GRAY

So many people around,
I had to keep assuring everyone I'd be all right,
I had to eat and make sure they noticed,
So they wouldn't keep coming to see me when
They had other things to do.
I had to comfort the children
And Sam's old friends who got scared
(If Sam could die, they could die, too).
I had to give his clothes away and pay the bills,
I didn't have time to think about how brave he was,
How sweet. One day,
Close to the end, I asked if there was anything I could do,
He said, "Yes, unpin your hair."
I said, "Oh Sam, it's so thin now and gray."
"Please," he said, "unpin it anyway."
I did and he reached out his hand—
The skin was transparent, I could see the blue veins—
And stroked my hair.
If I close my eyes, I can feel it. Sam.
"Please open your eyes," the therapist says,
You don't want to sleep the day away."
As I say, she means well,
She wants to know what I used to do,
Knit? Crochet?
Yes, I did all those things,
And cooked and cleaned
And raised five children,
And had things happen to me.
Beautiful things, terrible things,
I need to think about them,
At the time there wasn't time,
I need to sort them out,
Arrange them on the shelves of my mind.
The therapist is showing me glittery beads,
She asks if I might like to make jewelry.
Her eyes are as bright as the beads,
She's a dear child and she means well,
So I tell her I might
Some other day.[1]

As I read those words I am overcome with tenderness for my own Sam, also grayer and more vulnerable than when we too first let down our hair to each other,

but so much more precious to me because I now understand the human limited-
ness of our time together. I want to rush in to where he is sleeping and waken him
to celebrate the present moment which is slipping by with the liquid speed of the
Mozart piano nocturne I have playing on the phonograph. But we will waken
together to greet the sea and the morning, and that will be time.[2]

NOTES

1. Elise Maclay, *Green Winter: Celebrations of Old Age* (New York: Reader's
Digest Press, 1977), pp. 46–48.
2. Elizabeth Dodson Gray, *Green Paradise Lost* (Wellesley MA: Roundtable
Press, 1979), pp. 106–107.

8.

Non-Hierarchical Partnering

TOP Lecture, April 27, 1995
Theological Opportunities Program
Harvard Divinity School

8.

Non-Hierarchical Partnering

TOP Lecture, April 27, 1995

"Adam's World"

I am talking about *heterosexual* partnering, not because it is the only way to partner but because it has been my experience. And I am going to discuss *partnering,* not marriage, because I think partnering is what we are all really involved in. Today, at all ages, some marry and some don't—but they are together. So the issue is really partnering, not marriage.

Why is *non-hierarchical* partnering an important topic? Because the culture around us has assumed that heterosexual partnering, man to woman, is always implicitly hierarchical.

It is not accidental in our language that we have phrases like "lord and master" and "king of the castle" to describe husbands. These phrases describe the typical traditional patriarchal family structure, where the central issue has been who is in charge, who is in control. Men historically have been in control, and in the last decade or so we have been learning that inside that "castle" there has flourished a lot of abuse of women and children—physical and emotional and sexual abuse by the males in charge.

Originally men set things up so that only they got to vote; it took decades of protest and effort, by women, for women also to get the vote. Men traditionally also owned all the property; women almost never owned anything. It has been difficult until recently for women, apart from men, to get mortgages and loans and credit, so that a woman could own her own home or create her own business. Socially, the man has had the lead in ballroom dancing, the power to ask a woman out for a date, and the male customarily proposes marriage. A lot more women

71

would remarry earlier after they are widowed, I am convinced, except that men have traditionally held for themselves the power to initiate dates and marriage.

The whole tradition of marriage is summed up by the custom of the woman changing her name to his name after they are married. So when you get married, the man changes your life a lot. You as wife aren't expected to change his life very much.

All this, taken together, and its wider cultural expressions I have called "Adam's World." It is what sociologists call a social construction of reality. It is a bubble of assumptions that reflect the fact that everything in our culture has been thought of, imagined, set up, from the male point of view.

Naming Is Power

The gender experience of males is that everything is named, labeled, imagined, from *their* point of view. The assumed standing point is *male*. So each of us as individuals, whether born male or female, is socialized into Adam's world, and our experience is simply that "This is the way the world *is.*"

Until recently, we never even knew any other world. "Adam's world" was it. So when I was a student at Smith College, almost every book I read, whether in history, sociology, literature, philosophy, psychology, was written by a man. I did my graduate study at Yale Divinity School in the early 1950s, and it never occurred to me that every theologian and philosopher I read was male. Everything I was reading and learning about religion and our culture all had been done from this male point of view.

The Tilted Hill, the Slippery Slope

So when men and women come together to partner in Adam's world, it is like partnering on a slippery slope. It is like the slippery side of a mountain, a place where legally and economically and culturally men are always advantaged and are up, and the women are down. Jean Baker Miller in *Toward a New Psychology of Women*[1] talks of this experience using power terms, speaking of "dominants" and "subordinates" instead of about men and women. I consulted the dictionary, and a dominant is one who commands, controls, who prevails over others. A subordinate occupies a lower rank or class, and is inferior or submissive.

Being aware of these power dimensions of our partnering is important today because there is abroad in our culture now a lot of talk about partnering and offers of help with partnering. But it often ignores any power analysis. There is talk about gender war and gender peace, building bridges between women and men, increasing your awareness of male and female "styles of communication," and the different styles of male power and female power at home and at work. As a recent best-selling book title put it, "Men are from Mars, Women are from Venus."[2]

You would think that we are dealing here with just a little difference in style and way of operating. Forget it! We are dealing with power—the power of men, which is prominent in this culture, and women's *lack* of power, which is also prominent in this culture. Think *political* power, think *economic* power, think *social* power (for example, men's ability to initiate dates or propose marriage). Men have it, women struggle to gain a little of it.

So if you do not have a power analysis for how to get to a non-hierarchical relationship, you are going to be in big trouble! You cannot conceptualize a just relationship as simply a straight balance. It is not a simple flat playing field. You are functioning on a hill. So if you try to hold onto what you think is a symmetrical relationship, and it is on a hill, you don't get what you are looking for. You have to compensate for the tilt, for the hill.

Male Entitlement

All this, so far, has been about Adam's World, about the tilted culture between men and women which is all around you on the *outside* of your relationship. But what is even more difficult is what is on the *inside,* namely, that each man has been socialized to be a dominant, and each woman has been brought up inside herself to be a subordinate.

Put those two internalized socializations together, a dominant and a subordinate, and you have something at work in your relationship which is extremely powerful. We in the Theological Opportunities Program talk a lot about overcoming the disempowering effects of our socialization as women. We talk about "finding our voice," "taking ourselves seriously," "empowering ourselves," and so on. But seeing the need to do all this, I am saying, is to see only one half of our situation as women.

I would like to enumerate some of what it is we are interacting with when we partner with a male who has been socialized in Adam's World. My husband developed the following list of male entitlements for his own work with other males, to use when he wants them to understand what their "male advantage" really means for them in their everyday life.

David first started thinking about male entitlement after he heard our colleague Peggy McIntosh talk about "white entitlement."[3] Peggy realized she took quite for granted benefits she was experiencing from our culture, benefits which were different for her than they were for her black colleagues. She got unearned privileges, simply because she was white. She got these not because she earned these benefits but simply by having white skin.

Peggy McIntosh's work started David thinking about his *male* entitlements, privileges he got simply by being male. He realized that what I had been calling for several years "Adam's World" was actually his world of male privilege. This is how he sees it, and I am indebted to him for this analysis of male privilege "from the inside."

The Forms of Male Privilege

First of all, male privilege is the power that comes from being a member of a dominant group.

Male privilege is also the power to legislate institutional arrangements and what is, or is not, legal. Male power sets out the ground rules, the way the game is played.

Male privilege also comes from the power of the media, which are preoccupied with men, and exaggerate men's power.

Male privilege is also the power of physical size. Bigger is more threatening. And, as we all now understand, males use that extra physical size and strength sometimes to batter or kill their female partners.

Women have to be concerned about being alone in settings where they might be raped. But men, unless they are in prison, do not have this fear, and there is certainly male privilege in that.

Women, in addition to rape, learn to fear male violence of other sorts. On the other hand, it is a male privilege to have no need to fear female violence, for example, "castration." Lorena Bobbitt did not castrate, she just got the penis! Castration means removing the testicles. Even so, we all know the phrase "castrating female." The phrase exists in our language despite the absence of women actually castrating males in our culture. It is interesting also to note that there is not even a word yet for the often repeated male violence to women.

Males have the privilege of taking themselves seriously: "What I do is important—interesting." My husband David, for example, when I had major surgery and a long recuperation, took over all our meal preparation. This was something I had done for us for the previous quarter century. Suddenly David was learning how to do all the cooking.

David started inviting my friends to come to dinner so I could see them, and one of the centers of the conversation was how he was learning to cook. After this happened several times, I asked myself: when I was a young bride and learning to cook, did any of us new brides ever feel it was important dinner table conversation that we were learning to cook? I did not think so. After several such dinners, I asked David why he was doing it. *"Because what I do is interesting,"* he said, "and I assume our friends will find it interesting too." That assumption was his male entitlement at work!

There is male privilege in the males' social power to initiate, whether it is asking for a date, initiating sex, or proposing marriage. It is my impression that the younger generation which is my daughter's age has not changed this very much.

Living in a culture that treats women as "sex objects"—and not being treated as one yourself—is also a form of male privilege.

Reproductive freedom is also a male privilege. Men can have sex without getting pregnant.

There is certainly male privilege in men's power to focus on their own lives, their own careers, on their own expectations, their own orgasms. Can you imagine a sexual encounter with a man which does not result in him having his own orgasm? Never. He *expects* to.

"Having" children, without having to gestate them for nine months, give birth to them, and then invest much of the next fifteen to twenty years raising them—all this is certainly a male privilege. Do you know a man who was ever asked how he planned to combine having a career with his having children?

So males have the privilege of having children and not feeling guilty about not rearing them. Women worry all the time about how to juggle their multiple roles. That is not a worry most men have. Yes, Dads help with parenting and sometimes do baby-sitting. Males *assist*. But raising children is thought to be really a mother's job. So it is women who feel torn about this.

ELIZABETH DODSON GRAY

The Question Men Never Ask Themselves

Do males ever ask themselves, Where are all the "best and brightest" of women and blacks and . . . ? Do you remember baseball before Jackie Robinson, when it was all-white? Can you imagine today basketball or football as it once was, all-white? Would it be as good a game if it were again all-white? That is unthinkable now, because we know what sports can be when they are open to the most talented men of all colors. But the social controls of that other time kept all blacks out for many decades.

The purpose of such prejudice was simple. It was to protect white males from ever competing with *all* the "best and brightest." That same prejudice has also been at work to protect all males from ever having to compete against all the best and brightest women.

The Power of Backlash as a Male Privilege

David sees the current backlash against affirmative action as an expression of male power *defending* its male privileges. Many white males feel aggrieved about how their work-lives are going and do not see why they, as white males, should not always "get the job" and "get ahead." In this view it is perfectly all right that white males, *without* affirmative action, only hire and advance others like themselves—white males.

It is also male privilege exercising its power when males launch protests against women speaking out. When Phil Donohue and Oprah provided a television forum for women to be critical of men, the new term *male-bashing* was quickly coined by males in the media. Now when I lecture about my book *Patriarchy as a Conceptual Trap,* I must say that "I am really not male-bashing individual males" and that what I am describing is instead a *social system* which oppresses women and is called *patriarchy.* **Patriarchy is a social caste system, just as Apartheid was—except patriarchy is gender-based instead of racially-based.**

In the media and in politics, the term "family values" has been coined by male privilege to protest women's independence of men (meaning, "women not under male control"). The "family values" movement is not about protecting women from male violence at home, or in the media, or in the streets. Instead, it romanticizes the traditional patriarchal family of male control—at a time when what actually is happening is a rise in the frequency and even lethal intensity of male violence toward the women and children closest to them.

In the universities, the backlash against women's studies and multi-cultural studies in the curriculum is an unabashed defense of male privilege. This is the power of male backlash, now defending the exclusive preeminence in thought and history of "great dead white males."

Male Privilege is . . .

Males have the power to protest—and be taken seriously.

Males have the power to change female action and interaction, simply by a male being present. When a man is there, women are socialized to be concerned about him. "Is he interested?" they wonder, "What is he thinking?" "What will he say?" "What will he do?" My husband has found that his just being present changes the interactions among the women, and he often averts his eyes to disconnect, so women talking in a group will stop talking primarily to him.

Male privilege is the power to interrupt.

Male privilege is the power to be believed. When a man is in a back alley with another man and he kills that man and he says, "It was self-defense," he is often, though not always, believed. But when a woman is in an equally unwatched situation and says she was raped, she is hardly ever believed. It is the same with sexual harassment. Unless you have witnesses, the woman is hardly ever believed.

Perhaps the ultimate male privilege derives from the psychological advantage of going through life feeling oneself to be privileged, a member of the dominant group, the males.

"Sin" in Adam's World

Sin according to the Christian tradition is rooted in "superbia" or over-reaching, and has been labeled generically as "human pride." Augustine asked himself how original sin was transmitted from Eve to all. He decided it was by "concupiscence" or sexual desire. Whenever there was sperm going anywhere, there was also lust. So Augustine long ago decided that original sin was always present from the very beginning of every life. The equation for Augustine ran like this: "Original Sin = Eve = Sexuality."

Thinking about what Augustine had said, my husband David asked himself an interesting question: "What then is 'sin' in what Liz is calling 'Adam's World'?" David realized that there really has been no such theological diagnosis. The "original sin" in Patriarchy, he decided, is men's pride in their own being male.

Gender Socialization's Impact on Our Partnering

Men are socialized subtly and powerfully into all this male entitlement. They do not even know that they are; it is largely invisible to them. And women are socialized into viewing themselves as being *not* as important as men. Women learn that, as women, it is important to give themselves away, to sacrifice themselves on behalf of others, especially their families.

So when a woman partners with a man, the reason having a non-hierarchical relationship is so important is that you "move in" with that deeply imbedded and usually unconscious male entitlement. You sleep with it, you have breakfast with it, you try to split the chores with it, you parent with it.

The question, therefore, is *not* how to do *egalitarian* partnering, as though you were both coming to this as equals. You have to be concerned with *"non-hierarchical* partnering"—because **the problem you are dealing with is the tilt in the culture, a tilt which is also in him, and in you.**

What Non-hierarchical Partnering is NOT

Let us be clear, first, what non-hierarchical partnering is *not*.

It is not "two souls becoming one." Trust me, it is not, because when "two souls become one," they become male. That is a fact. I married in 1957 amid that kind of theological rhapsodizing. It is a mythology which has perpetuated male dominance in partnering.

It is also *not* "allowing the man to become the center of the woman's identity and life." This is something which has happened a lot in the past, and the culture has tried to assume it should always happen. We also know that this is seldom expected to happen to a man. My David came to it only after I had been ill and he was faced with the possibility of losing me. It was only then that I became the highest priority in his life.

The cultural message to men is to compete, to excel, to choose a life work, to contribute, to change the world, to be successful. Incidentally, a man is also supposed to find a woman who will care for him and bear his children. But certainly she is not to be the center of his life. The culture has expected women, it seems to me, to wrap themselves around their male partners, and make his life the center of her meaning and purpose in life—not only take his name but move every time his career requires it, and so on.

What Is the Appropriate Center of a Human Life?

I tried recently to find a paper I wrote at Yale Divinity School about the religious dimensions of women and marriage. I was looking in my collection of papers from that era, and I find it interesting that I saved a lot of others but apparently I threw this one out as one of my "not so interesting" papers!

I now view that paper as one of the most interesting papers I wrote, and I would love to know today exactly what I said then. What I remember I said, was that Ultimate Reality, God, the great I AM of the universe, is the real center of each human life, and not any other human being.

I had the theological acumen in seminary to realize, and to say in this paper, that if a woman makes a man—in this case her husband—the center of her life, she is committing religious idolatry. She is putting another human being in the place in her inner core where her relationship with Ultimate Reality should be.

I saw, even then, that this result is not good for anybody. When a man (and additionally the children) are at the center of a woman's life, it radically de-centers the woman from what really should be her center, namely, her own relationship to Ultimate Reality or the Spirit of Life. When that happens, a woman is radically pulled away from her own calling in life, so that she does not act out of that empowered woman-core of her own relationship with God. So therefore, living that kind of partnered life, in which the man is at the center of your life, *betrays* the sacred potential of a woman and her life.

Realizing this was enormously helpful to me as an insight and would guide me as I went on with my life. A few years later, when I moved into partnering with David, it meant I was very clear that he was not the center of my life, and he never would be. David was also very clear about that, as he will tell you!

But a woman's putting a man at the center of her life also betrays her male partner into illusion, and delusion, so that he thinks he is more powerful, more favored by the universe, more in control, and more wonderful than he really is. Power corrupts. Having a human partner almost totally devoted to furthering your life is very corrupting. It distorts the dominant one into pride, arrogance and insensitivity.

So a hierarchical heterosexual partnering is distorting and destructive for *both* female and male.

What a Non-Hierarchical Relationship IS

What is the sacred essence of such a relationship? First I need to point out what each of us brings to such a relationship.

I have a deep conviction that the Great I AM who is Creator of the universe, has created each of us as humans to be marvelously special and one-of-a-kind, totally unique. Each of us is a flower of amazing particularity, able to unfold into a myriad of gifts and talents that are only ours alone, talents which are possible only to our own personal, unique and one-of-a-kind DNA.

Let me tell you that I knew about DNA years ago. But only very recently has it begun to dawn upon me that any individual, when her DNA is formed at the time of her conception, is a truly random selection of the DNA of *all* of the people in her genetic history, everyone in previous generations in both her mother's and her father's genetic background. It is not possible for all of the richness of that DNA potential, randomly selected, containing who-knows-what-genius, to stop over this woman's head and say, "Ooops, there is genius here. I can't drop it in this *woman's* body; I've got to wait for a man!" Biologically that is not possible. So half of the genius in math, in music, in literature, in writing, in everything, is in *women's* bodies. It has got to be, biologically. It's got to be.

So I have a very "high" theology of human personhood. As Marnie Heizmann has said, "If the core of this divine image in us is free will, then isn't choosing and re-choosing a very sacred human act?" I think that is right, and I would go on to say now in this context, that God gives each of us our incredible uniqueness, and it is a holy, a sacred, gift. Matthew Fox has called it "original blessing"—as opposed to "original sin." It is this uniqueness that brings to us God's intentionality and God's possibility for us.

Pepito's Discovery of His Uniqueness

I want to share with you one of my favorite children's books, *Pepito's Story,* [4] by Eugene Fern. Pepito is a little boy living in a small Mexican town, and he is unusual because his favorite thing to do is to dance. The great love of his life is not stereotypic for boys; it is not bulls, or being big and macho, but dancing. Pepito feels very alone because the other children do not dance with him.

When Pepito is sad and unhappy about "being so different" from the others, and being laughed at, he would go to his grandmother and she takes him in her arms, and repeats this little rhyme. "If every child were like every other, you wouldn't know who was your sister or brother. If every flower looked just the same, 'flower' would be each flower's name." The book says "Pepito didn't know exactly what this meant, but somehow it always made him feel better."

Then one of his friends, a little girl, the daughter of the mayor of the town, gets sick. And everybody brings her presents, hoping she will get better. But she doesn't.

Pepito wonders what he can do to help her. So he goes to his grandmother, to ask her. She says, "No doll or toy will make Estrellita well. What she needs is something very special—something you alone can give." And she repeats the rhyme.

Suddenly Pepito has an idea. He goes to Estrellita's sickbed and he starts to dance for her, his unique gift. He dances and he dances. She sits up in bed, and her face brightens, and she starts to laugh, and she claps her hands, and then she gets up and both she and her father start to dance with Pepito. She becomes well, and can play again with all of her friends, but most of all with her friend Pepito.

The book closes with these words about Pepito. ". . . he was happiest of all, for he had learned that his dancing could bring people joy. He knew that each one of us has something all his own to give to the world, and at last he understood what his grandmother's little rhyme meant: If every child were like every other, you wouldn't know who was your sister or brother; and if every flower looked just the same, 'flower' would have to be each flower's name.' And he thought to himself, How dull that would be! I am glad I am a dancer! I am glad to be me!'"

God intends for each of us, women as well as men, to blossom into our own special, unique and amazing selfhood. Therefore, **to become our most authentic self is our most holy work as persons.** You, in your particularity and individuality, are God's gift to the world, and if you don't become yourself, the most you can be, that gift will never be expressed in the world.

My friend Carol Goldman tells a marvelous story about a Jew named Susha who wants to be like Moses. When he dies God says to him, "I really don't want to know if you were like Moses. I only want to know: were you the best 'Susha' you could be?" That question is for us too; are *we* being the best of who we are, blooming our flower to its fullest?

Partnering as a Holy Vessel

This is where non-hierarchical male-female partnering comes in. Non-Hierarchical partnering is a holy vessel which makes possible the full unfolding and blossoming of the woman, because non-hierarchical partnering is dedicated to the full flowering of the genetic potential of *both* of the partners—with the sense that this is a holy process because it is a sacred unfolding of God's genetic intention and possibility for these two humans.

Thus non-hierarchical partnering is a structure which makes possible the emerging of both female and male into the flowering which the Spirit of Life has intended for both sexes, both genders.

Sacraments of Non-Hierarchial Partnering

I am going to name now what I will call the "sacraments" of non-hierarchical partnering. Clearly we are into new names here. I am aware what the ordinary meaning of the word *sacrament* is, but I am going to use that word now in a new way.

By sacraments I mean some of the processes by which the adventure of non-hierarchical partnering works itself out, some of the processes I have experienced in my partnership with David these past nearly-forty years.

Transparency

I must speak first of *transparency*. This means no secrets. It means total openness of feelings. It means revealing our deepest and most authentic selves to each other.

What such transparency gives to me is a feeling that I am always really myself in our relationship. I could not be in a relationship in which I could not be totally myself. But it also gives me incredible support, a sense of my being loved for who I really am, rather than for who I am pretending to be. It means no role-playing, no posturing, no masks. David knows who I really am. He knows when I am being nice, and he knows me when I am being nasty, tired, fussy, and so on.

I think Jill Ker Conway writes about such transparency when in her most recent book, *True North,* she describes what she calls "the more profound experience of knowing and being known by another person whose mind and spirit complemented mine."[5]

Mutuality That Heals

A second sacrament I would commend is *mutuality.* By this I mean interacting in each other's lives in such a way that you can help heal the distortions in your partner. Note that the mutuality which does this is between *partners who are radically equal and equally active.* I do *not* mean the kind of mutuality in which the more dominant male interacts onto the less dominant female, and then she responds. The female has to be enough of a powerful and integrated locus of energy—activity, thinking, talking, doing—that fully half of the energy in the mutuality is coming from her. Otherwise it is not really mutual.

If you interact in each other's lives in this really mutual way, I am convinced you can help heal the distortions in each partner. This is the healing that comes when in our transparency we provide support for each other. This brings a real healing of our personal mental pain, or anxiety. And as anxiety diminishes, the distortions in our personalities which are rooted in that anxiety are diminished. We become more secure, more confident, more fully ourselves, and more loving, more able to reach out.

Healing through Mutual Correction

There is a healing which also comes when, in our symmetrical interaction, we can act to "correct" and modify the other person's excesses, hard edges, weaknesses, characteristic "failings" and biases. Here is an example from early in our relationship when we were engaged. David says to Liz, "You learned to pout from your Mother. I hate it. Stop it." He wanted to hear from me directly what I was feeling—without a pout. I stopped pouting. From that same period of our engagement, Liz says to David, "You think efficiency is the only priority in any situation, and I can't live that way. Don't expect me to. Get off my back about it!"

ELIZABETH DODSON GRAY

This process of mutual correction has helped our parenting enormously. Liz says to David all through our parenting: "You are using your Old Testament voice," meaning "your harsh, judgmental, totally righteous voice." I would continue, saying, "Our children are going to hate that. Stop doing it." David would change how he was talking.

Another time, we are riding in the car with the children and David says to Liz: "You are really in a bad mood today. Please be quiet." I recognized he was right. He was telling me I was being destructive in that situation. I knew he would then carry the conversation with our children for us both. David was saving me from one of my own worst moments with our children, and I was grateful to be rescued and be quiet.

Sometimes we haven't even had to speak to each other. The mutual correction can happen more quietly than that. David, watching me with the children, realized that my basic response to a child's request for anything was to say, "Yes"—and David's basic inclination was to say, "No." The contrast he saw was that I would have to think very hard to get to a "No." David decided that mine was a better parenting response than his and that he wanted to change his primary stance of "No" with the children instead to a "Yes."

When I was doing parenting, I had the experience of realizing that at the end of each day as we were getting into bed, I reviewed what I had and had not gotten done on my day's To Do list. Let me note that I did not count child-rearing as an accomplishment; it was just something I did all day that I didn't think accomplished anything except keeping my children alive for another day. It was really not what I felt called to do, I was called to ministry! So I had these little lists—write a card to somebody, clean a little bit of that, do something. I usually had five things on my list. At the end of my day I was lucky if I had done two. So I was in a stew about laying down the day with three of the things on my list still undone. It made me feel horrible.

David however would ooze into bed, saying, "Ooh, this is the best hour of the day!" At first, I thought this was weird. After a while I began to think that my own lists were even more weird. So I began to want to change. When you realize that some of your partner's responses are healthier than some of yours, you want to start to change, to leave behind your own deeply embedded neuroses and to move into some of the things you perceive are not his neuroses but his health.

In our marriage David said to me, "I would like the sinks wiped off every time you use them." My response was, "You must be kidding!"

Next, I need to tell you that I am still trying after almost thirty-eight years of marriage to get David consistently to respond verbally to me when I talk to him. I do not think that is an excessive demand, do you? But he still thinks so, and he claims he can't find that change button inside to make it possible. Well, we are working on that. [Someone from the audience says, "What about the sinks?" Response: "The sinks are unwiped, except when he wipes them."]

ELIZABETH DODSON GRAY

Trusting the Observer

Our personal mutuality of correction has involved trusting each other to play the role of "observer" when we are leading groups. When one of us is leading, the other is empowered (and trusted) to read the situation, to assess the variables, and to intervene if necessary to change the topic, the dynamic, whatever. The assumption is that the observer can see more than the person leading the group. Then the intervener must take on themselves the responsibility and the power to lead, and start a whole new train of thought or discussion. And the other person subsides.

When we interrupt each other, we trust each other as observers to perceive more than the one leading can perceive. So we give each other the power to interrupt. And we trust each other to use that power wisely.

We often lecture together, simultaneously, the two of us giving one lecture and talking from the same visuals. When we do this we interrupt each other frequently and create a very dynamic learning environment. What we have discovered is that it does not bother an audience when he interrupts me, but they get concerned when I interrupt *him.* We have learned to introduce ourselves at the start of our joint lectures, calling attention to the differing reactions to male-interrupts-female and female-interrupts-male, and saying we are going to both interrupt each other "lots"—and it does not bother *us,* so we hope it will not bother *them!*

The Power to Say YES and to Say NO

Trusting each other as observer also has a role when David is editing my books. I do *not* trust David to know my writing better than I do. But I do trust that he as an editor can improve my writing. It took me all of July one summer to do the final rewrite of my first book, *Green Paradise Lost.* Then we spent all of August while David went over every sentence, editing it. And we argued about every sentence!

What keeps me in the argument—I always could throw him out—is the realization that while my writing is good, it is better if he edits it. But it took intense confrontation between us to get him to edit my sentences into better "my sentences" rather than into "his sentences." I have long sentences with cadences and dependent clauses, and his first editing response was to chop it all up into little sentences. That was "war" between us for several years, until he recognized that he could learn to edit my flow into a better "my flow." We still struggle over his editing but not nearly so much.

Marge Piercy, in *Cries of the Spirit: A Celebration of Women's Spirituality,*[6] writes of "The Sabbath of Mutual Respect, . . . the power to say Yes and to say No, to open and to close, to take or to leave. . . ." This interaction of a fully empowered YES and NO, going back and forth between partners, is genuine mutuality.

Only Secure Males Can Do Genuine Mutuality

Because of this "mutuality of correction," David has been preserved from a lot of the illusion and delusion which is potential in male socialization and entitlement. He would be the first to tell you this is so. I should also add at this point that non-hierarchical partnering is not for men with fragile egos. Let me give you some examples. Perhaps the most obvious is Bill Clinton. He is not only strong enough and secure enough to have been attracted to a woman like Hillary, to have married her and then stayed married to her, but he put Hillary in a power position in his first term, out front and in charge of its major domestic proposal, the now-failed Health Care reform proposal. Neither of them has fragile egos.

Then there is the story my brother told me once when he called me in outrage about his wife and how he was going to divorce her. My brother is now dead but at that time he was a prominent psychotherapist in Los Angeles and a well-known writer and speaker. He and Grace had been away together, he told me, at a conference where he had been the principal speaker all weekend. He was having trouble when they got home opening their front door with his key, and Grace had said, "Here, let me do it. You never were very mechanical." Now I've got to tell you that my brother was brilliant in many ways, but neither he nor my father could even drive a nail straight; they were totally unmechanical. Yet my brother was outraged at this glimpse of truth, and he had called to tell me about his sad story, to tell me he had never heard of such a "castrating woman." I said something to the effect that, if that kind of remark was the worst thing I said to my spouse in a day, David would call it a *good* day!

Subordinates Won't Tell

Jean Baker Miller, in *Toward a New Psychology of Women,* says, "Members of the dominant group are denied an essential part of life—the opportunity to acquire self-understanding through knowing their impact on others. They are thus deprived of consensual validation, feedback, and a chance to correct their actions and expressions. Put simply, subordinates won't tell."[7]

Women talk of preserving the male ego. When they do, it is an example of "Subordinates won't tell." Sad to say, this is as bad for the male partner as it is for the female partner. There is a saying, "It is as hard to see oneself as it is to look backwards without turning around."

The Gift of Seeing Oneself

A totally honest partner gives you that real gift, an opportunity to see yourself as others see you.

It is unfortunate that many men (and also women) do not really understand the priceless gift that comes with feminism—the ability to see male culture as it cannot see itself. Potentially this is a great gift. And the sacrament of genuine mutuality between a woman and a man who are radically equal and equally active has within it that same gift.

The mutuality of correction fine-tunes and hones each partner into greater wholeness, health, and integration—if they will trust the other person and let it happen.

Synergy

Synergy is still another sacrament or sacred process of partnering. Synergy is the creation of more together than could ever be created by two individuals separately.

ELIZABETH DODSON GRAY

My personal thinking and writing, plus David's editing and publishing, have created a series of books, a body of work, that neither of us could have accomplished alone. Also, David and I "spark off" of each other, dreaming up many more ideas, projects, feminist rebellions, and defiances of our cultural contexts than either of us could imagine alone, or have the courage to do alone. The two of us together can generate more energy, more productivity, and more courage than either of us could do separately.

Likewise, my writing, when we wrestle both it and each other, is better than his writing or my writing alone. This joint work of confrontation is itself a creative act, a synergy of the energy of two being more than the energy of one plus one.

The Two Sides of the River

I want to close with a benediction. Often when I finish speaking, women come up and give me things to read later, and unless there is a name or a source I have no idea where they come from. This benediction came to me in this way, so it is "anonymous."

> The Spirit of Life calls to all creation
> to shake out our colors in the sun;
> The Spirit of Life walks with the poor and the oppressed
> and calls to the oppressor to relinquish and be free;
> For each part is a part of each other;
> We are all part of one another.
> On either side of the river grow the trees of life;
> and someday both sides of the river shall flourish.

NOTES

1. Jean Baker Miller, *Toward a New Psychology of Women* (Boston: Beacon, 1976).

2. John Gray, *Men Are from Mars, Women Are from Venus* (San Francisco: HarperCollins, 1992).

3. Peggy McIntosh, "White Privilege and Male Privilege: A Personal Account of Coming to See Correspondences Through Work in Women's Studies," Working Paper 189 (Wellesley, Mass.: Wellesley College Center for Research on Women, 1988).

4. Eugene Fern, *Pepito's Story* (New York: Ariel, 1960).

5. Jill Ker Conway, *True North* (New York: Knopf, 1994), p. 77.

6. Marge Piercy, in *Cries of the Spirit: A Celebration of Women's Spirituality,* ed. Marilyn Sewell (Boston: Beacon, 2000), p. 43.

7. Jean Baker Miller, M.D., *Toward a New Psychology of Women* (Boston: Beacon, 1976), p. 10.

9.

A New Balance of Power:

Dependence, Independence, Interdependence

Elizabeth & David Dodson Gray
TOP Lecture, October 16, 1986

9.

A New Balance of Power:
Dependence,
Independence,
Interdependence

Elizabeth and David Dodson Gray
TOP Lecture, October 16, 1986

I. POWER

David's Power

What power did I bring into our marriage?

I brought to our marriage the power given to me by the tilt of our culture. Simply being a male gave me power. So as a male I had the job out in the world, and with that job I got the money I earned in that job. I also came into our marriage assuming (as did Liz) that I could have children and have them raised for me. There was power in this assumption, because it meant I would never have to choose between having children and having my work, my job, my ministry. That was a choice which had confronted Liz but not me. She had had to choose whether she would marry and be my wife and the mother of our children, or would she continue her own calling and ministry? I should note that my male power with regard to this went totally unperceived by us at that point in our relationship.

Now there were also some personal powers and capacities that are relevant to our future relationship. I had particular skills which give me power. Math is easy for me. Technology is easy for me. Maps and following directions are easy for me. More about all this later.

Also I had been in psychoanalysis for three-and-a-half years while I was in Divinity School. I had the power to take emotions seriously. Emotions are real for me rather than seeming irrational. This was to be a very important power that I brought to our relationship and marriage as they developed.

I was to find that I both had power *and lacked power* because I forget things. Forgetting things makes me feel *less* powerful. But Liz perceives this forgetting as a part of my capricious power over her. Living with me, she says, is like walking through a minefield which may explode at any minute. Only five minutes hence, or two hours hence, I may forget what she said to me (or I said to her). I forget arrangements I have made with her. I forget where I put things or filed things.

For the first twenty years of our marriage she lived with my forgetting, "lived nastily with it" she would say. Then one day she decided she would "kill" if I did it once more. And of course I for-got—and forgot again and still again. My forgetting is a continuing source of rage and outrage in our relationship. We have both concluded that it is a part of who I am—and, as such, it is a source of a kind of power in our relationship that I don't much like.

Over the years I came to develop other powers. I discovered in doing this that I could empower Liz in important and positive ways. This has come to be very important to both of us.

I have done this by publishing her books. By typing all her papers. By being her editor. By designing publicity for her books and conferences. And I have evolved over the years into Liz' support staff for her work with the Theological Opportunities Program.

I have found too that with my skills in spatial relations I can create visuals that summarize complex ideas, visuals that both Liz and I use widely in our lecturing.

Liz' Power

I perceived I brought into our marriage the power of an equal education. I was a colleague in graduate school with David and we viewed ourselves as both radically peers.

At the time of our marriage I did not perceive that I had the power of my own family money. My parents were both older when I was born. Early in my young-adulthood my parents died and I inherited my own financial independence. But I was true to my times, the 1950s, and I was only concerned at that point that my family money and economic independence of him might threaten David. I was delighted when it did not.

It was not until the 1970s, when I talked with a lot of my friends who were unhappy in their marriages, that I perceived my family money as power. I asked my friends why they didn't get out. And they told me they couldn't because they would starve to death if they got out. Suddenly I realized I knew deep down I never faced that. I also knew (and I knew David knew) that in a very solid and real way that our relationship had to please me as much as it pleased him. Or I would walk. Not only with my education and my own ability to get a job like his. But I would walk with my entire money intact.

We were both subliminally aware of my family money, and there was enormous power there. All the money is gone. We have lived on it, educated our children, done good things with it. But while it was there it was an enormous power.

About my particular powers and capacities, I have to say that I realize the power I have in being able to stand up for myself. This is the power of my own anger. I don't know the psychology of where that came from, but I do know that it is accessible to me in relationship to David and to other people. As a matter of fact I taught David how to get in touch with some of his own anger toward parishioners, toward the bishop, and so on.

As a part of this—but larger than this—I have access to my own feelings, something which is allowed to me as a woman in this culture and which is incredible emotional power, whether we choose to recognize it as that or not. And because of that emo-tionality I also have the power, negative power, to throw us both into an emotional abyss. This happens by my getting angry which gets David angry—and suddenly swooowish we are going down, down into that emotional abyss.

David's Other Powers (As Liz Perceives Them)

Over the years we have replaced a simple camera that I enjoy-ed using, and a simple phonograph that I could work, with supposed improvements involving much more complex technologies which only David can operate. Recently we got a VCR I dearly love but which involves so many options that even David can barely operate it.

Since I am a total klutz with technologies, I feel surrounded by things that disempower me and make me dependent. And when David doesn't do them right. Or forgets to do them. Or mucks them up by doing some little thing wrong, it makes me furious with him and with the whole technological complexity that I've come to depend on but really don't like and can't do.

I also resent David's power that is expressed in his proclivity lots of times for making unilateral decisions that affect my life, without consulting me. That feels like capricious power over me and I rage against that. And over a period of time I have persua-ded him that unilateral decisions are not a good thing to do. They are not good for our relationship.

I also perceive that David has the power not to take my objections seriously, to override me unless I really throw a fit.

There was a pattern early in our marriage in which David would say he was going to do something and I would say that I really didn't think that was a good thing to do in terms of human relationships—and he would go ahead and do it anyway.

When later it didn't turn out well, I would say, "I told you I really didn't think we should do that," and he would say, "I didn't hear you say that. Did you really say that?" And, "Well, speak up. Why don't you make me take what you say seriously?"

This happened three or four times. So, the next time, instead of saying calmly, "I don't think we should do that," I said strongly, "I AM THROWING A FIT, DO YOU UNDERSTAND? I DO NOT THINK WE SHOULD DO THIS." (David comments at this point, "Our private life can be very dramatic.")

So now there is sort of a balance. I have the power to throw a fit and David will hear that if I do it; I also know that if I do not throw a fit, sometimes I do not get his attention and he may not hear. (David comments at this point: "You have heard about having to hit a mule between the eyes with a 2x4 to get its atten-tion?")

David's Perception of Liz' Power

I have always been deeply fascinated by and attracted to the power of Liz' personality. I find her a fascinating awesome person. I like that a lot.

I am also very aware of the power Liz has with words, with ideas, with emotions. I have always been impressed with that, and I like that.

Also Liz has always been more emotionally sensitive than I. And that is another kind of power. I knew emotions were real, a reality. But Liz read emotions better, faster, sooner.

II. DEPENDENCE

As we thought about dependence, the problem with it is power that is not under your control.

But I also feel that dependence can feel good. For example, for the last three years since I've been sick, I have depended upon David to bring me breakfast in bed each morning. It makes me feel pampered and taken care of. I love it.

Or, depending on how you perceive the power in the relationship, dependence can feel bad. What's bad is really the power problem in being dependent.

Within our marriage we have, without thinking about it, interpreted dependence as "dependence on"—how we depend on each other—and it has been a good category in our relationship.

How David Perceives Himself As Depending On Liz

First of all, I depend on Liz to draw out my emotions, to help me figure out what I am feeling. I come from a family which was not Scandinavian but there was a lot of German in it, and my feelings were largely inaccessible. They were bouncing around somewhere in the nether regions. This was the case even after three-and-a-half years of psychoanalysis.

My feelings not being accessible to me has been of concern to me and has been something I welcomed help with. I have depended on Liz for this. Liz helps me pull my feelings out, to get in touch with them.

Second, I have also depended on Liz to bear our children and to do a major part of our child-rearing. I was not aware for a long time that I was taking that for granted. But every man needs to know that he cannot have children by himself, at least not yet. And most men do not intend to rear their children by themselves.

With our children I depended upon Liz' unconventional and deeply intuitive parenting skills. I did not want to be a father of the sort my father was to me. I perceived Liz as a great help to me in that, and indeed she has been. Today I have a relationship with our children that I like a lot and that I think our kids like a lot—and that my father never had with his children.

Third, Liz selected what we ate. This is trivial but very important too. We ate what tasted good to Liz. I discovered when Liz was sick and I was cooking that we ate what tasted good to me. And then we started to negotiate what we ate. We had never had avocados when Liz was cooking, for example.

However we did not live in a home Liz alone had decorated. We enjoyed doing that together, we shared that. We also made all our money decisions by consensus—except for one large unilateral slip that I made after we'd been married about ten years, which our children and my wife will never let me forget.

Fourth, until recently Liz managed and planned all our social life. It has been Liz who has maintained our network of at-a-dis-tance friends through letters, through phone calls, through Christmas gifts and Valentines. Liz has also over the years bought Christmas gifts and birthday gifts most of the time, even for my side of the family. (Liz comments: "On the day before David's mother's birthday, David would say, 'What are we giving my mother?' And I would say, 'It's all wrapped!'")

Fifth, I depend on Liz for emotional intimacy. I have never found emotional intimacy with men. I also depend on Liz for access to women friends, as many of our friends know.

Emotional intimacy means to us being emotionally transparent to one another, being completely visible to each other. It also means being each other's best friend.

You know about code *words*; well, we have code events. Here's a code event that illustrates what we mean by "best friends." Our daughter and her friend Willy Jay are two-and-a-half and they are playing all morning at Willy Jay's house. They squabble all morning for the first time, and after Lisa has left, Willy Jay's mother asks her son, "Why did you and Lisa fight all morning?"

Willy Jay looked shocked—and uttered the unforgettable words, "Me no fight with Lisa, she my best friend!" That is the way Liz and I feel. We fight all the time but "Me no fight with Liz, she my best friend." And perhaps because we have fought constantly in a dynamic tension all the years we have known each other, we are still best friends.

Sixth, when Liz got sick, I realized looking back that I had depended on Liz' good health, her vitality, her emotional stability, her rationality, her energy, her vigor. All these I—and we—had taken for granted. Until suddenly they weren't there.

Liz' Perception of David's Depending On Her

I perceive that David is dependent upon my professional advice. On how to preach—I taught him how to preach after we were married. I taught him how to do college work. I first tried to teach him how to outline, and then decided I would outline for him, that he just didn't get that one. (David comments: "Years later I learned how, and now I outline for myself much, but not all, of the time.")

I really in many ways also taught David how to do group work in relation to the parish, because I had led groups in college and he had not. I feel David also depends on my advice about when to take a stand in the parish, when to take a stand on justice issues and put his job at risk. (David comments: "If we're going to hang, we might as well hang together.") Yes, we'll hang on things we both are clear it is worth hanging for. So I realize he depends a lot on my emotional support and professional judgement, as professional peer, comrade and colleague.

David also counts on me to bring newness into our lives. A lot of the things we have done are things he would never have thought of. One day I said I wanted to go to Europe next summer with our children, who were then 11 and 8. David said, "Why do you want to go to Europe? We already have a summer place." I said I don't want to miss going to Europe just because we have a place we usually go in the summer. So I understand that bringing newness into our lives is part of what I do in our relationship.

I also perceive that David depends upon me to move him out of the monochromatic emotions that he grew up with, in which, as he says, there were no highs and no lows and the emotional fires were kept damped and greatly restrained all the time. My life, on the other hand, is always sort of emotionally charged up all the time (David interjects: "It's like that hair-raising roller coaster ride you see in the TV commercials just now!")—and I understand that David perceives the way I move him into heights as well as depths is a good thing in his emotional life. Well, that's a part of our dependence on one another too.

How Liz Sees Herself As Depending On David

I depend incredibly on David's steadiness, on his reliability. It feels in an incredible way as though I have a part of the Rock right here in my life.

I perceive him also as always supporting me, respecting me, and enjoying me, my talents, my professional ability, my role as wife and mother. I never have to feel that I can only be *part* of who I am in order to make it somehow all right with David. I feel as though he enjoys *me*. The better I feel about my life, the more contributions I make, the more I can enjoy myself and be myself— he thinks that's terrific.

I remember a dream I had sometime five or ten years into marriage. I was back at Yale Divinity School and it was very familiar and great to be there and I was seeing all my friends. And finally I realized something was missing—and that something was David. I asked someone about David Gray and they told me I'd broken up with him, I wasn't dating him any more. I had this great sense of sadness, and I knew that in a very deep way just having him in my life was a very, very special thing. We conceptualize our lives sometimes as always doing a dance with each other, and just having David there to do the dance with, whether we are fighting or whether we are enjoying one another—I really depend on that.

I also depend on David for always affirming the erotic dimensions of my body in our lives. That's just a kind of constant that's always there that I count on in a wonderful way in terms of our sexual life. As we moved on into our erotic relationship, it was always David who was sure that we could find a way through whatever problem we were dealing with and get on sexually into the relationship we wanted to have with each other. I've come to count on that through the years from our honeymoon on, so I was not at all concerned about what was going to happen to our sexuality when I had my mastectomy. It was simply not a matter of concern to me because we have already weathered through a whole lot of things.

Now I turn to tangible things. I count on David for muscle for moving furniture. Some of you know we rearrange our lives and our decor every two or three months to match the seasons. So muscle is necessary.

I also count on David to do the gardening. I plan gardens and David does them. I want a yellow plant here, I want a purple plant there. We go out and buy them and David puts them in, does it.

I count on David to do the typing, which he does. His typing of all my manuscripts and books has been huge! I write on yellow pads, and if David could not translate my rapidly-written scrawls, I could not have written and published as I have. Without his pub-lishing my books and designing marketing brochures for them, and creating Roundtable Press, I would not have had the satisfying career I have had in my middle years.

I count on his support for my Theological Opportunities Program lecture series (TOP), which includes typing of my letters, typesetting our TOP program brochures, and creating and maintaining our TOP computer database. That's a lot! He also manages the technologies (camera, audio system, automobile, VCR) which I cannot do. Thanks to David, we can live in the modern technological world!

And since my mastectomy three years and four operations ago, I have depended on David as my primary caregiver. For all cooking and cleaning. For breakfast and dinner in bed, and sometimes lunch also. For physical therapy, which my physical therapist taught him to do. For constant chauffeuring, because I could not drive. For walking me for an hour late every night to help me sleep. For helping me do my special exercises. And for "emotionally standing with me" in all my terrible feelings, includ-ing the anger and depression of healing after the serious trauma I had gone through. He did this without lecturing, without pious cliches, without artificially cheering me up—just always being there. Letting me cry all day if that's what I felt I had to do, holding me and just always being there.

But I've got to say that I did not see that as *"bad"* dependence. I know this sort of dependence would make a lot of people crazy. But it did not bother me; I feel that after all I've done with David I deserve *ten* years. Yes, I love it. He says he's going to bring me breakfast in bed for the rest of our lives—and I adore it!

III. INDEPENDENCE
David on How He Is Independent of Liz

I run our financial records system and payments system. And I run a book publishing house. All with Liz very glad that she is not involved in any of it. I am independent of Liz in relation to all the various technologies in our life.

I feel now, after three years as Liz' primary caregiver, that I am more independent because now I have my own household skills. I can run a household by myself now; it is not a big deal any more. If Liz isn't there because she's away on a trip, dinner goes on the table without my really thinking about it a great deal. I can cook, I can iron, I can handsew, I can shop and plan meals. I can keep a refrigerator functioning efficiently and manage a freezer so things don't get lost for months at a time. I can plan our social life and cook for guests. I can do the laundry; actually I've done the laundry for many years. And I do all the cleaning and have done it since early in our marriage.

I am independent also in my own reading. I read things that Liz would never dream of reading. I love to read about geology and about the history of science and about science policy.

I am currently writing two books, which are quite apart from Liz. One is about my relationship with my mother, who has Alzheimer's disease. The other is about being male; as I have come into my late fifties I find I am really thinking a lot about why we men are the way we are, and I am trying to write a book about this. The working title is *Emerging From The Half-Life*. I am writing it in the largely anecdotal style of Gail Sheehy's *Passages*, and I think it is going to be an interesting book. I am loving writing it and some days I'll write a chapter in the morning and a chapter in the afternoon. It is very exciting to be about.

Liz' Perception of David's Independence

I am impressed by the fact that David has independently devised and put in place the systems of order that keep track of our lives—the lectures we do, all of our finances, and the thousands of books we sell. He does all this despite the fact that, when we were married, I really felt David could not do anything to keep our lives in order. But he has managed to organize an awful lot and I haven't done it.

I also perceive in David a tremendous independent urge to move in to help out, when there is a need. My favorite story of this is when we were still in parish life and were driving a group of teenagers back from the Cape. We came over a long hill and at the bottom of the hill around a curve there were people who had just had an accident. Literally the accident had just happened, and they needed flares to warn other cars so another car wouldn't plow into their stopped cars. David reached down under our front seat, pick-ed up his flares, and told me to hand them out the window to them as we went by. I cranked down the window and we handed them to these very surprised people standing there and we just swished on into the evening. He does that in just all kinds of things.

Liz' Perception of Her Independence

I perceive the absolute basis of my independence is my deeply centering spiritual life. Marriage and children are not the center of my life. I remember writing a paper my third year in Divinity School saying that I was very clear that for a woman, if your husband and your children were the center of your life, you were involved in idolatry.

I probably would not couch it in those Old Testament terms at this point in my life. I don't know whether it is true for everyone else, but for me it is true that David and our children are not the center of my life. The center of my life is my relationship to God and my sense of my life as ministry. This made it difficult rearing my children because I did not feel I was born to rear children, I was born to do ministry. And I wondered why the hell I had chil-dren if it meant that what I was to do with my life was to *take care* of them.

So taking care of our children was a problem for me. But I think it has also been a freedom—in that I did not *need* this mothering to be at the center of my life. That has been very freeing for my children as well as freeing for me.

I also perceive my own intellectual life to be incredibly independent of David. I am interested in ecology, feminist theology, the things I work on in my head. And that has very little to do with the things he works on in his head (although our feminism does overlap). I have written two books, *Green Paradise Lost* and *Patriarchy as a Conceptual Trap*, we have written two books together, and I am working on a new book about new images of God, post-anthropocentric images of God.

ELIZABETH DODSON GRAY

I also perceive that I am independent in terms of my relational instincts, expressed in my networks of friends and my patterns of sending cards, gifts, Valentines. This is something that originates in me and that is not at all dependent on David; it is just the way I live my life.

I also find it fascinating as a sign of our mutual independence that we both still pronounce certain words differently. I say "INT-resting" while David says "in-TER-esting." Over the past 35 years we haven't changed!

David's Perception of Liz' Independence

I'm very aware that Liz has her own spiritual life, her own emotional life, her own intellectual life, her own friends, her own will.

IV. INTERDEPENDENCE

As we thought about the ways we have conceptualized our interdependence, what we could focus on were two very broad principles or guidelines.

The first is what might be called **the principle of radical specialization.** Whoever does something best, or does something most easily, does it.

Sometimes the results are sterotypically male or female—and sometimes they are not. For example, Liz knew how to cook when we got married and she likes to cook, so Liz did all the cooking until her operation several years ago. And David did all the cleaning up after meals.

Liz outlines best, much the best. So for many years she outlined all David's sermons, all his papers as well as her own papers, or anything we write together. On the other hand, David has always done all the editing for whatever either or both of us write. We both write, separately and together. But David does all of the typing for both of us. It is so easy for him, and rapid and almost mistake-free, that there is no point in Liz wasting mutual time with her "ordinary" skill at typing.

The second principle is that **we give each other the power to be the observer of the other in our speaking, in parenting, in social situations.**

Being the observer of the other happens in two forms. One is to give feedback later. The other is that we have given each other the power over the years to interrupt and to change the direction of any moment. This means that if the other person starts to say something, we have agreed that the one who had been speaking stops by simply bringing that sentence to an end. And then the person who has stopped lets the other do whatever they feel they need to do.

The assumption is that the person observing you can see the situation better than the one who is busy speaking. Perhaps you are going on too long. Perhaps you are alienating the children. Perhaps there is something which is not right.. The observer has the power to cut it off immediately. And we trust each other to play that role for one another when we are leading groups, when we are speaking, when we are parenting, whenever. Again, the assumption in this is that we cannot see ourselves accurately, and we trust that the other person needs to play that role for us.

ELIZABETH DODSON GRAY

Radical Decisions

For us it was a decision from early on in our marriage to inter-lace our lives and our activities as much as we could. Our lives felt better to us as we did this as much as we could in every hour, every day, every week, and every year.

We try to spend as many hours together, awake or asleep as possible in a lifetime—so we can spark off of each other in our thinking and in our doing. That's been our great joy, and we've done it in our preaching, in our parenting, in writing, in program planning, in our group leading, and in our lecturing. For us it has been a superb way of doing our lives. Other people, we know, would find it sends them up the wall. You know the old line about, "I married you for better or for worse, but not for lunch." That is not where we are.

We have developed along the way a high tolerance for conflict. If you are going to spend this much time together, you have to be able to deal with the ways you drive each other buggy—and we do.

In conclusion, we have tried to see ourselves through the years as trying to create a relationship in which we were radically equal and equally active.

For David from Liz on Valentine's Day 2004

My dearest Valentine,
Lover of my life,
Companion of my days,
Your love has brought so much good into my life:
a long and deepening marriage,
the gifts of children and grandchildren,
the editing and the publishing of my books,
the enabling and support of my ministry at Harvard,
your unfailing joy at my success,
your unfailing pleasure when I am most truly my best
and my most talented self.

Your faithfulness and steadiness
has been the solid foundation of my life adventure
for lo these last 46 years.
And I am always grateful for your willing heart
and total loyalty.
Your last words at our every nap and night
—about waking you if I need you—
never fails, as I am falling asleep,
to wrap me in your love and concern
within the sweet little cocoon you have helped me into
in my couch-bed.
Our lately improvised "pillow talk" is very special to me
even while it is not as sensual as was
our cuddling like spoons for so many years.
The synergy of our creativity,
which results in great achievement,
never ceases to amaze me
as year after year it blooms in our lives
bringing great satisfaction to us both.
And I take so for granted
your never-faltering feminism which inspires you
to labor so tirelessly
to produce and enhance "women's voice"
in TOP pamphlets.
Through these years of my own feminist journey
your own feminism has given me
such deep and sustaining companionship.
I have never had to drag you along
but you have always been bounding
along beside me,
reaching ahead with your own

profound commitment to justice.
Whenever we have an ethical decision to make,
we are always together in
perceiving the justice dimensions of the decision,
and making it together.
And, finally, the sweetness of our long evenings
—alone together after our nap—
watching television with all the phones turned to "off,"
is so very precious to me, night after blessed night.
We are indeed "en-veloped in the generosity of time
and health" in these days of our lives.
I am deeply grateful for the magic of our intimacy
and the steadfastness of our commitment to each other,
so that we have grown into these mellow years together.
And so, my lover, my friend and my companion,
I salute you on Valentine's Day 2004,
and I dare to hope and dream that
we may be blessed with many more years together.
All my love, Liz

—David, 2006—

Dear Love of My Life for All These 48 years:

When we first walked down Edwards Street through those crisply dried leaves, little did we realize that we were starting such a journey of companionship and loyalty and mystery, all compounded with pregnancies and children and their marriages and then their own children.

There has always been about us a lovely penumbra of erotic attraction, which we have certainly exploited and enjoyed immensely.

But, beyond that, it is the companionship and loyalty and mystery we have found in each other which truly stands out in my memory's eye and in my heart. After those bumpy years of start in St. Louis, we have chosen together to weave our daily lives very closely, proximate in space and focus (even if I so often don't speak or respond—I regret this aspect of my being in our relationship). But the loyalty and the mystery are without apology or qualification.

And I think you know that I use the word mystery as Allen O. Miller taught us: Mystery is that which, the more you go into it, the more you know there is still to know. It goes on and on in a continually fascinating mode of living and loving.

And the loyalty is so mutual. We seem constantly to be helping each other be our very best and most complete and capable selves, and, where either of us is lacking, the other tries to fill in or make up that difference.

When we stepped into our marriage on Tuesday, July 2, 1957, what more could either of us have asked for? My memory of that day is so vivid and present, yet so far away and also populated with those we love who are now long gone.

This is the shared vision of having loved-well one another and our lives. Thank you so much for this great gift of all these years and days shared, and projects and loves begun and brought to various fruitions.

Happy Valentines Day from your beloved to his beloved.

Valentine's Day 2004

For Liz-Love from David-Love

O my great and grand love,
I am filled with a profound sense of
"sun-rise, sun-set,"
And like the Fiddler on the Roof,
I am in awe of the cumulative dailyness
which God,
and our own ways of loving and living,
have squandered upon us
in a wonderful "generosity of time."

Yes, we have lived for decades aware
that the Damoclean sword
hung always close over our head.
But we clung to each other
and to life and to our love,
and we have loved and lived as though it were
no impediment but instead an incentive:
"Faster,"
we would whisper to each other.

Thank you, once again, for this wonderful gift
of companionship,
friendship, clarity and transparency,
yes, for the full measure of loving.

In July Each Year, I Celebrate

Along with brilliantly oranged Day Lilies
and dancing patches of Queen Anne's lace
in July I celebrate—
brilliant sunshined sky-blues,
the occasional power of hurricanes
churning leaf and waves,
the sometime night appearance

ELIZABETH DODSON GRAY

of St. Elmo's Fire
as trued-in bolt of lightning glow—
and the
even rarer and more precious
July-experience
of life with you.
Yes, northwest breezes,
barbequed-chicken,
cherried Jell-O & pineapple chunks,
gulls soaring,
children's screams of delight,
a horizon-full of glimmer—
we have topped up
our hearts' July memory.

And each July, again, I get to
sing Happy-Birthday-to-You,
and pray for Many-Happy-Returns
of this your birthday!

love yourself

for no one
can be closer
or share more time
with you

be patient
and kind to yourself

value your attributes
appreciate your gifts

let go of the past
retaining only
its/wisdom

remain aware
for you are now

new

Corita

10.

Walking My Yellow Brick Road

Part 1.

TOP Talk,
November 10, 1983

10.

Walking My
Yellow Brick Road
Part 1.

TOP Talk, November 10, 1983

My Yellow Brick Road begins in September of 1972. I am sitting under a tree at Harvard Business School, crying all morning. David and I had left parish ministry a few months before and we were just starting an issue-centered ministry, a Colloquium on Ethics and Investments in the downtown-Boston financial community. It was a new beginning for us, and we were now auditing courses at Harvard Business School and Harvard Divinity School to prepare ourselves better for it. But I was crying because this new beginning felt to me like another shattering of my identity.

The Rubber-Band and Plumb Line

I had felt called to the ministry very early in my life—perhaps prior to high school. As early as I can remember my own consciousness, I had felt myself in a special relationship to that Ultimate Other in my life, whom I had been taught to call God.

In my teenage years I imaged that Ultimate Other as the one who pulled on the other side of the rubber-band of my identity. And I soon discovered that, for me to be whole, centered, rooted in my own deepest identity, then the rubber-band of my relationship to that Other must be centered and in place also. Through trial and error I had discovered that, when I moved away from that plumb line in my soul, I soon felt unreal, shallow, fragmented and frenetic—literally out of touch with myself.

So that plumb line had guided me through college and then divinity school at Yale, into college ministry in Harvard Square, and finally into marriage with David and into having our two children.

Reworking My Identity to Include Mothering

But with parenthood my sense of that plumb line came to feel confused. I had felt deeply *called* to my religious ministry. And my marriage to David, an Episcopal minister, seemed part of that religious calling. But I did not feel called in the same way to rear children, only deeply socialized and commanded to do so by my culture.

It took me several painful years to put together a new identity that worked for me—which included mothering as well as such things as the League of Women Voters. What I came up with was a larger and more diversely conceptualized sense of ministry.

It was very much like taking a long, thin, graceful bud vase of clear glass holding a single rose, and reshaping it into a shorter, rounder, many-colored vase holding many flowers from roses to daisies. I learned to project my ministry-identity into League-of-Women-Voter meetings, UNICEF collections at Halloween, adult education, and sermon-writing with David—as well as into children in the sandbox or on swings. In my small town, my church, my family, and among my friends my ministry-self and personal-self extended in all directions. It made sense to me and I finally felt comfortable in it.

Crying—and Beginning to Remember

And then David and I decided to redirect our lives from a parish-centered ministry into the issues of corporate social responsibility, and ethics, and investments—what later we were to characterize as an issue-centered ministry. And there I was under the tree at Harvard Business School, crying.

It was the fall of 1972. Our children were in school every day. Investments were more David's "bag" than mine. We left our small town every morning together for all-day in Boston. And once again I felt I had stepped off into nothingness. No, more than that, I felt that someone had taken a hammer to my laboriously constructed second vase and shattered it. Suddenly now my ministry and my identity and my selfhood (which were all somehow one and the same) were in pieces around me again. And so I sat under that tree and cried and cried and cried.

But finally I began to remember. I had been through this process before. After all, I had reconstructed a tall, clear bud vase into a shorter, rounder, many-colored vase. What I had to do now was do that over again, only differently.

So I picked myself up that morning, and started walking up Boylston Street into Cambridge—and started walking what I have come to call "My Yellow Brick Road."

Finding My Yellow Brick Road

I felt like Dorothy in Frank Baum's fantasy about *The Wizard of Oz*. I wanted to get back to my equivalent of Dorothy's Kansas, back to where I was whole and focused and myself again. But, unlike Dorothy's experience with a yellow brick road, *my* yellow brick road has never just stretched out before me, each yellow brick gleaming in sunlight. Oh no! My yellow brick road was (and still is) very elusive. It only appears in front of me at what seems to be one brick at a time.

The first brick I found at Episcopal Divinity School. It was a notice on a bulletin board about a Women's Studies course I then decided to take. It was aptly entitled "Women's Liberation and the Value of Human Being," and was brilliantly taught by Olga Craven Huchingson. I started reading my first feminist books.

The second brick arrived in the mail, sent to me by my friend and former apartment-mate Connie Parvey. It was the brochure for the first Theological Opportunities Program lecture series about "Self-Denial and Self-Fulfillment." And I started walking.

Now, more than ten years later, you may ask, What was (and is) this Yellow Brick Road? From today's perspective I would say that the Yellow Brick Road is the movement of the Ultimate, the Creator, in your own life. It is the movement of the Ultimate, calling you forward into the acting-out of your own deepest convictions and goals. It is the Ultimate, confirming you, sustaining you, encouraging you—yes, impelling you onward to the vision of the Promised Land prepared for all that the Ultimate Creator is birthing into being.

"Celebrate your existence!"

William Blake

Liz/David Dodson Gray

2008

11.

Painting the Seasons Sacred

Written in 1988 as a chapter in *Sacred Dimensions of Women's Experience* Revised in 2008

11.

Painting the Seasons Sacred[2]

A chapter in *Sacred Dimensions of Women's Experience,* 1988

A Theology of Seasons

It all started when our daughter Lisa was about two or three years old, and I realized that she was "living in two worlds." She went to the Episcopal church where David was a minister and there she lived at times in liturgical seasons called Advent ("waiting for Christmas") or Lent ("waiting for Easter"). There were different colors and different hymns and different moods for each of these seasons. They were special "times." But when she came home, there was no Advent or Lent time. There was only the day-by-day "ordinary time," except for Christmas and Easter and birthdays.

I wanted our children to experience a whole reality in which there was continuity between what happened in church and what was happening in the world. How do I explain to my child that Advent or Lent are seasons in the church year, but only happen in church? When Advent and Lent are celebrated with special color and activities, but only in church and not at home and not in the surrounding secular culture, the result is a splitting apart of reality. It seems to me akin to expecting a child to learn that two plus two equal four—but only in church; at home or elsewhere, two plus two equal five, or three. So my husband and I decided to bring the church's liturgical seasons of celebration home with us. We would make these seasons come alive and be real in our home space as well as in our church space.

I began in Lent with color. If purple was the color of Lent (and Advent) in church, perhaps I should figure out a way for purple to be front and center at home for that time. Now, I didn't decorate much with purple, so I hardly knew where to begin.

One of David's old girl-friends had given us some pale-lavender place mats for a wedding gift. But since I wasn't thrilled with her, I had buried them beneath my more colorful place mats. Now I got them out and started to use them. I also bought some small square purple pillows for our long black sofa, and I looked around for *anything* to put on our walls. Thus began my decorating our home for the seasons.

After I brought Advent and Lent from church into our home, I realize that I felt an even deeper need to bring the natural world inside. How could we ignore the flaming leaf-colors of autumn, or the magical pinks of the flowering cherry and magnolia trees in spring, or the bright yellows of jonquils or the delicate chartreuse of the new young leaves on big trees?

The church seasons celebrated the past and what God had done there. But I knew that God is also incredibly active and present right now. I saw it every day as I participated in our ever-changing New England seasons on this part of planet Earth. To my religious sensibility at least, God as that Ultimate Reality and Presence in all our lives is also fundamentally revealed in the day-by-day processes of creation. I saw (and see) God's "hand" in the processes of earth and soil and air and rain, the processes which maintain all life on this planet. It is these processes which make themselves partially visible to us in the changing all around us of the natural seasons of hot and cold, wet and dry.

Responding to the Wonder

To those who have eyes to see, life on this earth is filled with wonder. In our New England setting that wonder changes from the flaming golds and reds of autumn leaves to the quiet soft white of snowfall to the born-again newness of springtime crocuses and flowering trees. We decided we wanted to celebrate this wonder of the ever-changing but ever-steady revelation of the creativity at the heart of the universe. We wanted to bring that wonder inside our home. We wanted to be in touch with its variety and its changing nature, and to have our lives resonate to its changing rhythms and colors. We would try to live and move and have our being within its pervasive power.

So we began changing the house with the changing natural as well as liturgical seasons. In mid-autumn, as the days began to shorten and the nights lengthened, we put down under our coffee table a cozy long-haired Greek rug in powerful deep orange tones. Over the years we made or acquired pillow covers in gold and orange, like gold and orange leaves of the season, to go on our black-and-brown tweed sofa. We also got similar colors for napkins, table mats and tablecloths. The deep orange of bittersweet was picked up not only on the dining room table but also in the candles over the piano. It seemed natural to decorate the dining room sideboard and the piano with fall leaves and flowers. In this season we bring out pictures that convey the mood and fruitfulness of the harvest. We found reproductions of Cezanne's apples and Millet's "Harvest of the Grain." One year I created a wreath of nuts and artificial fruits that each autumn adorns our front door. All this leads to and culminates in our celebration of Thanksgiving Day.

But after Thanksgiving there is a stark change of pace. We strip our house to its barest components and during Advent as we prepare for Christmas we again only decorate with purples and blacks and whites. So in Advent (and Lent) purple becomes the color of the accent pillows, the candles, the table mats and napkins.

We now have etchings in black and white that go up on our walls in this season: faces, bare trees, drawings of children and parents by German artist Käthe Kollwitz. Our house seems hushed and expectant—waiting like Israel for Emmanuel to come.

Christmas and Deep Midwinter

Then on the day of Christmas Eve, all of the Advent things are put away. The house is thoroughly cleaned, and Christmas bursts forth in it. The house is adorned in the bright reds and greens of Christmas through the Twelve Days of Christmas until a party with a neighboring family on "Twelfth Night" ends the Christmas Season for us with charades acting out the story of the Three Kings as well as the dismantling of the tree.

In our part of the country in midwinter we see around us in the outside world a soft and muted wonder. Browned shrubs and barren black tree trunks stand in brilliant sunlit contrast against fields of white snow. It is subtle and very beautiful, and we try to bring that white and brown and black patterning inside in January. Bold brown/black/white patterns adorn tablecloth and sofa cover, and sculptures of wooden birds stand out on the surface of a white Formica coffee table as though it were a field of winter snow. The brilliant area rugs of autumn and Christmas are gone now, leaving only the basic understated gray-green rug beneath to continue the soft muted theme. In this understated season of warmth and chill we ponder the providence of God which hides underneath the cold blanket of snow the potentiality of seeds and spring and life-renewal. Midwinter is in many ways life pausing and waiting, waiting to begin again.

By the time we have gotten to February it is still very cold outside in New England but our spirits thirst for the strong colors and sentiments of Valentine's Day. David and I have created a new and passionate season of riotous red hearts around Valentine's Day. It is neither natural nor liturgical but something celebrated in our secular and commercial culture as only the romance of heterosexual love. We have recaptured Valentine's Day and made it serve our own purposes. All the blacks and browns and whites of early midwinter are now replaced by masses of hot-pink and red in hangings, in pillows, in art work, in table coverings. This is the season when for many years we created homemade Valentines to value our friends, working with what in nursery school they call "beautiful junk." We are down on our hands and knees on the floor, playing with rug remnants and scraps of fabric and bits of paper lace, fashioning with red construction paper and Elmer's Glue and odds and ends special messages of friendship and affirmation for those we know need such encouragement and companioning this year. When in late February we are finally ready to lay down our home-made Valentine Season, we find ourselves filled with the warmth of the many relationships in which we nourish and sustain our life.

But the after-effects of my first cancer surgery made it impossible for me to use my arm without pain, and we reluctantly agreed we had to move to a different kind of creativity for our Valentine. We decided to design a printed Valentine greeting which we could send to *more* of our friends. Our previous customized Valentines had been so personal and so closely adapted to each individual's life journey. The question now became: "What one message is worth saying to more people?' We searched and then I saw in a weekly-engagement calendar by Abbey Press the following quote:

*Life is short
and we never have
enough time
for gladdening
the hearts
of those
who travel the way
with us.
O be swift to love!
Make haste to be kind.*[2]

The first line of "Life is short" resonated deeply in me, because once you have a cancer diagnosis, the threat of dying hangs over you like the sword of Damocles. The injunction to "gladden the hearts of those who travel the way with us" made enormous sense to me.

"That's it," I said triumphantly, and David had them printed. This was thirty years ago, and we have enjoyed sending out what has become a kind of mantra-for-the-year, celebrating "being alive" and "the gift of time" and "the glory and the wonder of the natural world."

Many friends have spoken of their appreciation for our "Valentine connection." But the major effect of that first printed Valentine was upon me! It changed the way I thought about relating to my life-journey companions.

With my cancer I had stopped identifying with the healthy in the world and I had begun identifying with the wounded and the sick. I saw *myself* in the wheelchair and behind the walkers. I needed to reach out to connect, to affirm, to empathize, to reassure, to "notice," to try to "gladden the heart." It was a profound turning point in my psyche, which I owe to that one particular Valentine.

A Rich Fabric of Meaning

Now I want to tell you about our rainbow wall. Out of the blizzard of paper that moves through our professional lives, I found myself several years ago wanting to save and savor some of the expressions of feeling which from time to time friends, colleagues, relatives and our children send to us—especially those which use in their card-design the symbol of the rainbow which, about a decade ago, we chose as the logo of our Bolton Institute for a Sustainable Future. I began taping some of these letters and cards up on a wall in our living room. That wall now overflows with a visually-rich montage of rainbows and hearts and birds and butterflies and flowers and even faces of our friends.

Then one August, after a National Peace Day march in Concord, Massachusetts in which we had carried Crane Trees made of fifty multicolor origami paper birds, we decided the rainbows of cranes were too beautiful to stow away. Since then they have cantilevered out over our rainbow wall in a cascade of moving, flowing, wind-shimmered, colored birds.

I find now that no matter what my mood, whether up or down, I look at our rainbow wall and I feel immediately woven about with relationships of love and caring. It has become a rich fabric of meaning which delights my eyes, lifts my spirit, and nurtures my heart daily in my living/working space.

"Spring Training" for the Soul

But then again the season turns and we are ready to strip our souls down to the bare necessities of Lent. We are back to the royal and penitential purples.

My search for good purples through the years sometimes has led me in odd directions. One day, shopping in a department store and very tired of my old purple things, I happened upon some gorgeous deep-plum-colored bath towels. I fell in love with them and decided to buy one towel for the center of my dining-room table and buy matching wash-cloths for my napkins.

I proudly decorated the table with my new acquisitions before Lisa, age 8 or 10, came in from school. The route from the back door to the stairs and up to her room, led through our small dining room attached to our kitchen. Lisa stopped, took a long look, and then said,

"Mother—That is a *towel.*"

"Yes, Lisa, I know."

"Mother—Those are wash cloths."

"Yes, Lisa, I know. But aren't they a wonderful plum color?"

"Mother, *nobody* puts towels and washcloths on the dining room table."

"Well, Lisa, they don't now but I suspect I am starting a new trend." She gave me a long look and continued on her way upstairs.

Finding the Right Art for Each Season

For many years we searched for appropriate black-and-white art for our walls. We now have two pieces of art which are so emotionally powerful that we do not want to live with them as icons in our lives for too long a period. One is a large etching of Jesus' head with crown of thorns, by Georges Rouault. The other is Käthe Kollwitz' "Mother searching the battlefield for her dead son." We fill the silence of the black-and-white house with Lenten music. It seems a time of more quiet and meditation, and in our dining room an enlargement of Fritz Eichenberg's "Christ of the Breadline" reminds us of our commitment to justice and bread for the poor, the hungry and homeless "street people."

Celebrating the Breaking-Forth of New Life

After the silence and darkness of Lent comes the bursting forth of Easter. The joy, the liberation, the triumph is all mirrored for us in the born-again quality of nature's resurrection in the coming of springtime.

Inside I find it in the colors of yellow and orange. So these colors radiate from sofa pillows, table covers, and from our walls. A large serigraph by Corita Kent, "Yellow April," focuses the theme in our living area. Guests for Easter dinner bring yellow and orange tulips to fill the house with the rejoicing of flowers. Purcell's Trumpet Voluntary sounds out the season for our ears. At sunrise on Easter day a champagne festival-breakfast gathers friends and family to rejoice together in a liberation celebration. We join at Easter in celebrating newness of life in both our liturgical and our natural seasons.

ELIZABETH DODSON GRAY

The power of changing your home cannot be underestimated. One year, when Easter came very early and the natural spring outside came very late, I overheard in a supermarket line women lamenting the dark, dismal rainy springtime and the lack of colorful flowers. As I listened to them, I wondered why I had not felt those feelings. And then it dawned upon me that our personal family spring had come early with Easter, and our house was filled with the sunshine of yellow flowers and Corita's "Yellow April" and the rejoicing of the "Trumpet Voluntary." My indoor reality had blossomed into light and joy even though the natural reality outside was late in coming. Your senses take in color and sound, and your mood is permeated by those senses. It reminds me of an Easter hanging we use which has the poetry of e.e.cummings:

> I thank You God for
> most this amazing day:
> for the leaping greenly spirits of trees,
> and a blue true dream of sky;
> and everything which is natural
> which is infinite
> which is yes.[3]

After Spring Comes Summer

But what about summer? Ah, summer is different. We do not "paint"—instead we respond!

When Hunter was 18 months old, David and I bought with my money a small house on the water in Connecticut. In Baltimore where I was raised, "by the water" was called "the Eastern shore," so our family always called our house by the water "the shore house." In the summer David could only be there four days a week because he had to be in Westboro for Sunday services and then early in the week for hospital calls, counseling, and church administration. But for three glorious months the kids and I had every day at the shore.

So in the summer we do not "paint" or decorate. We respond to the nuanced moods of the sun and wind and rain. Each morning we wake and can't wait to get to the deck, facing the water, to respond to the invitation of the day. When the sun greets us, we hasten to the beach and the water. When rain pours down, we huddle inside, play Monopoly and toast Somemores. Or sometimes we pile on rain gear and go for a day to the nearby natural history museum.

We are enveloped in the mystery and the wonder of the natural world—the gift of the magical sun, the wind so we can sail our small sailboats, the nurturing rain which refreshes the flowers and the earth.

Summer seems endless to us. It is endless time by the sea—in which to play, to swim, to sail, to explore, to BE! What a gift, what a life, what a dance of companionship with the elements! It is a time of wonder, of renewal. Weekends we have as our guests friends who have children who are compatible with ours. We delight by day in sand and sea, the glimmer of the sun on the water, and the sounds and shouts of children playing. When the kids are bedded down in the evening, we adults ponder what, in the mystery of living, it means to be our age.

On our screened-in porch, in the midst of our circle of young parents, we are accompanied sometimes by the glimmer of the moon on the water and always by the light of a hurricane lamp on the white-and-round dining table. As we compare notes about life, we are resetting our moral compasses.

Summer feels endless to us, each day flowing seamlessly into the next. We are secure in the knowledge that we have three whole months, free of school, free of commuting to schools, free of commitments.

It is a very special time for us, bathed deeply as we are in the rhythms of the natural world. How could I *not* become an eco-feminist?!

Resonating to the Rhythms of Life

Our movement from season to season is a pondering of the presence in our lives of both change and stability. In the natural world we are savoring the changing moods and dimensions of the seasons, which all take place within the stability of God's care. And with our family we are celebrating the changing feelings of love, anger, fear, joy, and tears—all of which happen within the *unchanging* stability of our relationships and our being available for each other.

This celebrating is a way of life, a kind of sacred order repeated over and over in the sacred space we have created in our home. What we experience in our home is a flow of rich images and deep rhythms which surround each day in its uniqueness and difference and undergirds it. Such celebrating helps to open the eyes of the soul to look within the mysteries of the seasons not only of a particular year but within the mysteries of the seasons of our lives. What we are learning to find there is the deep and pervasive presence of God, the Pulse of Life. Then life begins to glow, to light up from within.

We Live in Sacred Time

The passing of the seasons reminds us that we live in sacred time. The movement from the glory of the autumn to the bursting-into-bloom of the spring makes visible the incredible gift of life we participate in on this planet. The high excitement of the celebration of Christmas and Easter contrasts sharply with the somber and subdued times of Advent and Lent. But taken together they form changes of mood which lead us through the passage of each year. The interweaving of the "liturgical seasons" with the "natural seasons" helps us live in both worlds, as they interpenetrate in our human lives.

Painting the seasons sacred has become for us a sacred task, because it helps us embody our gratitude for the gift of life and the gift of time which the Creator of all that is, has given us.

NOTES

1. For a book-length treatment of the "theology of seasons," see Elizabeth and David Dodson Gray, *Children of Joy: Raising Your Own Home-Grown Christians* (Wellesley, Mass.: Roundtable Press, 1975).

2. Henri F. Amiel, 19th-century Swiss philosopher.

3. e.e.cummings, *Complete Poems 1904–1962,* ed. George J. Firmage (New York: Liveright Publishing, 1994), p. 663.

12.

Color:
A Meditation on
Our Daughter Lisa

—May 30, 2008—

12.

Color: A Meditation on Our Daughter Lisa

May 30, 2008

Color As A Way of Perceiving Life

She was in the back seat as we traveled. She was five and she was playing with an "Etch-a-Sketch" erasable sketch pad, and, as five-year-olds do, she drew a stick figure. She looked at it for a long time, erased it, and never drew another stick figure.

Instead she reached for her crayons and a blank piece of paper, and she began drawing horizontal bands of colors, different colors, across the page. I remember this because she began asking me, "What color should be next?" She questioned from a deep urgency as she struggled to discern what color should be next.

Color became for Lisa a major prism through which she viewed her life. Her primary family relationships came for her in colors. Mom was yellow, Dad was green, she was pink, Hunter was blue, and Mrs. Thayer was purple.

Lisa became passionate about colors. Colors "spoke" to her, and she matched them up with people and experiences. No one else named people in color, but Lisa did. And her choices of color were deeply intuitive and quite correct.

As Lisa grew up, everything had to match. Hair ribbons, turtlenecks, striped socks—everything. In high school, when everyone absolutely had to wear blue jeans, Lisa matched the colors of every item of clothing which was not a blue jean. Even the many colors in a striped turtleneck (all the fashion) had to match the colors in the striped socks (equally "in") and the color of the hair ribbon on her pony tail. It was her way not only of "seeing" the world, it was her way of expressing herself in that world.

Precocious and Easily Bored

She had always been a bright and precocious child. She bored easily, and she had to be constantly involved and challenged. I remember when I was pushing her stroller, she wouldn't even let me read a book. I had to gaze devotedly down at her while I walked and I pushed.

When she was a nine-month-old and just crawling, I "bought" myself fifteen minutes to do the breakfast dishes by stringing a path of interesting "objects" on the floor and under tables and chairs from her bedroom to the kitchen. When she got to the kitchen, if I was lucky, I had finished the dishes and was ready to gather her up for our all-morning walk.

She learned language early and would use it delightfully. I remember at age nearly three when she astonished two older ladies at a Thanksgiving service by standing up on the pew cushion and singing (perfectly) the first stanza of "Come, Ye Thankful People, Come." And she dismayed a lady at the Christian bookstore in Advent when Lisa answered the lady's nice question about what she wanted from Santa, by asking "Who is Santa?" (We didn't teach Santa to our children; Christmas was Jesus' birthday.)

But it was color, not words, that she was passionate about. She was not an artist or painter, so clothes became her paint and her canvas. They were what she chose to use to express to the world her dynamism, her energy, her moods, her sense of beauty.

Life Filled to "Over-Full"

Boredom was her threat, and when she was old enough to make her own decisions about time, she always chose to fill her time "over-full." As a junior in her private high school, she was taking five honors courses (her classmates took one or perhaps two). She also had a part in the play, a place on the field-hockey team, and a week-end boy-friend in Connecticut.

She was adamant that she wanted all of this in her life and she refused her teachers' attempts to convince her otherwise. She had no intention of "trimming down" her life. We often likened her life to a girl riding a bicycle on a tightrope, holding a parasol in one hand, and balancing with the other.

But since our view of child-rearing was not to "shape" them into our preferred image of them, but to support them as they emerged into their own unique genetic possibility, we did not discourage her from living out the lifestyle she was choosing for herself.

I remember once in Washington, D.C., when we were there professionally, Lisa called from home at 10:00PM. She was a high-school junior, and she wanted my advice on "prioritizing" her next several hours. She had to study for a test, and do something else urgent and important (which I have forgotten), and bake a home-made birthday cake for a good friend. She resisted my suggestion that she buy the cake at the store the next morning; she *had* to bake it herself for this best friend!

ELIZABETH DODSON GRAY

Learning to Speak Lisa's Language of Color

Lisa's passion for color was not only a compelling theme in her life—as well as a way of expressing herself in her world. Finally color, with all its vibrancy and nuances, came to symbolize Lisa for us.

Color is alive. It actually comes "at you" in bright colors, and it retreats "away from you" in dark colors. Color can be nuanced into delicately different shades of aqua and turquoise and sea foam, just as there are many shades and intensities of black.

David felt finally that he had to learn the "language of color" so he could take part in phone conversations with Liz and Lisa when they were talking about the intricacy of distinguishing and "naming" distinct and subtle variations in color.

I think Lisa's absorption in and fascination with color helped us perceive and appreciate her "emerging genetic personality." As she expressed that emerging personality in her own style of vibrant color and living life to the "over-full," we were made powerfully aware of her absolute uniqueness, and that our job as parents was not to shape but to support that emerging dynamic person which was—and is—Lisa.

13.

Motion:
A Meditation on
Our Son Hunter

—2008—

13.

Motion: A Meditation on Our Son Hunter

2008

Reveling in Constant Motion

He was always most happy when he was moving his body. When we went to any park, he rushed to the climbers, ignoring the swings. He needed to use his legs to climb. As a toddler he learned how to bounce his highchair across the floor. On walks he ran out ahead.

Until we invested in a wooden climber which could also fold up to store, Hunter climbed the chairs and tables of our living and dining rooms. The climber was a four-foot cube of ladder-like rungs. It had a door and a window-opening, suggesting it be used also as a playhouse. It came with a six-foot slide to hang off any top rung. There were also two boards (four-foot-by- two-foot) which could be put in place to make a top-layer (or a middle-layer, or into half-layers at the middle and the top).

We put this climber in one whole end of our living room as a gift for him but also for us. The climber became the constant outlet for his prodigious energy and need to move his muscles.

He would watch "Captain Kangeroo" on the TV while climbing *up* the slide with a rope he had installed himself at the top of the climber. With its plank-boards inside the cube-climber, the climber became a house, or a church (his father was a minister), or a school, or a fire station.

I remember at age four his "fireman" birthday party with pre-school and neighborhood friends. All of the six kids climbed on the "fire house" wearing red-plastic fireman's hats and for their fire hose they used the long tube from our cannister vacuum. That climber stayed in our living room until we moved when Hunter was ten.

ELIZABETH DODSON GRAY

Getting Out Ahead

Hunter had a way of "getting out ahead" of a situation. Once I remember teaching his Sunday School kindergarten class when we were sitting nicely lined up in chairs, pretending to be flying over Africa on a "missionary journey." All the other kids were cooperating nicely in the fantasy, dutifully looking out of imaginary windows at the ground below. Suddenly Hunter shouted "Geronimo" and "bailed out" of the airplane!

I also remember, in that same year, when I was leading the class on an imaginary "Lion Hunt" in which you move through imaginary tall grass, over a bridge (accompanied by appropriate sounds and gestures), until you discover the eyes of a lion staring at you in the dark cave. You scream, and RUN, retracing your steps over the bridge and through the tall grass (complete with sounds and gestures).

Now I had led this "exercise" many times, with adults and children of many ages, and I had never experienced what happened next. Seconds after we screamed and started running, Hunter shouted, "Boom, I shot him!"

Of course, we would have had guns with us, and of course someone could always have shot the lion. But no one before had ever thought to do that!

Living for His Sports

As he grew older, his moving legs led him to love sports and excel in them. He needed to run but he had an athlete's "toeing-inward" which we spent months trying to "fix" with orthopedic shoes. The orthopedist finally said, "Well, most good athletes don't walk straight either." Hunter played soccer, hockey, and lacrosse and literally "lived" for his sports.

I despaired of getting him to read and enjoy reading, until I watched him avidly reading the sports page during our early morning drive to his private school half-an-hour away from our home, and I realized that he would devour every sports book I gave him, which he did!

His passion finally settled on hockey. When Lisa discovered at age eight that all of her friends could ice skate and she couldn't, we sent her to a figure-skating class. Hunter got to "tag along," so at age five he learned to figure skate and he loved it! He learned to skate backwards as fast as he could skate forwards—an ability which later gave him an amazing competitive "edge" when he skated defense for Deerfield Academy and he could skate backwards as fast as the charging forward could skate towards him. He therefore never had to turn around, and so his prowess in preventing goals by other teams was truly awesome.

I will never forget the evening when Hunter in fourth grade was trying out for our town's junior hockey team. Because he went to school out-of-town, and nobody knew what he could do, he was put in a very low group to try out. The coach lined up all the boys on the ice and then he skated down the ice and told the boys to skate towards him until he blew a whistle—and then stop. Hunter executed a beautiful figure-skating stop, and looked around in amazement to find that everyone else had resorted to "falling down" in order to stop. The coach made Hunter his star forward, which of course Hunter loved.

I will also never forget how one morning a week all winter the whole family had to rise up at 5:00AM in order to be at the hockey rink half-an-hour away by 6:00AM for Hunter's weekly practice time with his town-team. Lisa huddled in the back seat of our car beneath quilts and tried to sleep while David and I warmed up with hot coffee and cocoa before we had to drive an hour in the opposite direction, past our home, to their schools for 8:15 and 8:30 opening bells. It was difficult for the rest of us, but Hunter was *so* happy that it was worth it for us all.

I also remember a fabulous birthday party when he was in fifth grade. We rented an entire hockey rink for an afternoon time, so Hunter and his pals could play hockey on a real rink for an hour. At the end of that hour David took a picture of Hunter in his Bruins shirt and hockey helmet, looking so exhausted that he was closing his eyes even as David photographed, but with an ecstatic smile on his exhausted face!

What Price Hockey?

I can remember Hunter in seventh and eighth grade attending Fessenden School and people asking us why we spent money to send Hunter to a private school. I remember replying "Would you believe we do it because Hunter can spend two hours every day on the school's hockey rink?"

I knew hockey made Hunter happy, as nothing else in his life did. I also knew that *if* he was happy, he would make good decisions about his life, including decisions about drinking and drugs and cigarettes. And that has proved to be true.

So Hunter's need to "move" opened up a pathway before Hunter that he was thrilled to walk—or should I say *run* and *skate*. But the thrill for his parents was to watch how graceful he was "in motion," whether running in soccer and lacrosse or skating in hockey. He had some of the grace of a Michael Jordan, some of the dedication of a Tiger Woods.

He was passionate about what he loved, and it gave meaning to the rest of his life, including the school work which he tolerated, and only studied enough to keep his athletic options at Deerfield and at the University of Vermont. It was a privilege for us to discover his "yellow brick road" and to help him walk in it. The terrible fork in the road for him was when he realized that he was not good enough to play professional hockey. But that is another whole story.

14.

Raising a Non-Sexist Son

—Mop and Glo Ads Are Not for Women Only—

An article in *Parents Together: A Newsletter for Parents of Adolescents* (Greenwich CT), 1988

14.

Raising a Non-Sexist Son

—Mop and Glo Ads Are Not for Women Only—

An article in Parents Together: A Newsletter
for Parents of Adolescents
(Greenwich CT), 1988

The Good Work

I have a favorite cartoon which summarizes for me some of the issues in rearing a non-sexist son. In the cartoon the mother is vacuuming as the eight-year-old boy passes by on his way outside to play baseball. Tossing his baseball in the air and casually catching it in his mitt, he speaks to his house-cleaning Mom in immortal words as he passes by: "Keep up the good work, Mom!"

There you have it. Mothers work to remove dirt, while boys (who will grow up to be non-housecleaning men) play! And they exhort their mothers to continue their good (women's) work.

It is no accident that when boys attain the ripe old age of 18, and have never been asked to scrub a floor, dust and vacuum, or scrub the inside of a toilet or tub, they understand at some deep level that they are "privileged persons." They intuit that they belong to a superior caste of humans for whom *someone else* will always remove the dirt. It is clear to me that children of both sexes at a very young age understand the power implications when Dad brings home the money (which is highly valued in our culture) and Mother (or some other woman) removes the dirt.

Raising Boys

So what does all this mean for raising boys? Well, I can only tell you my experience at this. We have two children, a daughter Lisa who is three-and-a-half years older than our son Hunter. When Hunter was about ten I attended an academic lecture late one afternoon at Harvard Divinity School.

During the question period following the lecture a surprising question was asked about how the speaker and her husband handled the housekeeping chores. This evoked from her a story of family conferences to distribute chores evenly between not only the parents but also the children.

I'm sure I was not the only attendee who charged home to implement this great new idea! My husband and I have always shared the chores: I cook while he does the cleanup, I dust while he vacuums, we both shop for food. We had both roared with laughter when Hunter, then newly walking at nine months, had staggered around brandishing the long metal tube from the vacuum cleaner, imitating his father. "Wait until he discovers that the vacuum cleaner tube is *not* a symbol of male virility in this culture!" we said to one another. But despite this, we had *never* thought of expecting our kids, now ten and 13, to *share* the chores!

So we did as that speaker suggested. We sat around the table together and drew up a list of all the chores: daily, weekly, monthly, whenever. Then we all spoke up for what we *wanted* to do, and then we distributed what remained between the four of us. And we set up a rotation system so no one would get stuck forever with something they really hated.

I'll never forget the day when Hunter came in with real dismay and "new learning" in his voice and said, "They're *all* terrible! When you and Dad or Lisa were doing a chore, I figured it had to be more pleasant than what I was doing. But they're all terrible!" I am afraid I responded in real amazement: "You mean you didn't know that?"

We tried to be casual at first about quality control. I remember the time I found Hunter doing his first dinner dishes. He was dipping the dishes with one hand into icy cold water. When I said the water had to be hot, and soap was necessary, and how about using two hands, he said very seriously, "Oh, I didn't know that."

From then on I tried to imagine, as best I could, the mental context of "no idea about how to do anything" which he brought to housecleaning. From that starting point I would try to come up with very basic directions before he did something new. Sometimes this earned me a scornful, "Oh Mother, I knew *that!*" But other times I am sure that it helped.

Uncovering the Male Cinderella Complex

I also remember the day Hunter scrubbed his first kitchen floor. He had a friend visiting for the day so they were both down on their knees pushing a soapy scrub brush back and forth when Hunter turned to his friend and said seriously, "I don't know about you, but I feel like Cinderella."

Now that was a wonderful comment, because Cinderella is the heroine who is only cleaning the hearth because her wicked stepmother is being mean to her. She is really *not* supposed to have to do that sort of thing, and she would not have to if her *real* mother and father were functioning properly.

You can see that progress had been made in Hunter's consciousness when he asked us several weeks later to buy "Mop and Glow" when we next went to the supermarket. When he had recently seen a "Mop And Glow" commercial on television, he had not seen the ad as addressed to some faceless army of scrubbing mothers or women. *Now* that ad was addressed to him, and he wanted to claim whatever help there was in a new product *for himself.* He now saw himself in the cleaning role—a major step forward.

And then there were the months when every time he settled in to do his bit of housecleaning, he complained—which elicited my "Feminist mothers of the world, unite" speech. He finally said, "Mother, please don't give me that speech any more." And I said, "I won't, if you stop complaining!" So we made a pact.

Making It to Home-Plate

Finally, about a year later, we reached what I considered "home plate." He knew how to do all the housecleaning work, he could do his share quickly, without speeches of victimization, and without reminders of when it had to be done, and without outside quality control. We had made it "home."

What had we gained by all this? In addition to a lot of help for ourselves during busy years when our children were teenagers, I feel we had done something important for our son. Without our daughter Lisa's even sharing in the family chores, the culture and women's role in it would have made sure she knew how to do housecleaning. But the culture by itself will never do that for a young man.

We had made it possible for Hunter to enter adulthood as a liberated male. If he did not marry (or until he married), he could occupy his own living space without trauma. He could marry a woman and not expect her to remove all his dirt. In his gut he knows that these chores are not gender-specific, that "Mop And Glow" cans do not have only female names on them. His sense of virility and masculinity will never rise and fall on who is doing the cooking or cleaning. And I think, *I know,* this is a great gift to him.

Hunter is 26 and married now, to a wonderful professional woman. They are both gifted athletes and live in Park City, Utah, in order to ski while they earn their livings. I know Hunter cooks more than Sherry does, and I never hear them discuss the chores, so I guess they are not an issue. And that in itself is a triumph, I think, for a couple. The chores should not be all done by women, or by parents, and they need not even be an issue—of power, of control, or of oppression.

After all, it is only dirt!

15.

Grieving My Mothering Self

—Mothers Day 1979—

15.

Grieving My Mothering Self

Mothers' Day 1979

I woke up alone in the strange room and was still deeply into the throbbing feelings of my dream. In the dream I was angry and crying, hitting at my daughter who had mutilated a beloved object and screaming at her: "You took things from me and never even asked!"

I lay on the bed with those hurt, angry feelings still resonating inside me, and I realized that I had been having a Mothers' Day dream.

After Twenty Years, Mothers' Day

It was Mothers' Day and parents' weekend at our son's boarding school. My son, reminded by his father, had dutifully produced a card signed: "Love, your son." That was an improvement on last year when he'd been too busy to purchase a card conveniently available at the school store.

Our daughter was hurriedly packing up her belongings after exams. It was the end of her Junior year at Smith College (which is where I also went to college), and she had to be out of her room by a deadline. I knew that nevertheless sometime today she would also have at least a card for me. She always cared about such things even when it was a busy time in the schedule of school or college. It really wasn't their fault that there wasn't much space for long celebrations of Mothers' Day.

But in that strange stripped-down guest room in her college dorm into which I had awakened from my dream, I started crying again, this time wide awake.

I was crying for myself, my mothering self. I was crying for all that those years of mothering effort had meant. Did they know? Could they ever guess what the time and energy and concern invested in mothering them had cost me?

139

ELIZABETH DODSON GRAY

Motherhood and Social Convention

I suddenly didn't know whether I hated more the absurdity of the cultural ritual of Mothers' Day, or the terrible fact that without that one day's mock bow toward motherhood, the culture would never even notice the "service" of mothering at all.

It is the social conventions that lock us into "the women's room," as Marilyn French was saying the other night at a Radcliffe lecture. What social convention is more powerful than that all-compelling assumption that children are the responsibility of the mother?

How I had hated the social dictum that prescribed that *I as a woman* must give up my professional career so that *we as a couple* could have children. It never seemed fair to me that on top of the burden of pregnancy and childbirth now it was mine alone to renounce my career and ministry so that we could have children. Always the cost was mine, even though the benefit was to us both.

Convention dictated it. And my kind, but culturally- conditioned husband, accepted the convention. He accepted the gift of those years of my life as something due him by the nature of things. "Accepted"—that's what got to me. Everyone accepted. My culture, my husband, my children—all accepted without question that the cost was mine. It was as I shouted in my dream: "You took from me, and never even asked me!" My acquiescence was assumed. That's how life has been for women.

And Nobody Knows

My obedience to conventions had been assumed. Now on my twentieth-anniversary Mothers' Day, how could anyone possibly know what that mothering had cost me?

My husband, eyes blinded by convention, had had a hard time taking seriously the pain of my experience. How then, could he now understand what my mothering had cost me? Our children don't remember anything except the recent years. They don't remember the crying, the teething, the sleeplessness, the boredom, the strained patience, the feelings of being caught in a Never-Never Land that would never end. The appreciation expressed in their cards on Mothers' Day came only from the recent years they do remember.

But the mothering of the recent years is such a small part of what I have invested. How, I asked myself, was it that nobody knew the real cost? How was it possible on Mothers' Day that nobody really cared what it had meant to me to do the mothering all those years?

They Think Mothering Comes Naturally to Women

I looked across the room at the red cardboard cupids someone had stuck onto the bare dormitory wall by an unshaded light bulb. Then I looked at the faded red streamer running across the ceiling from corner to corner. Wistful remnants of some old Valentine's party, I thought. They seemed like harlequin reminders of the illusions of romance that, pied-piper-like, lead women into marriage and family, only to vanish like the dew in the dailyness of diapers and kitchen table and dirty floors.

What a crazy place to wake on Mothers' Day, I thought.

How could nobody know? I asked. How could nobody really care about all the pain and sacrifice of self that went into my twenty years of mothering? Marilyn French had said women's work couldn't be taken seriously by our culture and that you couldn't write seriously about it. So too with mothering, I thought. There's no way to write about all that pain of sacrificed self.

Husbands, people, society, couldn't believe it. You must be a terrible person, an unnatural mother, to be saying or feeling such things. They all think mothering comes naturally to women. *And because there is nothing else for women to do, then in all those years of mothering there could be no sacrifice of other identities. To other people mothers seem to have no other identity.*

The Twenty-Year Ache
What did they know or care of the pain of talent unexpressed for years? Of sermons and speeches not given, insights never shared, writing and thinking never done, creativity never expressed? What did anyone know or care of the ache for what might have been?

Now they wanted to sum all that up with one Mothers' Day card. Twenty years of that ache captured in the saccharine verse and pale flowers—and they wonder why you cry.

You're crying for yourself and for your mothering friends, now newly divorced by their husbands in mid-life crises. You are crying for all those dutiful women who followed apple blossoms down the aisle and now wonder who they are when they're not being wife and mother.

Motherhood demands losing yourself, pouring yourself out in twenty-four-hour-a-day concern. And so you give until you've forgotten how to imagine an identity of your own. And then suddenly you find that you've become the Devouring Jewish Mother who can't let go. What a cruel trick to program women to have the control button stuck on *Give*—and then suddenly in teenage to change all the rules and demand that mothers take their hands off and pull away from the children they've invested so much in.

The Invisibility of All You've Done
Take your hands off and go elsewhere, they say. Elsewhere? Where is there to go?

Go into a working world that's gotten along for twenty years quite nicely without you? Into a society that insists mothers have not "worked" in twenty years or acquired any skills? Into a society that has giant cadres of economic second-class citizens known as secretaries, store clerks, and the like? Go—go where?

Go anywhere, they say. But turn off that mothering switch because we don't need you any more.

I wept for all of us who had mothered at great cost to ourselves, and who now were remembered on Mothers' Day, with a card.

16.

A Feminist Meditation on Motherhood

Mother's Day Sermon,

Brookline Unitarian Church
1983, revised 2010

16.

A Feminist Meditation on Motherhood

Mother's Day Sermon, Brookline Unitarian Church 1983, revised 2010

Lullaby: "Lullaby and goodnight, save some fun for tomorrow"
On November 23rd, 1958 my daughter Lisa was born. I remember singing lullabies to her, as I rocked her to sleep in our newly-purchased maple rocking chair. I was older (28) and I was trained as a minister when we were married, but the decision to have children was not considered and thought out as it is today. It was automatic: "Of course we wanted children!—probably six," we planned on our honeymoon. But with a little more caution I decided we would have them one-at-a-time, and we would rethink that decision as we went along.

Lullaby Written to Lisa

> *Little love, little love, little Lisa-love, (2x)*
> *Little Lisa Gray, O little Lisa Gray.*
>
> *I want a little kiss from my littlest Miss, (2x)*
> *Little Lisa Gray, O little Lisa Gray*
>
> *I want a little hug from my little love bug, (2x)*
> *Little Lisa Gray, O little Lisa Gray*
>
> *I want a little cuddle from my little snuggle-buggle (2x)*
> *Little Lisa Gray, O little Lisa Gray*

The last verse always made her giggle!
Two-and-a-half years after Lisa we planned another baby. Lisa and I were "growing babies in our tummies together," she decided.

Then I had a miscarriage, and I cried for three straight days, in the midst of which Lisa said, "But Mommie, don't cry! I'll give you mine when it pops out:" Which, of course, made me cry all the harder!

Lullaby written to Hunter

Hunter-Bunter, he's our boy. He and Lisa are our joy.

About a year after that I did have another child, a boy we named Hunter. We were amazed when my husband's mother said, "How wonderful you have both sexes. Now you can stop." We wanted at least another child. But you'll remember I had said I'd decide one-at-a-time. Well, our son Hunter finally slept through the night for the first time when he was two-and-a-half. We've often laughed and said Hunter accomplished the ultimate in sibling rivalry: he eliminated all the siblings who might have followed him.

What Do I Say about Motherhood in Those Years?

I had chosen it freely—I thought. But I was far more coerced by internalized social expectation than I thought. I did wonder (and resent) why I was expected to give up my professional vocation of ministry (with all the heartbreak and psychic denial which that giving-up involved) in order to rear "our" children 24-hours-a-day—and my husband was not!

Motherhood itself I found exhilarating and exhausting. Deeply demanding of patience and nurturing. Deeply satisfying at many moments of incredible closeness between mother and child. And deeply boring in its thousands of moments of trivia and routine. And deeply demanding of the sacrifice of self on the part of the mother.

Now I am older. I'm not sure I'm wiser, but these are my latest reflections on the gender-dimensions of the cultural institution of motherhood.

The High Cost of Parenting

I now see that *in this culture women alone pay the high personal cost of parenting.* Men feel they have the God-given right to conceive children and have women bring them up for them. A recent study shows that the average father parents each child a total of 8 minutes each day.

It is women who do the work of socializing children not to electrocute themselves around the house and not to get run over by cars in the street. Women do the social work of raising children not to be ambulatory variables but to fit into society. It is women who teach children their first language and how to eat, how to smile, how to respond, how to play, how to sing, how and where to go to the bathroom, how to please and why to care about pleasing.

In short, it is women who teach all of us *first* about intimacy and relationship.

ELIZABETH DODSON GRAY

The Invisible Is Not Valued

This societal work of motherhood is so invisible it is taken for granted. It is unpaid; it doesn't count in the GNP. *It is not even called work.* "When did you start working?" they ask you, when you reenter the "workforce."

I was reading John Naisbitt's book *Megatrends,* about "the ten new directions transforming our lives." I was startled to note that even as he discusses women joining the labor force in ever greater numbers, he still assumes that somehow women are going, nonetheless, to continue this invisible work of mothering the next generation. He says more women are working, going to college, studying law, medicine, starting new businesses, and having children later. *But Naisbitt never discusses—anywhere—the problem of child-care.* If women are doing all these things, who will raise the children? Will men?

Naisbitt assumes, apparently, women will continue to perform this deeply-taken-for-granted function, even when women are also doing other things. And society seems to have no intention of helping women out in significant ways. Women doing their own child-care is assumed. It is assumed in the same way we have assumed free air and free water.

We Will Never Know . . .

We do not mourn what mothers might have contributed to the culture if they had not poured their lives into motherhood. One of us might have been another Gandhi, or another Martin Luther King, Jr. We might have led the world out of war; as Randy Forsberg and Helen Caldicott are trying now to do.

We do not mourn the symphonies that were not written, the art that was not painted, the poems never written, the architecture and drama and sculpture never brought to fruition, the social policy never shaped by those women. All this we do not mourn.

The On-and-Off Switch

Then there is the on-and-off-switch syndrome. "We need you! Turn yourself on!" David Suskind once said, "Men are takers and women are givers, and I'm glad I'm a taker." So turn yourself on, givers. We are ready for the good cooking and the clean floors and the laundry done. We are ready for apple pie and Mom's kisses and cuddles. Who else will teach America's children the proper values? Be sure to be there with cookies and milk after school, and carpool to music lessons. Don't forget the PTA and Brownie troop. Don't forget the dentist and the doctor's checkup. Pour the Kool-Aid and supervise the hose in the summer. Mom, we need you. Who else will teach the girls to be girls and the boys to be boys?

But later on, Mom, let's remember how old your children now are. Let's not be one of those castrating mothers who won't let their boys grow up to be Men. Let's not hover over them like the stereotypic Jewish mother who never fades away. Of course, Mom, it's your fault if they're on drugs or on police records. Not enough of the right mothering, everyone says. Nobody ever suggests that it might be for the lack of right fathering.

Find the off-switch, mother. No one needs your giving any more.

I find that I get very angry at this societal demand that I as woman/ mother be turned on—and turned off! I am expected to turn my life inside out to care for others when nobody else wants to do it. And then all of us mothers are later expected to turn all that caring *off*, on cue, and find something else to do with the personality that often now knows no other identity beyond nurturing.

At this point I had it easy. I did have difficulty learning the "being" mode after graduate school and a professional life of "achieving." But for me, sliding back into a professional career was like putting on old familiar clothes.

But for millions of women that is not the case, and we have called them "displaced homemakers"—displaced from home by children growing up. Sometimes they are displaced by divorce. And sometimes by the death of a spouse. And what of the millions of women who are single parents, who struggle for endless hours each day both to earn the daily bread and also to parent. And most of them get the low wages paid to women in this culture.

These women and their children are now the fastest growing part of the new poor. The *"feminization of poverty"* we are now calling it. Studies show that the biggest loss for children of divorce is not the loss of the father's love and presence but loss of the father's income. I have a lapel button which reads: *"Sexism rewards motherhood with poverty."*

Sexism Rewards Motherhood with a Card

Sexism also rewards motherhood with a Mothers Day card and a plant. Twenty years of my life—for a Mothers Day card? Twenty years of my life to hear that tone of voice saying: "Oh Mother, stop worrying." "Oh Mother, stop clinging." "Oh Mother, stop caring."

Society rewards motherhood with that awful mixture of saccharin and hostility which the image of "Mother" evokes in our society. Only the image of mother-in-law is worse. "You're so dear to me, Mother"—when you do what I want. When you don't get in my way. When you are independent and not a drag on me in your old age. How come you live so long in your nursing home, and expect me to visit you when I'm so busy? Don't you know that you're not supposed to expect anything from me, now that I don't need you any more?

To all of us who are children I want to cry out: Have you heard about elderly abuse? Have you heard about homeless old women? Have you heard about "bag ladies" who have become invisible to us?

Socializing Your Daughter into Fear

The final irony is that in a patriarchal society motherhood means socializing your children to live in a society which hates women. By that I mean, ours is a society that constantly subjects women of all ages to battering, rape, gang rape, incest, pornography, sexual trafficking and the pervasive threat of physical and sexual violence.

It was another Mothers Day, at Battell Chapel at Yale, that I got up at the concerns time to protest my anguish that my daughter the previous afternoon had been freaked out as a fifteen-year-old by a radio account of a girl her age who had been raped, sprayed with lighter fluid, and set on fire.

I found I was very angry that I had to socialize my daughter to be paranoid about the possibility of being raped, in order to try to protect herself against that experience.

Do you know what it does to a mother to have to socialize her daughter constantly to fear being raped? I feel like a Chinese mother of old who is binding her daughter's feet so that she might someday be married.

Susan Brownmiller in her book *Against Our Will* says that we socialize our women to be victims. Question: Do we, as she also suggests, socialize our boys to victimize? To rape? Or do we only socialize them to expect someone, Mother or Wife, to devote their lives to male well-being?

Dorothy Dinnerstein calls this phenomenon "live female will in captivity." Is that what our daughters are growing up into? These are hard and disturbing questions about how we socialize our children. But these questions must be faced.

What do I make of all this?

We Could Change the Shape of Parenting

Parenthood is a deeply meaningful relationship and commitment. But within patriarchy we have distorted the female form of parenthood—motherhood—all out of shape by the too-heavy demands placed upon it. We have said to women, "It's all your responsibility, Mother." We have said, "Do Motherhood one-hundred-percent of your time with no respite, no days off or nights off, and no vacations."

Now I want to tell you that there's no way that such psychological overload as that will not nearly destroy both mothers and children.

There has to be a better way to live out what is obviously a necessary and deeply satisfying mode of human existence. Perhaps we can all repent of the past. Perhaps we can join together, as both males and females, and perhaps we can find a better way really to *co*-parent our children as mothers and fathers together, in real mutuality—so that men can learn "being"[2] half-time and women can be free to "achieve" half-time. As one who has been and is a wife and mother and daughter, I devoutly hope so, because it will be much better not only for women but for men—and most of all better for our children, who need a balance of achieving mothers and "being" fathers in their lives even more than they need milk and doctor's checkups.

Lullaby: "Go to sleepy, little baby"

Whether parents remain together in marriage or not, children need fathers' attention, love and financial support. *Evidence is mounting that boys who do not have significant fathering, especially in their early years, feel insecure about their masculine identification.* And women who receive inadequate fathering have emotional needs which distort their adult living.

Society Needs to Parent

Beyond the so-called nuclear family of Mom, Dad and two kids, we need to expand our parenting to new extended-family groupings. Single parents, non-parents, good friends, multi-generational groupings, are choosing to live together in households which provide to children a wider circle of parenting relationships.

---

[2] See chapter 36 for a full discussion of "being."

Even beyond these wider parenting groups, we must expect our *society* to parent—and stop leaving it all to Mom. Nurturing children is a serious and wonder-full business. But it is not God-given only to women.

If we take seriously the vulnerability and also the possibility of the next generation, our whole culture will nurture its children. This is certainly *not* happening now.

How could single-parent women and children be the rapidly increasing-bulk of our poverty population, if we really cared about our children, not to mention our. women?

How could many of our divorced men be permitted by the culture to avoid their child-care payments, if we as a culture really cared about our children or about the single-parent women who struggle to support those children on women's low-paying jobs?

Society must care about adequate and equal wages for working women, because many of these women are the only support for children. We must demolish this idealized image of the breadwinner father and come to grips with the reality of what-is in our culture. And that means seeing women as breadwinners also, and paying those women as the sole-breadwinners which, in many families, they are. Society must also care about day-care centers for children of those working mothers.

Society must listen, pay attention, and stop child-pornography, pedophilia, child-abuse, child-incest, and child-rape. How can we say we care about children when we duck these dark realities in many children's lives?

In today's society, the threat of violence hangs heavy over our children—from the threat of nuclear war to the imminent possibility of drive-by killing or street violence among teenage gangs. If we cared about children, if as a society we *parented* our children (instead of leaving it all to Mom), could we not do better than this?

Sometimes I feel that Mothers Day itself is a giant "con" to get mothers to do what our society refuses to do—namely, *care* about our children.

So on Mothers Day I feel like saying, "Forget the cards and flowers, folks. Forget the pedestal for good old Mom. Forget the sweet talk and give me some good solid legislation which cares about women and children.

I'll take the passage of the Equal Rights Amendment to the U.S. Constitution for a Mothers Day Remembrance. I'll take legislation which adequately finances day-care centers and rape-crisis centers. I'll take the nuclear freeze and a war-free world for my children for Mothers Day. .

Instead of flowers this year I'd like to see thousands of "Men Against Rape" groups. I want financial support for mothers and children in poverty. I'd like national legislation which will make it impossible for men to flee their payments for child-care by disappearing across state lines.

So—don't pacify me with flowers and verse. Don't tell me how much you love women who are nurturing. I'm tired of "words, words, words" on Mothers Day. I want you—men and society—to care about women and children *every day* of the year. Stop the rape of women. Stop the battering of women inside marriage. Eliminate the so-called "feminization of poverty." Stop the child-pornography!

And then you can try me on a Mothers Day card. Then— and only then—I might believe you, and not choke on my card.

ELIZABETH DODSON GRAY

In this season of hearts, we offer to you new prayers for our hearts, prayers which understand and affirm women. May they bring you new ways of blessing the gracious and nurturing mystery of the universe.
With love, Liz & David   *(2005)*

Mothers Day Prayers
by the Rev. Thomas McKibbens, 2002
First Baptist Church, Newton Centre, MA

ADORATION

O Great Mother of the Universe, who birthed us into being and has nurtured us along the way; you have guided us in right paths; you have warned us when we have strayed, taught us when we were perplexed, and blessed us throughout our days.

PRAYERS OF THE PEOPLE

Holy God, your labor gave birth to a universe, and we now focus our minds and hearts on the deep need to express thanks for the myriad ways you have nurtured us through the years.

Today we thank you for all those who nursed and cuddled us, who kissed our hearts and helped us find our wings.

Thank you for those who loved us when we rebelled and thus showed us the meaning of faithfulness.

Thank you for those who expected great things from us and so helped us discover our strengths.

Thank you for those who showed us how to pray and thus helped us to know how to trust.

We thank you for those who did the best they knew how, even if we wish they had done differently.

For all the mothers and mother-figures in our lives, we pause to give thanks. Through Jesus Christ our Lord.

Gentle God, we pray today for those who are trying to have children but cannot. Thank you for the abundance of love you have poured into their hearts.

Direct their steps to someone who needs that love as desperately as they need to give it.

God of strength, we pray for those who are frustrated and exasperated with being parents. Give them patience and discernment to see the unique treasures of growing children and the wisdom to nurture wholeness in a complicated world.

We pray for those working mothers who struggle with the demands of their professions and the love of their families.

Be especially near to those who must raise their children alone, giving them extra measures of stamina and humor, that both they and their children will be whole.

Bless those who have chosen *not* to have children and to direct their love and commitment to other worthy ends, and who find fulfillment in other loves.

Finally, we pray for mothers we name silently in our hearts. . . .

Help us all, dear God, to become bearers of your redeeming love to all the young lives we touch, to all those who are our children by affection or by birth.

Help us as a church to raise our children with a firm foundation of healthy faith, so that in them the world may see the strong and tender love with which you, O God, have loved us from the beginning. Amen.

BENEDICTION
Go in peace, and may the blessing, power, and peace of God, cosmic creator, ascended Christ, and enabling Spirit, be upon you always. Amen.

17.

Choosing the Family You Want

TOP Lecture November 9, 1995

17.

Choosing the Family You Want

TOP Lecture, November 9, 1995

Choosing Family beyond Blood-Family

It was a party at our house when our daughter Lisa was seven, but it was not a birthday party. It was a "choose your own godmother" party, and Lisa had chosen her beloved first-grade teacher of the previous year, Mrs. Castellani, and a dear family friend, Polly Marquis. Lisa already had two "official" godmothers from her baptism seven years before in St. Louis where she was born. But she had not seen them for years, and it had occurred to us that perhaps she needed to choose two more godmothers who lived close to us and were therefore more accessible for a real relationship.

We may have gotten this idea of "chosen godparents" from the fact that my husband David had at age 12 chosen his two godfathers from among his family's best male friends, all because David had not been baptized as a baby. Those two chosen godfathers, Karl Jones and Tom Johnson, had been very important male figures in David's teenage and young-adult life, even though his own father was also "on the scene" in those years. It had seemed to David really neat to choose these special adult figures for himself, so perhaps this is how we got the idea of Lisa having a similar experience. There is an 8x10 picture of Lisa at that party, with Mrs. Castellani next to her, beaming at her.

I volunteered to speak for today's topic because I have come to realize that in my life I have *often* chosen new family members for myself and my family. But I rarely, if ever, *thought* of what I was doing in those terms. Instead I simply accepted that your blood family *was* your family—and that was it.

ELIZABETH DODSON GRAY

Twenty-two Years with Mrs. Thayer

But even in my teenage years, I experienced an expanded "chosen" family. My parents were older when I was born— I had a brother six years older than I, and my mother was 40 and my father 46—so my parents were dealing with illness when I was teenager.

I was a sophomore in high school when my father had his first stroke, and my mother hired a widowed lady just her own age, "Mrs. Thayer," to live with us and help out as housekeeper, cook, etc. This was Baltimore, Maryland, right after World War II and in good Southern fashion I was taught always to call her "Mrs. Thayer," and I was to obey her with the respect accorded adults but not always given to hired employees.

So Mrs. Thayer became a fixture in my home, through my high school and college years—including my father's last illness and death when I was a senior in college—and on through the years of my mother's widowhood. This continued while my brother and I were away at graduate school and into our young-adult years.

After I married in 1957, I moved to St. Louis and Lisa was born. My mother was not well and we felt it necessary to move both Mother and Mrs. Thayer to our home in St. Louis, where my mother died the next year, at age 72. By now Mrs. Thayer, who was also 72, had made her home with my family for the last 14 years and she was truly "a part of the family." So Mrs. Thayer continued to live with us, now in the second generation of our family, and my two children, Lisa and Hunter, grew up for the next ten years with a grandmother-like figure in residence, until Mrs. Thayer died at age 82.

In the opening days of first-grade Lisa was asked to draw a picture of her family. She drew me and David and younger brother Hunter and Mrs. Thayer. The teacher asked, "Who is Mrs. Thayer? Is she your grandmother?" Lisa was clear that she was not. "Is she a servant?" the teacher asked. Lisa knew she was not a servant. The following year Lisa encountered this same exercise at the start of second grade. This time she solved this conundrum very creatively. Lisa came home from the "Draw your family day" triumphant: "I just told them that she was 'a Mrs. Thayer'!"

Lisa, now 36, had a baby boy (her first) earlier this fall. And she is now searching for her own "Mrs. Thayer"!

Mrs. Thayer made my life as clergy-wife and mother so much easier. When she first arrived with us in St. Louis in 1970, her only responsibility was to care for my mother. She soon found that Sunday "dinner" in our house consisted of soup and sandwiches, since we had spent all morning at church. So after one or two Sundays of soup and sandwiches, Mrs. Thayer inquired whether we would mind if she cooked Sunday dinner—because she herself really "missed" Sunday dinner. We said, "Help yourself!" And soon we were settling in to enjoy what would be years of full Sunday dinners consisting of Mrs. Thayer's roasts of beef and lamb and pork (meals I had *never* cooked) and Mrs. Thayer's lemon meringue and cherry pies!

Soon thereafter she asked if we would mind if she did some ironing while my mother napped. In a few weeks she was ironing everything in sight, including all our sheets and underwear. It turned out that Mrs. Thayer really *liked* to iron. After my mother died, Mrs. Thayer and I settled into a pattern of my making the cakes while she made the pies—and for about three nights a week Mrs. Thayer did her kind of cooking (roasts, twice-baked potatoes, pork chops baked in escalloped potatoes), while for the other meals I did my kind of cooking (casseroles, pizza, omelettes, quiche).

What *really* helped me out as a clergy wife was that Mrs. Thayer cooked the festival meals for us. She did the big meals for Thanksgiving, Christmas, Easter. This meant I could devote myself to the children and the church on those days, and not give a thought to what we would eat afterward as the big meal, until it appeared on the table!

Our agreement was that Mrs. Thayer *never* cleaned. Cleaning and straightening up was our job. And in our always too-busy household David and I only set to cleaning when guests were coming, and then always in a desperate flurry of activity. Mrs. Thayer, seeing all this as she went up the stairs to her room, would call over her shoulder, "It wouldn't be this bad if you'd clean a little every day!" And David and I would rush to the stairs and call up to her retreating form, "We'd rather *die* than clean every day!"

My only real problem with Mrs. Thayer in our lives (besides the understandable loss of privacy) was that Mrs. Thayer was Germanic in background. She had strict Germanic child-rearing tendencies which were very different from my Dr.-Spock-era ways. Because I had been carefully trained as a young person to treat Mrs. Thayer as an adult figure to be obeyed, it was hard for me to shift gears and now be her employer (Yes, we still paid Mrs. Thayer for her work with us).

I now had to lay down carefully and clearly what were *my* child-rearing guidelines. What I did not want was for Mrs. Thayer's child-rearing propensities to damage my children, as I could so clearly see she had already alienated her own then-midlife son. And I also did *not* want to be forced over this issue to "sever our connection."

I think it was clear to her and to us that, for all our sakes, we wanted this to work. But changing the terms of our relationship was not easy for either of us. But she and I both managed to do it, and Mrs. Thayer living with us continued to be an "all-win" relationship for us all.

My children will always, I am sure, remember coming in very cold after they had been out playing in the snow and being called by Mrs. Thayer into her room to "soak their feet in hot water," her way of helping them warm up again quickly.

Choosing a Sister for Myself

During those same years I came to realize slowly that Louise, my brother's first wife, had become as close to me as a sister. Neither of us had blood sisters (she was an only child), and as the years went by, despite their divorce, Louise and I realized we had many common sensitivities and personal and professional interests in psychology, religion, the environment, feminism, and *life!*

Then in the early 1980s Louise had colon cancer and I had breast cancer. Again we were walking similar journeys, she in Los Angeles and I in Boston. We were both trying to deal with our anxiety about the cancer coming back.

Hers finally did come back as metastasized liver cancer, and she had three years of living amazingly well with infusion chemotherapy, even to being able to fly from California to attend Lisa's first wedding. Louise kept me company in the family pew at the wedding, both of us with beautiful big hats, as Hunter walked Lisa down the aisle and David performed the ceremony.

Louise died on Christmas Day two years later. And I knew I had lost a precious companion of my entire adult life, who could not have been closer if she actually had been born to my mother as my blood sister.

Discovering Another Mother-Figure

Sometimes it seems that the tapestry of life opens up and allows you the opportunity to live deeply in relationships that are out-of-the-ordinary and become deeply precious. I lost my parents early in my young-adulthood. Recently I have acknowledged the mother-like quality to my always expanding and deepening closeness to my older friend Mary Turner Lane, of Chapel Hill, NC.

Purely by chance in connection with a speaking engagement in Chapel Hill, I stayed a long weekend with Mary Turner. I discovered then how much her feminism, and her total reaction to life (including her wonderful Southern accent), both charmed me and grounded me. When she spoke to the Theological Opportunities Program in the Spring of 1994, I introduced her saying that I trusted her feminist reactions more than those of anyone else I knew.

Mary Turner was widowed when her only daughter was 2½. She was, as she puts it, "nudged" by a male academic mentor from being a young Southern belle who was preparing to be a school marm, into what became her life-long academic career at the University of North Carolina at Chapel Hill. Along the way she started the Women's Studies Program at the university and for decades on that campus she was the major institutional advocate and organizer for women students and women faculty.

I am always inspired by Mary Turner's life and I marvel at where life can unexpectedly lead you. Today Mary Turner has a beloved very-grown and very-accomplished mid-life professional daughter as well as a very beloved granddaughter. Mary Turner and I now live in one another's lives by means of the telephone and our visits back and forth. This past June while she was visiting me at our shore place and tennis from Wimbledon began on TV, I discovered she even shares my great passion for Grand Slam TV tennis matches.

All this makes me feel "as if" I had a mother who could accompany me in my deepest passions and sensibilities, something my own mother never had the opportunity (or the vision) to do.

An "As-If" Grandfather

For our children's college and prep-school years, we also had an "as-if" grandfather. David's father died in 1971, and several years later his mother came from Florida to live in Rhode Island with her older first-cousin and life-long dear friend, Karl Jones, who I mentioned earlier when I was speaking of David's chosen godfathers. Karl's wife Bettie had recently died, and for the next decade Mommie Pat and Karl had a wonderful life together. From childhood on they had always been very fond of each other and these years continued that life-long companionship under one roof after their spouses both died.

In this decade our family gathered for our festival Thanksgiving and Christmas dinners at Karl Jones's home in Barrington, RI, surrounded by his fabulous 11 acres of rose gardens and the festival meals were now prepared by Karl and Bettie's long-time cook. (Mrs. Thayer had died about five years earlier.)

In my mind's eye I can still see us gathered with Mommy Pat and Karl at Karl's table, and Karl raising his sherry glass to celebrate his favorite toast, one David had heard since similar childhood festivals decades earlier:

Here's from me and my folks to thee and thy folks:
Never was folks that loved folks,
as much as me and my folks love thee and thy folks!

There was not a dry eye in the room when Karl finished. Except perhaps for Karl, who I think did not cry over such things.

Another Daughter, This One Chosen

I have also been privileged to experience two other "as-if" relationships—"as-if" another daughter, and "as-if" another son. My other daughter is Missi Stern, Lisa's best friend since age five.

Lisa and Missi met in kindergarten. And ever since they have been best friends: in first grade Lisa acted as Missi's "voice," and they shared everything with one another. Then in seventh grade they parted to go to different schools. But our families continued celebrating together Thanksgiving dinner and Christmas gift-giving at a festival dinner before Christmas. We also celebrated (with Mrs. Thayer's help) huge festival Easters together, complete with Easter egg hunts. Her mother and I celebrated Lisa's and Missi's birthdays at huge birthday parties which both mothers loved to give. The Sterns for many years visited us for a weekend during the summer at our shore home in Connecticut and Missi always stayed longer. There the girls as young children "played house" out on the big rock formation at the water's edge for endless hours. As teenagers and young adults they talked for similar endless hours as they sunned together on our deck.

After Missi graduated from Middlebury and Lisa from Smith, they worked in Boston. Within a year they shared an apartment in Charlestown until, four or five years later, Lisa moved to California. Recently when they were together, they acknowledged with awe that now, both at age 36, they have known each other *deeply* for some 31 years.

Thirty-one years is a long time for 36-year-olds to hold someone close in their heart—through Barbie dolls, studies, teenage dating, college years, young-adult careers, through Lisa's marriage, through Lisa's moving first to California and then Arizona, and now Missi's engagement. They have come to acknowledge that indeed they are like cherished sisters to each other, once again "as-if," but very real.

And through all these years I have been privileged to be an "as-if" mother to Missi. Her parents separated and divorced, her father was ill, and later as a mid-career young adult Missi went through a long period of unemployment. Each of these were prolonged and difficult periods in Missi's life, and David's and my support was very important in sustaining Missi through those trials and in bringing her out on the other side.

So when on Mother's Day I receive her "You've been like another mother to me/You are always there when I need you" card, I feel very blessed to have experienced in different ways *two* daughters' growing up. And I know that my bond as an "as-if" mother to this "as-if" daughter is very deep and very real, and very important to us both.

Our "As-If" Son

Then there is our "as-if" son, who came into our lives through another kind of opening in the tapestry of connection. In 1967 when Lisa was 8½ and Hunter 5, David took leadership in our community as the Episcopal minister to initiate a Fresh Air Fund program. In the Fresh Air Fund, white suburban families invite inner-city children to live with them and their children for a portion of the summer.

David had worked the summer after college in a church in New York City's East Harlem, and so we decided to work through the East Harlem Protestant Parish to do this. It was in this way that we made contact with two children of our own children's age, and they came to spend a portion of the summer with us at our home by the ocean in Connecticut.

This was how Tony and Margaret first came into our life. Margaret chose to go home early the second summer, but Tony came for a month the first summer and then all summer for the next ten years until he was 15.

I look back now at my son Hunter's adaptability and flexibility, because he and Tony became "joined at the hip" every summer. Tony would arrive, and immediately every experience Hunter had was to be shared with Tony. I do not remember any great fighting; they just shared their days every day all summer. What this meant was that Hunter had an instant "twin brother" for the summer.

Friends at the time said to me: "What do you think this means to Tony? You all have *so* much—and he is growing up on welfare in East Harlem with a single-parent mother and five siblings. What *will* he—what *does* he—think about life back there when he goes home at the end of the summer?" I would reply that I honestly did not know.

All I knew was my goal for the experience, for I craved for my own children to step out of their white suburban ghetto and to have black children who are really close friends. Tony and Margaret were giving to Hunter and Lisa that gift, of being their young black friends.

But I also hoped living with us could mean to Tony that later, when he grew up and went out from Harlem into a white world, he could do that with the security and confidence of having already lived these summers in a white world, in a white family who loved him and whom he experienced over time for 10 years. As later in life he faced that wider white world, he could feel that he has already been there and done that, and it is not all new and frightening to him.

You will see here pictures of Tony and Hunter, their arms across each other's shoulders and sharing one wet suit together, the top on Hunter and the bottom on Tony.

I remember when Tony first came to us at 5, he was afraid of the mosquitoes that appeared at dusk. I guess East Harlem does not have mosquitoes.

I remember Tony being scared of live lobsters before they were cooked. I remember being with him at the Museum of Natural History at Yale. We had rented headsets for Tony and Hunter, Lisa and Margaret, but not for ourselves. The headsets provided an interpretive commentary complete with sound-effects. And Tony at 5 was terrified when, standing beneath a gigantic skeleton of *Tyrannosaurus Rex,* he heard a great roar in his headset. Tony bolted, running off in an opposite direction out of the large hall with its great overarching skeleton. Suddenly I had four children moving off in opposite directions! But without a headset of my own, I had not a clue as to what had just happened.

As a five-year-old, Tony spoke with a rich African-American *patois* that often baffled us, despite David's summer in East Harlem. I remember David that first summer coming to me after having put Hunter and Tony to bed, rubbing both backs until they both had dropped off to sleep. "I'm not certain," David said, "but I think Tony told me that he was thrown out of a second-story window by someone and broke his arm."

I remember also Tony, even when young, having the fabulously muscular physique I associated with the world-champion African-American boxer Joe Lewis. I remember too how David had to learn to readjust the light-meter on his camera in order to take good pictures of Tony's rich ebony-black skin.

And most of all, I remember loving the sweet disposition of this little boy who had the courage at age 5 to get on a train in New York City to come for a month to be with total strangers who were white in 1967 in the middle of the turbulent years of the civil rights struggles. I admired too the courage of his mother who had trusted us as total strangers to take adequate care of her little boy, just so he could have a month away from the heat of the city.

I remember Hunter and Tony in a production of "The Music Man" in 1968 at the Charles River Creative Arts Camp. Tony was so proud of learning to sing and dance in the chorus. He also learned to play somewhat the violin and the trumpet.

The Twists of Fate

It was that musical experience at summer camp which led Tony to the Junior High for the Performing Arts in New York City and then to the Senior High for the Performing Arts (the school featured in the TV-series "Fame"), and then on to music and rap gigs after high school while he worked in a Fayva shoe store and later also as a paralegal in the Brooklyn District Attorney's office.

Then during our children's college years we lost touch, though we still sent Tony a check at Christmas time. But then, when Hunter at 25 was getting married, he wanted to invite Tony. We called his mother to find out where to send the invitation. His mother did not really answer but said Tony would contact us.

Finally we received a letter from Tony. I am sure it was a hard letter for him to write, for he was telling us that he was in prison for killing his girl-friend while he was on crack cocaine.

He wrote to me, "I'm sure you'll think this happened because I was poor and lived in a ghetto. No, Mrs. Gray, this happened because I made enough money with my music to afford cocaine, and did this terrible thing."

Tony went on to tell us that, when he realized what he had done, he felt he should be executed. But the lawyers plea-bargained a 6-to-10 year sentence, to which his girl-friend's family agreed in order to assure his punishment and avoid the risk of his avoiding any punishment on some technicality (or by a jury) in a trial.

Prison. I had difficulty imagining that the sweet little boy I had known for ten years could ever have hurt anyone.

In prison, Tony became a Black Muslim and he now calls himself Hasan. But he will always be Tony to me. He experienced some excellent educational programs. He learned to use a computer, completed a college education, and became literate in philosophy, literature, psychology. He also learned to write powerfully and started writing autobiographically, and wrote for the prison literary magazine.

After graduating in prison from college at the top of his class, he came back out into the world and he could not find a steady job. He held on for two years, until despair led him back into one drug episode. Then he sought out a drug rehab program, and now he is back into prison to serve the rest of his sentence for using drugs and so breaking his parole.

Looking into a Wrinkle in Time with Tony

When Tony was writing on his autobiography, he would send us the chapters one by one. He never could make it to describing how he had killed Lois; it was too painful.

His first chapter was about his mother. And that led to describing his memories of first coming to visit this white family in Connecticut at age 5. Can you imagine our feelings upon getting a totally unexpected glimpse into the remembered awareness of that 5-year-old-Tony experiencing his first summer with us?

Tony wrote of remembering that he was afraid, because his older brother called white people "devils"; but he comforts himself that his loving mother, whom he adores, has sent him to these people and he is going to trust her wisdom. "All I could do was think of my mother's eyes as she told me to 'be good and mind the people.'" I held onto that, he wrote.

"In those eyes lay the burning truth of her love. In those eyes, lighted for the whole world to see, was my mother's care: she made sure her children had a place to sleep; she made sure that they went to school; she made sure that the little brown animals that crept along the baseboard at night did not bite us; she made sure that I had washed myself good before I left; she made sure I had something to eat; she made sure I had clean underwear. A person who makes sure you have clean underwear won't just give you over to anybody "("Summer 1968," p. 7).

Tony had noted in East Harlem what he called "white spots," white people who came to East Harlem and stood out because of their (lack of) color. Writing about coming for the first time to be with us in Connecticut, he writes, "There were so many white spots. I had never seen so many. I asked myself, 'What did they do with all the black people?' This is when I realized that I was now the spot. A black spot in the Bermuda shorts, khaki pants and the Polo shirts the Grays had just bought for me, among that sea of blond, red, and brown heads of hair with all the green, blue, and gray eyes. Did they eat Chitlens? Did they have the same color blood as me? Are we the same?" (pp.7–8).

He concludes his first chapter with these words: "That was the spring of my life. Like a fresh flower erupting from its womb and reaching for the warmth of the spring sun, I basked in this light. On those memories it never rains. The sunflowers that stood in the middle of their neighbor's field, or the brook that ran through their back yard, or the moon glistening off the ocean as the waves gently rubbed against the shores, will always be a source of peace for me, a peace I thought I lost being behind these walls. Whatever happened to that little boy?" (Letters from a Prison of Regrets)

Only gradually as he wrote to us from prison did we begin to glimpse what those summers at the shore had meant to him. "As I told you before, life for me with you guys made a difference in my life, and it is effective even to this day. There were things that I was exposed to that I would not have ever been exposed to, staying in Harlem. As I hear (as I do now) the sounds of the beach, I also see this little boy playing baseball in a Yankees-suit in a backyard near a beach house. I also see that little boy reading a book called *Charlotte's Web,* and finishing it. Even though these are not seen anymore by my physical eyes, my mental eyes see all these sights with great detail. That little boy is still here inside of me, and I hurt a great deal knowing that I have trapped him inside of a prison of regrets, sorrows, and 'what ifs'." A little further on, he continues: "When I feel that I cannot go on, I often find myself focusing on the past. Looking way back in time to days of innocence. Learning how to swim, learning what the 'port side' and the 'bow' are on a boat. Learning how to play tennis. I look at that little boy, and he gives me inspiration to go on" (letter, March 7, 1991).

Seven months later, he wrote: "I want you to know that without you in my life at that early age, I would have been deluded into thinking that the 'white man' is the cause of my particular situation. But what you guys have shown me by taking me in, some twenty-five years ago, was that care knows no color lines" (letter, October 1, 1991).

Again: "There is only one sure thing that I know is true for me, and that is God. He has given me the gift of you guys, who have allowed me to walk on a beach, to ride on a bike, to read a book, to be. For without these memories, and the hopes that spring from these memories, I hate to think how I would have maintained myself during my times of drowning in the seas of sorrows that are my constant companions. . . . These memories are the beacons of light that guide me back to the sanctity and safety of knowing there just might be hope left for me" (letter, March 7, 1991).

A Sunflower Recalled

A year-and-a-half later, Tony wrote: "I am enclosing my graduation announcement. I realize that you're not able to come, but I know that you will be there with me in my heart. When I get up to make the Graduates' Address, as well as receive both of my degrees, you will be standing there with me in heart and mind. I owe so much to you, and it is so strange how life seems to come back around to the simplest things we thought we have long forgotten. I don't remember the name of your neighbors in Pine Orchard, but I do remember their sunflower. That sunflower has been a lifeboat in this sea of fortunate pain. I have said 'thank you' a million times for these memories. I don't mean to be excessively thankful, but here it goes for the one and millionth time. Thank you" (letter, October 5, 1992).

Today as I reflect upon these years with Tony, including his years in prison, I am awed by the tapestry of life. Who could ever have guessed how, in the providence of God, childhood memories so easily given by us could be so powerful a source of healing and hope in a terrible space of sorrow and regret and incarceration?

* * *

I come out of telling you these stories marveling at how interconnected we all are; how familiar and truly "family" we are to each other, whether we realize it or not; how much we hold each other afloat when we come to care; and how much *the threads of our lives are woven together into tapestries of relationships* that it sometimes takes us years even to glimpse or comprehend.

Mother's Day Cards

Mother's Day 1992:   Scottsdale, AZ

Dearest Mom,
I love you so dearly. Please always know this because your love and guidance has got me to this point. I count on your strength and make it my own—even when it is very tough to do (like now). Best of luck with your next trip.
Love and Hugs, Lisa
P.S. I am always thinking of you when you are on your voyages.

Mother's Day 2010—Card accompanying flowers

Happy Mother's Day, Mom!
You are a dynamite mother.
I could not be me
without you!
Your daughter, Lisa

Mother's Day 2008: Handwritten on Hunter's card

Dear Mom, Thanks so much for all you have given me my whole life! You and Dad and our family were such a great place to come from. I feel very lucky and blessed. Thank you!! I appreciate the sacrifice that I know motherhood was for you, but more I appreciate all the love and support you have given me and that you still do give to me.
All my love, your everlasting son, Hunter

Mother's Day 2009: Handwritten from Hunter

I love you so much, and of course I am very proud of who you are and all that you have accomplished.
Thanks to you and Dad for being such wonderful mentors as well as parents.
Love, Hunter

Mother's Day 2010: Card from Missi Stern
Liz,
In so many ways,
you've been like a mother to me—
and I wanted you to know
how happy and grateful I feel
having you in my life.

HAPPY

Mother's Day

This pretty much says it all!

How can I ever thank you enough for being such an important and supportive part of my life!

I love you!

Missi

Mother's Day 2011: Card made by Tony Linnen

Ms. Gray . . .

The words have been exhausted . . .

My appreciation is endless . . .

Your comforting words inspiring . . .

Your tireless actions transforming . . .Mother's Day Mother's Day

You've always been there . . .

From comforting me at night when I was 5 . . .

To comforting and guiding me through the many dark nights and storms my hands have created . . .

You've been there. Always.

Through all my births and transformations. I'm fortunate to have had two mothers in my life.

Happy Mother's Day,

Love, Tony/Hasan

18.

Walking
My Yellow Brick
Road:

Part 2

TOP talk
November 10, 1983

18.

Walking My Yellow Brick Road: Part 2

TOP Talk, November 10, 1983

The third brick in my Yellow Brick Road was, of all places, at MIT's business school. At MIT's Sloan School of Management I joined my husband David in January 1973 in a new interdisciplinary seminar about the issues of "Critical Choices for the Future." The seminar had been organized just that fall of 1972, following the UN conference in Stockholm about the human environment and earlier in 1972 the publication of the book *The Limits to Growth.*[1]

Suddenly I was reading and learning about energy and fossil fuels. About natural resources, metals, minerals, ecology, the environment. About population growth, food, agriculture, and hunger. And about technology, entropy, and exponential growth. I was learning about a whole world of issues that before I had not concerned myself with.

I discovered to my amazement that no one was steering spaceship Earth with any real foresight, any real looking-ahead in time. Not the corporate decision makers. Not the technological decision makers. Not the political decision makers.

I discovered we were (and *are*) destroying our life-supporting environment. Producing poisonous chemical wastes. Using up irreplaceable fossil fuels. And the wastes from burning all those fuels were causing what today is called the greenhouse effect upon global climate and oceans. I had not realized the human population had doubled while I was growing up, from 2 to 4 billion people, and would double again by early in the next century to 8 billion people

I was—I *am*—horrified at the cumulative effects of all our impacts upon this planet. And all this was even before our more recent and real concerns about effects of nuclear power and nuclear war.

ELIZABETH DODSON GRAY

My Psyche Became a Veritable Cement Mixer

I found myself at MIT increasingly wondering Why? Why were we doing all this to our earth and to ourselves?

How could we think we could do all this to the beautiful blue skies, to the rain, to the lakes, to the shimmering ocean I loved, to the sunlight, to the forests, to the plants, to other species? And as the MIT half of my brain was wondering in that way, with another part of my brain I was reading feminist theology at Harvard Divinity School and Episcopal Divinity School.

I began to see connections. Between the way male culture (and even indeed my own Judeo-Christian tradition) had taught us to think about nature and God and body and spirit and control and chaos. And mind and emotion and women and evil. And most especially how it had taught us about what I came to call "ranking diversity."

I began seeing connections in all this, and my reading and emerging thinking in feminist theology was for me a catalyst. I was coming to see how all this that was happening had something to do with *how we were thinking and seeing*—and *that* had something profoundly to do with how—and why—we were destroying our planet.

My image of the Yellow Brick Road receded for a time now. And as I walked around, I felt I was moving in a constantly rotating daze. My mind and my psyche, like a cement mixer, were constantly turning, and turning everything I knew upside down and around.

Twice a week I would stop my mixer at MIT and drop in the latest stuff from there. And in it would go, and the mixer would start turning again. Then I would drive around to Harvard Divinity School for the TOP lectures and stop again at Episcopal Divinity School and drop the latest into my feminist theological thinking.

And always the mixer would continue turning everything over and around.

Starting to Want to Change Our World

Gradually I found that my book (which would become *Green Paradise Lost*) began writing itself. I was writing other things too. But I thought I was writing a book about the line and the circle—about how all our disciplines were turning from linear thinking to circular or systemic thinking. It was a book I actually couldn't write, and which in 1982 Fritjof Capra wrote as *The Turning Point.*[2]

But I remember sitting on our beach in Connecticut, having just learned that each year in the United States 30,000 new books are published. And, of those, only a fraction appear in most bookstores. Even if I wrote a book full of ultimate truth, who could or would publish it? Even beyond that, how could you get people to read it, given that flood of new books each year?

I had begun—I trust you see—to want to change our world. In a major way, not in the minor way that people in the ministry seek to enlighten and comfort and uphold their own particular flock. No, I now wanted to change the way we think about nature in an entire culture. I wanted to save our planet from ourselves, and for our children and for the future. But how?

ELIZABETH DODSON GRAY

One Year Later . . .

Never underestimate my Yellow Brick Road. Could you believe that one year after my sad day on the beach contemplating the statistics of book publishing and authors, every member of the U.S. Congress would have been sent by the chair of a Congressional subcommittee an offprint of what later became the book, *Growth and Its Implications for the Future,*[3] which David and I and another MIT colleague co-authored?

In the late winter of 1974 as an outgrowth of our work at MIT, the three of us got the opportunity to write up the basic documents—the staff work—for ten days of Congressional hearings about the future. A larger two-volume version of that work using cartoons from my cartoon collection, was published by the Government Printing Office, would sell more than 10,000 copies that year (considered by the GPO a best-seller)—all without any advertising.

David and I got to lecture about our work to the Congressional Research Service and again at a dinner given for us and attended by members of Congress and their staffers, held at the Smithsonian Institution.

A year earlier all this was unimaginable, literally inconceivable. But suddenly, in the space of a year's work, people were reading what we were writing, listening to what we were saying in lectures at places we could not have imagined.

Suddenly we were started, launched, into a free-lance issue-centered ministry to the culture at large. It was not quite what we had two years earlier had in mind. But never mind. We had gone on to a more encompassing and awesome issue of trying to help an achievement-driven, consumerism-obsessed culture turn a mid-life passage into simple living in harmony with our home, the Earth.

A Road Compelling But Elusive

The urgency of our global environmental predicament came to be for us like the account in Jewish Scriptures of the Cloud by day and the Pillar of Fire by night which always accompanied and led the Israelites onward, out of the dubious luxuries of Egypt and slavery and through the Wilderness to an as-yet-unclear promised future. This urgency was (and is) always with us.

Yet we found the Yellow Brick Road not only compelling but also elusive. How to eat, pay the bills, and keep our children in college while we followed this road of no-regular-salary?

At one point David applied for admission to Harvard Business School. With an MBA he hoped he could become a consultant to corporations confronting limits-to-growth issues. Despite getting a grade in the 98th percentile on the Business School Admission Test, he was not admitted. We came to realize that few past 35 were admitted and none in their 40s: "too old."

But because David did not get admitted to Harvard Business School, we ended up teaching at MIT's Sloan School of Management where our MIT mentor Carroll Wilson, needed major assistance for two years while he ran a global energy project.

After leaving MIT in 1976, we taught at Williams College for a semester. We were learning never to underestimate the power of my Yellow Brick Road, however elusive or dimly seen it might appear.

ELIZABETH DODSON GRAY

Discovering the Power of Ideas on Paper

My cement mixer had finally turned out a full-length manuscript of a book, *Green Paradise Lost.*[4] What I had spent five years creating was rejected by successive publishers as too feminist, too religious, too ecological, or too much a mixture of all of the above!

David finally said, "We will publish it ourselves. What can be so hard?" Not in my wildest dreams would I have thought to do that. But he located a place where he could be taught how to type my book manuscript into one of the earliest computer-phototypesetters. He took it through all the book-design and business stages to manufacture and completion. He then designed color brochures to advertise my book by direct-mailings and figured out how to market it.

Suddenly, in addition to the ministry, we were also in the business of being book publishers as Roundtable Press.

Walking the road, brick by brick, other bricks have slowly emerged before us as we ventured out on the road. In 1978 we started a conference for professional women, which we did for the next six or seven Octobers.

We were, yes, *given* an incorporated, non-profit institute (Bolton Institute for a Sustainable Future). We became active in the U.S. Association for The Club of Rome (USACOR), furthering the concerns about limits-to-growth which have followed from the book *The Limits to Growth,* the first report to The Club of Rome.

In 1982 we published another book of mine, *Patriarchy As A Conceptual Trap*[5], a book based upon a lecture I had given to USACOR, a book unique in its 56 cartoons which illustrate my points. My daughter said, "Mom, you have footnoted it with *New Yorker* cartoons!"

David edited another book also connected with USACOR, and designed and took that book through all the stages of manufacture. *Making It Happen*[6] helped celebrate the 10th anniversary of the publication of *The Limits to Growth.*

All sorts of opportunities have opened up to us to speak at colleges, schools, churches, national conferences, and so on. From our point of view as it happens, day after day, month after month, it seems like a wonderful magic. I have likened these opportunities to speak to "messages in a bottle" which float in to us on the tide. We had no agent; we never knew who had recommended us. The invitations just floated in and we responded.

Our books have been read and used as required texts at more than 35 colleges and divinity schools all over the world—Australia, New Zealand, Canada, Europe, England and the U.S. I have just given permission for my latest book to be published in Poland where it has already been translated into Polish. By 1983 we have sold about 10,000 copies of *Green Paradise Lost* (my first book) and about 3400 copies of my book of 16 months ago, *Patriarchy as A Conceptual Trap.*[7] Who could dream that we could publish ourselves and have this response?

I think what pleases me most is that *Patriarchy* is being used by the national staff of the United Presbyterian Church in a study process by their denominational executives. They are using it as an aid in sensitizing themselves, both men and women, to the subtle issues of patriarchy so that, as they design their newly merged Presbyterian national structure, they might try to create a nonpatriarchal structure.

Not in My Wildest Dreams Could I Have Imagined

I want to tell you that, as I sat crying under that tree in 1972, it was not in my wildest dreams that I could have imagined the opportunities, yes the power, my Yellow Brick Road has brought me to help and to be heard in the processes for change in our world.

I have the amazing experience of hearing women I do not know come up to me after a speech and say to me things like: "Your book changed my life; its made me see my whole world differently." Or—"I've always felt about the world as you write about it, but you put it into words for me." Or again—"I always felt I was a little crazy until I read your book, but now I know it's all right, in fact it's better, to see the world this way."

When I hear such words, I am, frankly, amazed that somehow, in some way, my own crazy, unorthodox, often elusive but ever-beckoning-onward Yellow Brick Road has given me some power to change the world.

But I now know that I must follow its leadings, and I must take the risk to step out—even when I don't *see* another solitary yellow brick ahead of me. David and I have come to call it "walking on water."

Venturing Out

Rosa Parks did not know what she would generate. Certainly she did not know she would open the door to the Civil Rights movement, Martin Luther King, the Voting Rights Act, and a period of marked improvement in conditions for many people of color in the United States.

Nor, at the start, did Randy Forsberg or Helen Caldicott—the women who spearheaded anti-nuclear activism in the Cold War Years—know where their Yellow Brick Roads would lead.

All of them knew only that their own next step was beckoning. When they stepped forward into history, stepped out in faith and in courage to change their world, they created for us all profound new opportunities, opportunities which had not existed before.

We are all on a journey to justice, and a journey to peace on this planet. It is also a journey to justice and a journey to peace *with* this planet.

It will feel incredibly good to the human spirit to get there, to come into that land of justice and peace and to settle in there, and to dwell there. We were all created for that kind of harmony.

So I invite each of you to honor your own personal Yellow Brick Road by letting it move you—attract you—into risking your own journey into the power to change the world.

—SOMETIMES TEARS CAN CHANGE A LIFE—

From: danadurst@xxx.com
Date: April 25, 2011 10:40:39 AM CDT
To: Jean Gordon <jgordon@xxx.org>
Subject: Re: [Elizabeth Dodson Gray]

ELIZABETH DODSON GRAY

I met Elizabeth when she came here to Little Rock years and years ago (like maybe 30 or 40??) and spoke to some group that I no longer remember. I think it was religious-oriented. Anyhow, I was very young and just starting out in my career and had been indoctrinated into the banking world—and I understood that I would NEVER be a man. But I had better act like one. If I ever expected to be even marginally effective I should be tough, show no emotions, and—God forbid— NO CRYING!!!!

Well, Elizabeth gets up in front of a huge group and talks brilliantly about whatever the subject was and she then starts talking about Easter, which was coming up soon. And she started weeping about celebrating Easter in the home church of her childhood. And she was not the least embarrassed about it!!!!! She said she always cries when she talks about Easter, and she was so matter-of-fact and open about it and not the least bit uncomfortable.

I was stunned beyond belief, not to mention deeply moved. She was just so "who she is"—so authentic—and not the least bit concerned with how others might react. It blew me away. And knowing me as you do, you know that this had a permanent impact on me! Can you imagine me giving a flip NOW about how anyone (particularly the "establishment"—which men were at that time) reacts to any revelation I might give about my true self? Nope! I can't tell you the number of times in a year—still!—that I think of that moment.

NOTES

1. Donella Meadows et al., *Limits to Growth* (Washington, DC: Universe Books, 1972).

2. Fritjof Capra, *The Tao of Physics: An Exploration of the Parallels between Modern Physics and Eastern Mysticism* (Berkeley, Calif.: Shambhala Publications, 1975).

3. Elizabeth & David Dodson Gray and William F. Martin, *Growth and Its Implications for the Future* (Washington, DC: Government Printing Office, 1974; and Wellesley, Mass.: Roundtable Press, 1975).

4. Elizabeth Dodson Gray, *Green Paradise Lost* (Wellesley, Mass.: Roundtable Press, 1978).

5. Elizabeth Dodson Gray, *Patriarchy as a Conceptual Trap* (Wellesley, Mass.: Roundtable Press, 1982).

6. John Richardson, ed., *Making It Happen: A Positive Guide to the Future* (Washington, DC: US Association for The Club of Rome, 1982).

7. This talk was originally given in 1983. The number of copies of *Patriarchy* it reports sold are as of 1983. By the year 2012 when this talk was incorporated as a chapter in Elizabeth Dodson Gray's memoir, *Patriarchy as a Conceptual Trap* had by then been reprinted four times, for a total of 20,000 copies. 18,000 copies had been sold by the start of 2010.

19.

Reflections on a Double-Twenty-fifth Reunion

Smith Alumnae magazine
August 1976

19.

Reflections on a Double-Twenty-Fifth Reunion

Smith Alumnae magazine
August 1976

And gladly singing to you always
Our loyal hearts with joy shall fill.
O fairest, fairest Alma Mater,
You hold and claim us still.

—Smith College Alma Mater

The call to my twenty-fifth reunion evoked mixed feelings. I was very involved in a quite satisfying academic and professional colleagueship with my husband, needing to finish writing projects, with two teen-age children graduating from their schools, about to move to our shore house for the summer —and who needs a reunion in the midst of that schedule? On the other hand, one will never pass through that twenty-fifth celebration again. It is historically unique, and perhaps deserves to "have attention paid." Since the passing years have brought to me a keener respect for the unique moment in time which will never come again in quite that form, I decided to "pay respect" and attend.

But then we discovered that our two colleges had betrayed us! The Smith and Yale twenty-fifth reunions had been scheduled for the same weekend. Which of us would stay home and "mind the store" by ferrying the teen-agers about? And, if we solved that, how would we slice the two sets of festivities in half? Finally four days before reunion we settled all of that, and knew that in some form or other we were each "twenty-fifthing."

Driving to Smith I faced the fact that I really wasn't looking forward to it very much. I knew that except for my roommate (whom I was looking forward to seeing) my close dormitory-friends were not returning. I wondered what seeing more casual acquaintances again would mean—if anything. I was pleasantly surprised at the cocktail party before Class Dinner. I found that I actually enjoyed "interviewing" classmates with the "Where-are-you-living-and-what-are-you-doing?" routine, because many of their answers were so interesting that we were off and running into interesting conversations. To my surprise, when I finally connected with my roommate, I did not view her as an "oasis in the desert," and since I already knew "where she was living and what she was doing and thinking," I found myself even a little impatient to get back to interviewing other people. It was like opening boxes when you didn't know what was inside. So many of the boxes were delightful, and when you didn't find connecting interests, you just "moved on."

Class Dinner was festive, with many of us wearing long dresses and all of us (including some 60 of our husbands who were with us) wearing spectacular orchid leis which a generous classmate had flown in with her from her home in Hawaii. We discovered the next day that we were a prize-winning 25th reunion with the highest attendance. We also broke the previous record for giving Smith the largest 25th reunion gift ever. So we feasted. And talked. And sang. And listened to Push sing. And received Jill Conway's speech to us with delight and admiration for our new president.

Late that evening I reconnected with my roommate for the sort of deeply satisfying "relating in depth" which is possible when you have been close in college and have "kept up" through visits and letters. We sat around with a classmate who had driven up with her, comparing notes on how our consciousness as women has changed in these past few years. I was interested that I was not alone in my "consciousness trip" into feminism, and I was fascinated to hear about some of their experiences in their differing business situations.

Saturday morning we gathered on the chilly turf for Ivy Day. Here again I found myself surprised to be marching and feeling very much at home in the midst of the dormitory group I had lived with for only half of my freshman year. We stood, watched and cheered as the older alums marched past, admiring the spring in their steps and the zest in their faces, and chuckling with pure delight at the marvelous slogans on the sign boards they carried.

I found myself so grateful that even after all the changes which twenty-five years have brought in many things at Smith, the traditions of Ivy Day persist. Our daughter, Lisa '80, is beginning Smith this coming September, and I was glad that we would be sharing some similar experiences and memories.

As we watched the fiftieth reunion class (148 strong) march past, someone said, "Say, they're in pretty good shape after 25 more years than we have now! I wonder if we'll look as good as that?" Maybe we can do it, I thought, though 2001 still seems a long ways away.

I was marching with a very special friend from that other dorm, someone I always had felt close to in college but have seldom seen since and didn't know she was returning to reunion. It was she and I who, back in college years, had once met in the corridor of the library just outside the main reading room, and because we had not seen one another for months, we had sat down on the floor where we were in the hall, and while the traffic flowed around us for the next hours, we had a soul-to-soul conversation. And so it was for the Ivy Day march. As we fell in behind the class of 1946, we also fell into a deep conversation of sharing. As we marched along through the throngs of parents and spectators who lined the walkway on both sides, we had another soul-to-soul. In the midst of that wildly public scene, we had the space to be completely private and personal. Like most of the totally special and memorable moments in life, it was like "the alighting of a butterfly" — unplanned, spontaneous, and coming to you like a gift.

That afternoon our class gathered for a panel discussion by five of us on "where we've been and where we are going." I was particularly interested in whether my classmates had followed any of my own and my roommate's feminist pilgrimage in these last few years. I was pleased at the depth and honesty of the life stories shared by the panel members, and by the awareness of feminist issues which they expressed. One husband present said that last year at his twenty-fifth reunion he had found his classmates feeling like galley slaves, chained to the repetition of their jobs day-after-day, year-after-year. How come, he asked, we were expressing such a sense of freedom and of our widening choice of options in our middle years? (For example, one panel member has just started out as a playwright.) The panel agreed that as women were being liberated from their stereotypic role of staying-at-home, men could also be liberated from their yoke of economic bondage. Perhaps Mom supports the family for a year while Dad learns a new skill in midlife!

But as a feminist I was not cheered by the thematic content of the songs which the Smithereens so brilliantly sang to us Saturday night. They seemed to be of the old romantic genre in which a woman must have a man in order to survive. If the Smithereens were singing with tongue in cheek, I couldn't see signs of it. I also looked with a newly jaundiced eye at some of our own class songs from the 1940s, songs like "You can't get a man with your brain." I cringed. But singing our songs I was newly impressed by the talents expressed in them and the power of the memories they evoked. "This the House We Live in" seemed especially poignant with its sense of the past and my own expectation of the future of our daughter at Smith.

My husband had dropped me off at Northampton Friday afternoon and we had each gone to our own Class Dinners, his at Yale and mine at Smith. Late Saturday afternoon he had come back to Northampton for cocktails and dinner, and now we were driving back to Yale late Saturday night, for he was to have the prayers Sunday morning at the Battell Chapel Service of Remembrance. Since he was a member of the class of 1951 and we were also commuter-participants of the Battell congregation, it was particularly appropriate that he should do this. We were enjoying sharing our reactions to both reunions. Finally I said I had been struck by the comment made as the fiftieth reunion class marched by. I realized that those alums at that moment were providing important role models for us as women of 46 years living in a culture that does not respect aging. They were helping us be able to look ahead in life with confidence and expectation. This too was an unanticipated and spontaneous gift given to us at reunion by "those who have gone before."

David said that the Yale reunions didn't have quite that feeling because the reunion classes each met in separate residential colleges and, because of the large numbers involved, never did anything like march past one another. We agreed that my sense of the past and future at that Ivy Day parade—the past represented by the marching older alums and the future by my sense that our daughter would one day be here too—constituted a very true and helpful broadening out of the dimensions of the present. Our Bicentennial year has helped all of us in America do this same kind of remembering of our roots and our forebears, as well as helping us extend ahead the horizons of the future as we face questions about energy, pollution, population and food. It has become very apparent to David and me in our professional lives at MIT that such a tricentennial perspective, looking back to 1776 and looking ahead to 2076, needs to be a feature of present living, affecting not only our sense of living but also the choices and decisions we make now that affect the future. We need to be taking "soundings" about how deep the water we're in really is. Or it's like driving a car and checking in the rearview mirror as well as watching the road ahead. What else in our culture helps us do this?

Sunday morning I chose to sit in Battell Chapel in our usual spot in the second row, while David left to robe for the service. I was soon joined by two elderly Yale alums of the class of 1906, who were explaining to each other that their cataracts made it necessary for them to sit up so close to the front, and that their arthritis was bothering them. I was amazed to find myself feeling identified with them. I did not pull back and look at them as "old," for I too don't see well anymore without glasses and I have my own twinges of arthritis. They were part of me and I of them, for we shared together the human condition of aging. And like the sisterhood of feminism, we must support one another for we are flesh of the same flesh and bone of the same bone.

Just at that moment the opening hymn, *O God, our help in ages past*, began and I was caught up in the majestic panorama of the years expressed in

. . .

Time like an ever-rolling stream
Bears all its sons away.
They fly forgotten as a dream
Dies at the opening day."

Even the sexism in the word "sons" could not deter me from pursuing the tricentennial perspective begun in my own Smith Ivy Day parade, which was now flowing again like a strong current through this Yale Service of Remembrance. I realized that those Yale alums who attend this service of remembering —they gain this heightened and deepened sense of the meaning of the present and of their present lives. The preacher himself, remembering his father's graduation ('06), his own graduation ('41), and his son's graduation ('71), had a deep sense of his own place in the generations. But he also had a marvelous historical and bicentennial sermon with an open-endedness to the future as he recalled Robert Kennedy's "Why not?" and Martin Luther King's "I have a dream." We closed with my own David's deeply "remembering" prayer:

Under the arches of the years we pray to you, O God . . .
We remember the excitement of discovery, the mellowing of friendships, and the deepening of loyalties to people and causes, all of which have shaped and directed our lives.
So it is with gratitude as well as sadness that we mark both the passing of years and the passing of friends. We celebrate now the mystery of the gift of their lives . . .
Let the music of peace ring in our ears.
Let the drum beat of justice quicken our step . . .

ELIZABETH DODSON GRAY

Let the vision of human solidarity, sisters with brothers in their strengths and their differences, young and old, poor and rich, needy and needed, strengthen our resolve not to whisper on our own account, but to raise our voices in the chorus that shouts praise and glory and honor to God who made us different but made us for one another:

That the weak and poor might be lifted up and the mighty be brought low, that the hungry be fed, the sick made well, the oppressed given justice, and the privileged brought back to share the human lot that privilege obscures.

It was for me a marvelous service, for it was a non-sexist service. Even the Old Testament lesson, in the hymnal entitled, "Now Let Us Praise Famous Men," had been noticed and corrected. All five ministers who took part in the service spoke in terms of "sisters and brothers" and "her and his." David closed his prayer with the Lord's Prayer, beginning "Our Creator, who art in heaven, Hallowed be thy name . . ." The opening portion of the service was led by a woman graduate (Yale '71) who is an Episcopal deacon. After reunion at my own alma mater, where sexist categories in language and song seem not to have been seriously examined, it was thrilling for me to be able to experience a truly non-sexist service in which the categories of thought and language and symbol had not only been examined but also changed—and this in an institution with a strongly male heritage! It gave me some hope in the human solidarity for which my husband prayed.

Where in our culture do we enrich and enlarge our present with a deepened sense of both past and future? Certainly college reunions are one such place. I would urge all of us, male and female, young and old, to return and "pay respect" to the unique historic moment of our reunions. You will find people who in college were totally uninteresting to you and are now "lit up" by new concerns. You will find close friendships made more precious by further sharing. You will garner wisdom which another has learned in the fiery crucible of their own experience. You will gain a heightened sense for "those who have gone before" and those who follow after the human continuity in time. And finally and not least, you will find new and good models for aging in a culture which does not respect or value the aging process. These new models for aging offer us a new sense of human solidarity as we age in mortal bodies, and they remind us of our need to undergird each other in our various generations as we travel together through time and space. ■

Elizabeth Dodson Gray is writer and ethicist who graduated from Smith in 1951 and from Yale Divinity School in 1954. She is co-author (with David Dodson Gray) of Children of Joy: Raising Your Own Home-Grown Christians (1975) and (with David Dodson Gray and William F. Martin) of Growth and Its Implications for the Future (1975). She and her husband are two-thirds of the leadership team for a seminar on "Critical Choices for the Future" at MIT's Sloan School of Management.

Do not resent
growing old.
Many do not get
to have
this privilege.

Elizabeth/David Dodson Gray

20.
Ministry by Inadvertence: "Nudged" by God

50th Reunion Panel
Yale Divinity School

October 11, 2004

20.

Ministry by Inadvertence: "Nudged" by God

50th Reunion Panel, Yale Divinity School
October 11, 2004

This is a transcription of a talk I gave as one of four panelists at my 50th reunion at Yale Divinity School. Each of the panelists was asked to reflect upon their fifty years of ministry. *As the one woman on the panel,* I wanted to describe how a *woman* of my generation had to "work out her calling."

Each panel member's talk was preceded by a resume of their 50 years of ministry. Here is mine.

For the twenty years from 1975 to 1995 ELIZABETH DODSON GRAY was away two or three times a month lecturing in the U.S. and in Canada. In 1992 she lectured in Sweden for a day, and in 1993 for three weeks in the U.K. and the Netherlands. She was invited to campuses, to regional and national conferences, and to church-related settings. A proud moment for her was lecturing about the environment in 1990 to 2,250 people assembled for the prestigious Ware lecture at the Unitarian-Universalist General Assembly.

She also lectures with her husband. When they lecture together, they do it together—not sequentially one lecture and then the other, but together sentence-by-sentence and paragraphs one after one another. In their lecturing and in their life and work together they are radically equal and equally active. Both name themselves as Dodson Gray, using both their "maiden" names.

Liz' lecturing was an outgrowth of work she and David did at MIT's Sloan School of Management for a multi-year seminar on "Critical Choices for the Future." In 1973 they prepared with another MIT colleague the staff work for ten days of Congressional hearings in the 93rd Congress. This was published by the Government Printing Office as Growth and Its Implications for the Future.

Liz' own first book, Green Paradise Lost, *asked why we think we can treat nature badly. She speaks as a feminist theologian, an heir of the Judeo-Christian tradition who is a critic of the Christian theology of our divine right of human "dominion."* Green Paradise Lost *is now viewed as one of two classic eco-feminist texts and has been used in many colleges and divinity schools.*

Her second book, Patriarchy as a Conceptual Trap, *is footnoted with 54 cartoons, and condemns what from the Middle Ages Christian theology called the*

ELIZABETH DODSON GRAY

Great Chain of Being—the cosmic hierarchy which she finds rooted in the patriarchal "ranking of diversity" that begins with men ranking men above women. Ranking diversity IS the conceptual trap.

In 1988 she edited Sacred Dimensions of Women's Experience. *This book emerged out of the life of the Theological Opportunities Program at Harvard Divinity School, and was co-written autobiographically by 31 women, participants and friends of TOP. It is about the religious dimensions of those portions of the total human experience which males never experience and therefore have never named as sacred (for example, women bringing new life in childbirth). That same year the National Film Board of Canada released* Adam's World, *a 19-minute film made for television, about Liz's thought and work.*

In 1994 she wrote Sunday School Manifesto: In the Image of Her?, *contrasting the woman-affirming accounts of Jesus in the gospels with subsequent centuries of woman-denigrating Christian theology and practice. She notes that Christian theology and churches have never repented of this history of denigrating women. She asserts that Christians cannot have a children-friendly tradition until we have a woman-respecting tradition.*

Early in 2004 Liz was honored at the 30th anniversary of the Theological Opportunities Program at Harvard Divinity School, a series of ten Thursday half-day conferences each fall and each spring which she has coordinated and led for the past 25 years. The honoring included a Revere bowl with Harvard seal and a suitable inscription noting her 25 years leading the program at Harvard. Two years ago Liz was awarded the YDS Alumnal Award for her contributions in lay ministry.

Liz says her life has been incredibly blessed by the excitement and synergy of living and working with her partner, lover, husband, editor, publisher and YDS classmate David Dodson Gray. Together they are parents of two neat children, Lisa and Hunter, and four grandchildren.

MINISTRY BY INADVERTENCE— "NUDGED" BY GOD

This is going to be a rather personal reflection about the past fifty years since we all graduated from Yale Divinity School—and about what I would call my "ministry by inadvertence."

On Being "Not Serious" about My Life?

Mary Catherine Bateson in one of her lectures to the Theological Opportunities Program said that, when you look at her resume, you would think she was not serious about her life.

What she meant was that she had gotten professionally educated and trained. But then, like so many women, she had followed her husband from place to place, stepping out of her profession to bear children, and then as she raised her children she literally *improvised* a professional career within and around all of that.

Take a good look at the resume of my life, which was read introducing me. I did all of that *after* I was forty-five. But I ask you first to look at what I did *before* I was forty-five.

ELIZABETH DODSON GRAY

I left Divinity School *not* wanting to have a church, not wanting to be ordained. I wanted to do college work. I indeed did college work. I left Yale Divinity School to be the Associate to the Baptist Minister to Students in Cambridge and for three years I worked joyously. I loved it. Then the on-and-off relationship that David and I had had for six years finally blossomed into engagement and marriage.

What did I as a typical 1950s woman do then? I left my life in Cambridge and my job which fulfilled me, and I joined my new husband in his new job in St. Louis where he was to be low man on the totem pole of a large suburban Episcopal church—and I had *nothing* to do with my deeply felt desire to do ministry.

As many women do, I had children. I birthed and raised children in St. Louis for the next five years. Then we stopped back at Yale Divinity School for a year and we wrote a book together, *Children of Joy: Raising Your Own Home-Grown Christian.* Then we moved west of Boston to the small town of Westboro, where David was the Episcopal minister for the next nine years.

Through all of this I was like a highly-trained running horse, ready to run my race. But I couldn't get out of the starting gate. At some very deep level of my being, it made me very sad.

One of the great blessings of my life is that my children never felt my sadness. They tell me I was a wonderful mother. And they did not know then how very sad I was that I wasn't able to do ministry.

A Different Life

After seventeen years of parish ministry David left Westboro and we went in to Harvard Square to do things. We ended up at the MIT Sloan School of Management in an interdisciplinary seminar about "Critical Choices for the Future," which we ended up helping a senior faculty member run.

And here comes inadvertence.

I was sitting in that seminar (it had twenty-five guys and two women in it) and we were about to write our first papers. The man next to me, a friend, turned to me and said, "Why don't you write *as a woman* about the limits to growth?"

I thought, "How weird!" Not at Smith, not at Yale, not *ever*, had I ever written something as a woman. What could that be, to write something *as a woman*?

All this was happening very early in the Second Wave of the Women's Movement and at this point I had *no,* I repeat—*NO*— feminist consciousness. At Smith and at Yale Divinity School I had *never noticed* the masculine language about God. I had never noticed that 90 percent (or more) of the books I was asked to read were written by men. I had zilcho feminist consciousness. To write as a woman about limits to growth?—I had *no* idea.

But I had already intuited that what I would later call "masculine consciousness" was going to be a problem if we were going to limit growth. What did I mean by masculine consciousness? A major feature of masculine consciousness is extreme competitiveness. It is the bent of mind to climb every mountain—climb them simply because the mountains are there. It is the drive which says "I must do better tomorrow than today," and "Onward and upward." Are you going to try to sell "limits to growth" to that consciousness?—I don't think so.

ELIZABETH DODSON GRAY

The MIT professor told us all our papers would be collected and given to MIT Press which would perhaps publish them as a book. After several months an editor met with us and told us this collection of our papers was "not quite a book." But he said that the most interesting piece in the bunch is Elizabeth Dodson Gray's essay about "Masculine Consciousness and the Problem of Limiting Growth."

From then on I was golden. Whatever I did was taken very seriously.

In 1974 we did the staff work for ten days of Congressional hearings, and this became a book entitled *Growth and Its Implications for the Future*. Because I said it was important, it included a section on consciousness change. And it was also illustrated throughout with cartoons from my collection. The book was distributed that year to all the members of Congress. And during that session of the Congress it was the best-selling publication of the Government Printing Office.

Moving Deep into My Soul

Suddenly I was off and running, into something which was absolutely bubbling up in my soul, which I could not deny.

This book was writing itself inside my very being. I would be walking around Cambridge and suddenly I would whip out a pencil and paper and lean up against the fender of a car to write the words which were coming to me. I was writing what became the first half of *Green Paradise Lost*.

What I was writing was a critique of dominion. Once I got to MIT and knew about the environment, I asked myself, "How, living on this planet encircled by the biospheral cycles which moved through and enlivened and connected everyone and everything, did we ever think we could do whatever we wanted on the planet?"

And you know what? It is our own Judeo-Christian heritage which planted in our minds the illusion that we humans were *above* nature and in God-given control. Do you remember Psalm 8, "What is man that Thou art mindful of him? Thou hast *made him a little lower than the angels and put everything underneath his feet.*"

I am talking about that theology of dominion which by the medieval era had become the Great Chain of Being. It is that which has screwed the pooch for thousands of years. And we are the product of that.

So my passion became trying to convince everyone who had absorbed that concept of dominion with their mother's milk, convince them that the notion of our human dominion is a delusion. It is *not true*. And we are destroying the planet because we *think* this illusion is reality, and that we humans have a God-given status on top.

Tell Us about the Alternative

It was at this point that a friend of mine said something pivotally important to me. And you see here what I mean by inadvertence. The next steps in my pathway were being offered to me by other people. A friend said to me, "Liz, you tell me that hierarchical thinking—ranking diversity—is at the root of every problem we are concerned with on the planet. What," she asked, "would it be like *not* to think hierarchically?—how could we think? You need to tell us."

I thought, "What an interesting question! Maybe I can do that in the last half of my book."

ELIZABETH DODSON GRAY

One Summer by the Sea

We were about to go to our summer place. Bear in mind that we have two teenagers in residence. I am running a household, doing the laundry, doing the cooking, welcoming guests. And I think, *Oh I will write this book while I am here during this summer.*

In addition to what else I had to do, we had made a contract for the month of July to drive up to Northfield Mount Hermon School each week and do a Wednesday evening lecture on limits to growth. So that means we go up there Wednesday afternoon and come back Wednesday night, and Thursday morning I devote myself to my book until Friday noon, when I have to go to the grocery store to buy food for my weekend guests and they leave Sunday night, and then I start again on Monday morning to write again until Wednesday afternoon when we leave again for Northfield Mount Hermon. And I thought, "I think I can do that."

We went off our first Wednesday night to Northfield Mount Hermon and came back that night. Thursday morning I got up and I thought to myself, "There is *no way* I can do this! I am completely out of the mood. I can't do this. My God, what was I thinking?"

At that point inadvertence—no, I would say at this point, "nudged by God"—enters the picture. I feel like Joan of Arcadia (if you watch the TV series) because I felt nudged by God as well as by inadvertence.

Unexpected Fallout from "A Double 25th"

There in my mail that Thursday morning is a letter. And now I need to go back for a minute to explain to you that the May-before-this-July both David and I went to our 25th reunion at Yale and at Smith, and it was the same weekend.

For some unknown reason I decided to write up what I called "the double 25th," about the weekend that we both shared. I sent it off to my alumnae magazine—don't ask me why I did that, it was unsolicited. And I got back in June a response which said, "You know what? When your letter arrived with your little essay, our magazine for June was totally full. But it was so good that we threw something else out and we published your essay."

This was all happening in May and June, and now I am back in July opening this Thursday morning letter.

The letter is from a faculty member at Smith College in the English department (I did not know her), writing to a total stranger and saying to me, "I read your 'Double 25th' and you are a good writer and you must write."

Do you know how often it is that a faculty member at Smith writes to a total stranger to tell them they must write? Not often!—not often! And, believe it or not, like the TV Joan of Arcadia, I got the message. I recognized that it was a nudge from God—I needed to write that book.

So I went out and for the next month in those small spaces of time I wrote the last half of the book. Then David and I spent an intense August month editing the entire manuscript, fighting over every single sentence!

When David and I couldn't get it published by three or four publishers because it was either too feminist or too ecological or too religious, David said, "I will publish it."

I said, "Honey, you don't know how to publish a book."

And he assured me with that immortal male phrase, "What can be so hard?" So he published my books, coming up with these gorgeous color brochures to sell them to the people who teach religion, women's studies and ecology at all the colleges and universities around.

Like Messages in a Bottle

My books began selling and gradually, floating in like messages in a bottle, came invitations to speak. I had no agent or sponsoring organization. I didn't know where they came from. They just flooded in and I started a twenty-year career of lecturing around the country and at points the world. I did this with a passion because I really believed that ranking diversity in our thinking—in any way, shape or form—really *is* the root of the problem. And I really do believe that the theology of dominion is an absolute delusion and deception which will destroy us on the planet.

So those were two ministries I literally fell into by inadvertence and, perhaps, nudged by God. I did not set out to be an author. It took me two or three years to realize that I *had been* an author!—that I had written books and they'd been published and people were buying them and reading them and assigning them to their students.

And I certainly did not set out to be a lecturer. But one moment I must tell you about, because it represents to me a glimpse of what I hoped had been happening in my lecturing and books.

I was lecturing at Agnes Scott College in Atlanta as part of a panel and I had 15 minutes and I was trying so hard to do my whole "shtick." During the reception afterward a young man came up to me and introduced himself saying, "I am a member of the faculty in the philosophy department here." He paused and said, "I am bright enough that I never hear anyone say anything I have not thought before."

But then he paused again and said to me, "I need to tell you, I've never thought *anything* you said this morning."

I thought to myself, I must be doing something right because I knew this guy had *never* questioned the medieval Great Chain of Being—but at least he recognized that what I was saying was something totally new.

"Westboro?"

There is another anecdote which illustrates the cognitive dissonance involved in being a woman/author/lecturer. I was doing the major theological lectures at the weekend-long midwinter convocation of the Unitarian Meadville Lombard Theological School in Chicago.

There were between 50 or 60 of us when we gathered Friday night. One man looked very familiar to me and we ended up sitting next to each other at dinner. He said I also looked familiar and we began playing that game of "Was it here?" or "Was it there?"—all to no avail. So we gave up and just chatted. When he mentioned Westboro, I immediately said, "Do you know Westboro?"

"Yes," he said, "I was the Unitarian minister in Westboro for a few years in the 1960s." I responded that in those years "I was the Episcopal minister's wife in Westboro."

He dropped his fork and exclaimed to me in tones of utter horror, "*YOU* were the Episcopal minister's wife in Westboro?" Translated—he had spent good money on registration and traveled umpteen miles and hours in order to hear all weekend the Episcopal minister's wife from Westboro!

After dinner he retreated to the far end of the room, and we never spoke again. Yes, gender provides substantial cognitive dissonance between the condition of being a female and the role of being an authority worth being listened to and taken seriously.

Leading a Women's Faith Community

Okay, I've had a speaking career and a writing career which I finally came to recognize as ministries. But I must not forget my twenty-five years at Harvard Divinity School leading the Theological Opportunities Program, which I now recognize has also been a ministry.

We started out to do a lecture series fall and spring. But over the years we became a women's faith community where we could challenge any assumption, tell any secret—you know, incest, battery—weep any tear, celebrate any joy. And for those of us who have shared these twenty-five to thirty years together and others who have joined us, this has been such an incredible community, another ministry which happened by inadvertence, so to speak "while I wasn't looking."

In closing I want to say that it has been my experience that if you have a deep passion to do ministry, as I did, it is possible that the ministry will emerge, through inadvertence—emerge *in the mysterious interconnections of the complexities of your own unique life-journey.*

*The Dean of Yale Divinity School
and its Board of Alumnal Affairs*

present this Award for Distinction in

LAY MINISTRY WITHIN THE CHURCH
to
Elizabeth Dodson Gray '54

on this 10th day of October 2000

(Signed) Richard J. Wood, Dean
(Signed) Ian B. Strahan, President, Board of Alumnal Affairs

Elizabeth Dodson Gray is both heir and critic of our Judeo-Christian tradition.

A feminist theologian, her identity is deeply rooted in the Southern Baptist tradition of her childhood.

"I do not remember," she says, "a time when I did not feel a sense of the Divine Presence in my life . . . a deep sense of mystery and a passionate concern for justice." This sense of Presence and concern grounds her commitment to challenging racism, as well as her ministry of eco-feminism.

Elizabeth Dodson Gray joins these concerns in books like *Green Paradise Lost, Patriarchy as a Conceptual Trap,* and *Sunday School Manifesto* by developing a theology of creation sensitive to contemporary environmental concerns.

Ms. Gray earned a B.D. from Yale Divinity School in 1954. Her long-standing lay ministry is concerned with the limits of our finite planet and the values necessary for a sustainable future.

Harvey Cox portrays her ministry in the following manner: "Liz has always been interested in the 'voice' of non-academic women talking about their lives. . . . She has been able to nurture [women] into 'finding their voice,' telling their stories, and articulating [the] spiritual realities and depths of their . . . experience. Women 'doing theology' in their own lives has become a hallmark" . . . of her ministry.

Elizabeth Dodson Gray's life is a lived proclamation of God's call to radical change, her ministry—a life-affirming response to this call. In thanksgiving to God for Elizabeth Dodson Gray's faithful lay ministry, Yale University Divinity School is delighted and honored to recognize her with the Alumnal Board's Award for Distinction in Lay Ministry within the Church.

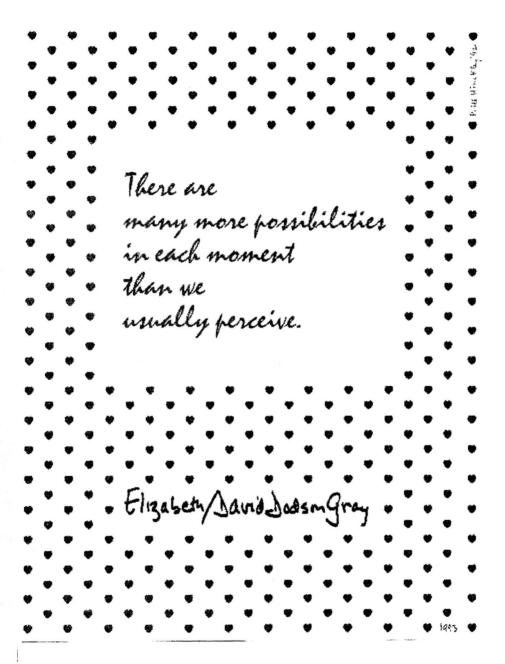

There are
many more possibilities
in each moment
than we
usually perceive.

Elizabeth/David Dodson Gray

195

21.

Come Inside the Circle of Creation:
The Ethic of Attunement

Lecture

Second International Environmental Ethics
Conference, Athens GA

Elizabeth Dodson Gray

April 1992

21.

Come Inside the Circle of Creation:

The Ethic of Attunement

Lecture, Elizabeth Dodson Gray
Second International Environmental Ethics
Conference, Athens GA, April 1992

The Old World View

Our view of reality is basic to our ethic. Behind every ethical system there is what Walter Lippmann has described as "the pictures in our minds of the world beyond our reach."[1]

Our Judeo-Christian tradition gave us one such picture, with its Genesis mandate of "dominion" (Gen. 1:26) which was fleshed out in Psalm 8—"What is man that Thou art mindful of him? Thou has made him a little lower than the angels and put everything else underneath his feet" (Ps. 8:4-6, KJV). What is envisioned here is a cosmic hierarchical pyramid of value—called The Great Chain of Being in the Middle Ages—a pyramid of value with "Man" on top, a pyramid based upon the illusion that you can "rank" the diversity of real life, putting that which is presumed to have more value "up" and in dominion or control over that which is perceived to be of less value and thus "below."

But I think the cosmic pyramid in our heads is actually in this simpler form shown here. This pyramid form is basic also to another more recent "picture in our mind of the world beyond our reach," the Evolutionary picture.

It is interesting that, a century after Darwin, the Evolutionary picture is fundamentally this same pyramid of value. But now God is removed from the top, and the human species is "ascending"—as Jacob Bronowski said in *The Ascent of Man*[2]—from the primordial oceans though the "lower" (simpler) species to the "higher" (more complex) species.

In the evolutionary picture we have confused our human uniqueness with superiority—even though any biologist will tell you that each species is one-of-a-kind, unique. We never asked ourselves if we, as a species, had the best eyes, or ears, or sense of smell, or fleetness of foot—because the answer would be "No." We never asked ourselves if what humans do is as remarkable as the photosynthesis that plants do. Instead, we convinced ourselves that "big brains" are the mark of a superior species. But recent research has revealed that cetaceans (whales, dolphins, porpoises) have an equally large and convoluted brain cortex. Cetaceans, by the sonar of echo-location, can detect sickness, health, happiness, sadness, and sexual arousal in fellow cetaceans. If we could echo-locate, we would be certain we were the superior species!

In both the Judeo-Christian religious picture of cosmic hierarchy and in the scientific evolutionary picture of species hierarchy, you can see manifest the self-serving nature of the game of ranking diversity. Always it is "Man, the ranker" who just happens to end up at the top of his own ranking!

Where Does All This "Ranking" Come from?

There is a cartoon in my book *Patriarchy As A Conceptual Trap*[3] which gives us a clue to the answer to that question. Two men are standing on a suburban lawn and the snow is gently falling from a domed sky. One man is saying to the other: "How do we know we're not inside someone's paperweight?"

The truth is we *are* inside someone's paperweight. We *are* within a bubble of assumptions, a social construction of reality, totally done from the point of view of the male and male life-experience.

We need to pause here to dip briefly into "the sociology of knowledge." In the period from 1909 into the early 1920s scientists then peering into the very heart of the atom were deeply puzzled. When they looked with the "eye" of one technology, light was a wave, but when they used the "eye" of another technology, the same light could seen just as certainly to be made up of particles. But how, they asked themselves, could the same light be two (contradictory) things at once?

There was nothing in their Western intellectual heritage to prepare them for this seeming contradiction. One of them reports they had to become like Zen Buddhists to deal with this phenomenon.

What these scientists finally concluded was that what they saw depended upon how they looked. Or to put it another way, the act of looking affected what was being looking at. What they had discovered was that the standing point of the observer deeply conditioned what the observer could know. Thus, **knowledge is standpoint dependent.**

Building on that realization, a philosopher wrote in the 1970s, **"Reason is standpoint dependent."** How you do your thinking depends upon what intellectual and cultural tradition you take as your standing point. Let us look at some examples.

We all learned in school that Columbus discovered America. Does that mean America was "lost" until Columbus "found" it? That has indeed been our Western view. It was not until the World Council of Churches' General Assembly in Vancouver in the late 1970s that a native American told the gathering that, "From the Native American point of view, Columbus and his men were a few white sailors lost at sea." And they were! They were looking for India and they had stumbled upon a continent they had not known existed. When they got there, they did not know where they were. And they did not appreciate what it was they had found.

So "lost"-ness and "found"-ness is standpoint dependent, profoundly so. Jan Struther in her book of essays, *Mrs. Miniver,*[4] writing about travel makes a perceptive observation that the first few days of returning home are difficult because you as the traveler know you took the center of the world with you. But the people at home quaintly feel the center of the world stayed behind with them. Precisely!

The sociology of knowledge, therefore, tells us that anyone's reasoning will be deeply affected not only by assumptions like these but the realities of race and class and national, ethnic and cultural origin. But it has only recently begun to dawn upon us that reasoning as a standpoint-dependent activity is also deeply affected by sex and gender. The sociology of knowledge teaches us that all of us live within a social construction of reality I have named "Adam's World."

Adam (the male) can say, as is said in Genesis 1, "I've named everything, thought everything, from my point of view." And we, men and women socialized into Adam's World since birth, feel the first line of the caption: "This is the way the world is." We have never experienced another way.

It is no accident that the pervasive "ranking" of reality, imaged in the pyramid, came into being within what I have called Adam's World and what feminists call "patriarchy." I define patriarchy very simply as a slanted society in which males are valued highly and females are valued less, in which men's prestige is "up" and women's is "down."

Margaret Mead said that when she journeyed in her anthropological studies from tribe to tribe she discovered that it did not matter what was done in a particular tribe—it only mattered who did it. If the weaving in a particular tribe was done by men, it was an occupation of high prestige. If twenty miles away weaving was done by women, it was of low prestige. The important thing was which sex did it.[5] Think of cooking in our culture. If it is done by women at home it is no big deal. If we go to a fancy restaurant, we find "gourmet" cooking done by a highly paid and honored "chef"—who almost invariably is male.

We all live within that slanted "Adam's World," and it should not surprise us that this world view, done by men, ranks and rewards highly what men do.

Patriarchy has been and is a problem for humans on this planet because it has been the seedbed of our near-fatal cultural need to "rank diversity." Patriarchy's need to value men above women has set the obsession with comparison flowing in our heads within patriarchy. Patriarchy has given us all as our intellectual heritage a mindset of comparison. Men look at women and ask, "Which of us is better?" Whites look at people of color, straights look at gays, developed countries look at developing countries, humans look at trees and plants, earth and water—and ask, "Which of us is better?"

Thus the problem which patriarchy poses for the human species is not simply that it "ranks" and oppresses women—that's bad enough. **But patriarchy with its obsessive need to rank diversity (beginning with male and female) has erroneously conceptualized and mythed "Man's" place in the universe. Thus by the illusion of dominion which this has legitimated, patriarchy has endangered the entire planet.**

The Ethic from the Old World View

Now, if you were an ethic born of this world view, what would you look like? From this hierarchical view of reality was born the human ethic that we could "do" anything we wanted on the planet, and that whoever and whatever was "below" us—animals, plants, nature—would accommodate to our human wishes.

This anthropocentric illusion about our human species and our "place" on planet Earth has unfortunately been the basis of Western science and technology. We never ask whether a particular invention or scientific "advance" "fits in," because we have only conceptualized ourselves as "above," never "within." Mark Twin has a great saying: "It ain't what you don't know that gits you into trouble. *It's what you think you know that ain't so!*"

This also has given us an atomized ethic of self-interest. When you take isolated, autonomous entities, and rank them into pyramids of value— some "up" and "into control," some "down" and "supposed to obey" and otherwise accommodate—then within that world view, self-interest can be imagined as stopping at each human person's skin. I can maximize my

self-interest—go further up the pyramid of status, power and privilege—and never be touched or hurt by whatever happens to other entities.

Again it is cartoonists who state this ethic of self-interest most sharply
for us. David Pascal in one of his cartoons depicts a landscape of
transparent bubbles, each occupied by a single individual. There is one
person without a bubble who has crawled on hands and knees to a bubble
and is apparently asking its occupant for help. "I'm sorry," says the person
inside, "My responsibility doesn't go beyond this bubble."

Wenzel makes a similar statement in a cartoon in which a door-to-door
interviewer responds to a sportily clad gentleman who has come to his door:
"That's your answer, sir? 'I got mine, the hell with everything'?"

Within such an atomized self-interest, it is of no concern to whites in the
suburbs what happens to Blacks in the inner cities. Men are unconcerned
about the pervasive male violence to women and children. Overstuffed
Americans ignore the reality of hunger in their own country and in Third
World Countries. Those with homes step over the homeless on the way to
work or to the theater. We send pollutants up the stack into the air, and we
think we breathe in air made on some other planet.

The New World View
Into such a world has come new revelations about reality brought to us
in the sciences of ecology and sub-atomic physics. In a multitude of ways,
each of these disciplines has put out the startling news—"Reality is
different than you have imagined it!"

Item: "You can never do just one thing." Life is like sticking your finger
into water; you always produce ripples.

Item: "There is no away to throw things to." Even garbage ends up
somewhere. So do social outcasts and people in prison.

Item: "We humans are within—not atop—life; and life is a system of
interconnections where everything is ultimately affecting everything else."

Item: "We are actually like a fetus, maintained in life by the biospheral
cycles which, functioning like a placenta, bring us our nourishment and also
carry away our wastes."

Item: We are like 'who's' in Dr. Seuss's classic *Horton Hears A Who!*[6]
We dwell within the five-mile high 'fuzz of life' on the tennis ball of the
living Earth.

We are living today (and have always lived) within an interconnected
system. But we do not yet perceive or understand such systems very well.
We have a hard time thinking systemically, partly because many of these
systems are so vast, but also because all our training teaches us to break
problems down into "manageable" parts rather than to see them and deal
with them whole. Our entire formal education consists of experiencing
knowledge divided up into departments and specialties. We are taught to
hold a tight and narrow focus and to value the intense tunnel vision of
educational specialties, disciplines and departments.

But the major problems of our day—whether they involve the health of individuals, the well-being of the economy and our society, or the environmental viability of the entire planet—suggest a new and different world view. We are being compelled by the complexity of these problems to re-imagine the character of our world and to look at reality *whole* rather than *in parts*.

From within any of our specialties, we are being forced increasingly to construe our biological and social existence as a vast system, or system of systems, an extensive and complex network or web of relationships.

The Ethic from the New World View: Is it "Stewardship"?

Now, if you were an ethic born from this new world view of Interconnected System, what would you look like?

Some have advanced an ethic of Stewardship. This is the new attempt within Christianity to deal positively with our environmental crisis. Those who espouse Stewardship seem to be saying, "Yesterday we interpreted dominion as domination. We see now that was a mistake. But we do not repent of the illusion of dominion. We are still secure in our conviction that we have been given by God a primary place of authority and control as humans. But now we will wield that authority with care. We will be good stewards of the world entrusted to us. Tomorrow our hearts will be pure, and we'll do it right!"

Stewardship is still steeped in hierarchy and paternalism. It takes for granted that we know what is right to do. Stewardship assumes that we both perceive and understand the intricate web of life which is complexly organized into ecosystems—of which we humans are constituent parts.

Nor has Stewardship yielded up one iota of patriarchy's illusion of dominion and superiority and smug self-assurance about its own goodness and good intentions. Stewardship is an ethic for those who will be good "husbands" of what is entrusted to them. This is still the old patriarchal tradition, in which males used to "own" their wives, "own" their children—as today we "own" cars and animals and trees and farms and nations "own" continents and even the 200 miles of adjacent ocean, with all that is in it.

Stewardship leaves these illusions of hierarchy, ownership and dominion safe in our heads and hearts. "Taking care of" nature from "above" is not the ethic we need, because we simply do not know enough to do what is promised in the words "taking care."

An Ethic of "Attunement"

What ethic do I think is an adequate ethic to express today our true situation of interconnectedness and relationship?

Instead of Stewardship I would speak of Attunement.

In place of dominion, in place of illusions of control, I am suggesting, yes, Attunement.

Write it on your hearts. It means that we are to open ourselves, we are to listen and look, we are to pay attention.

Why? **Because we are within life,** not above it, and we see life incompletely and often dimly, and we cannot afford not to attune ourselves. Not Paying Attention to our life-supporting systems in the Earth's biosphere will no longer work for us.

Is it possible to attune ourselves to trees and rivers? After all, they don't talk. Christopher Stone, writing in *Should Trees Have Standing,*[7] said ". . . Natural objects can communicate their wants (needs) to us, and in ways that are not terribly ambiguous. I am sure I can judge with more certainty and meaningfulness whether and when my lawn wants (needs) water, than the Attorney General can judge whether and when the United States wants (needs) to take an appeal from an adverse judgment by a lower court. . . . For similar reasons, the guardian-attorney for a smog-endangered stand of pines could venture with more confidence that his client wants the smog stopped, than the directors of a corporation can assert that 'the corporation' wants dividends declared."

What Stone is proposing for "natural objects" is similar to what parents do when they "attune" themselves to the non-verbal body language of infants. All of life is not bound up in words. Body language speaks volumes in parenting, in sexuality, in friendship. The Earth also has non-verbal body language, as Christopher Stone points out. When the air smells bad, when the trees on the crests of hills and mountains die, when the waters are fouled to the eye and nose, it does not take a genius to know that we are doing something wrong—and to stop doing it.

Paying Attention When We Hear Crying
Shortly after my daughter was born I discovered that she cried intensely every time I tried to put her in water to bathe her. So I stopped bathing her that way and kept her clean with baby oil and cotton. In that era of correct child-rearing I didn't talk about this with anyone, I just did it.

My daughter's body language was absolutely clear to me and, attuned, I accommodated. Her hair didn't fall out, her skin didn't rot, and she grew up to be an athletic young adult who takes at least two showers a day. But as an infant bath-water was not for her and I "attuned" myself to her crying.

"What we most need," says the poet Thich Nhat Hanh, "is to hear within ourselves the sounds of the Earth crying." Can we hear the plant in the tropical rain forest, the plant which may have the cure for cancer or for AIDS. Can we hear that plant calling out just before the bulldozers reach it? The extinction of species is as silent as the holocaust furnaces were for individuals. We did not hear a cry then. Can we listen now? Can we hear and attune ourselves at all?

NOTES

1. Walter Lippmann, *Public Opinion* (New York: Macmillan, 1922).

2. J. Bronowski, *The Ascent of Man* (Boston: Little, Brown, 1973).

3. Elizabeth Dodson Gray, *Patriarchy As a Conceptual Trap* (Wellesley, Mass.: Roundtable Press, 1982).

4. Jan Struther, *Mrs. Miniver* (New York: Grosset & Dunlap, 1940), p. 269.

5. Margaret Mead, *Male & Female: A Study of the Sexes in a Changing World* (New York: William Morrow; Morrow Paperback, 1975), p. 159.

6. Dr. Seuss, *Horton Hears a Who* (New York: Random House, 1954).

7. Christopher Stone, *Should Trees Have Standing:? Toward Legal Rights for Natural Objects* (Los Altos, Calif.: William Kaufmann, 1974).

—SOMETIMES THERE ARE RIPPLES FROM A LECTURE—

From: "Anne Blackstone" <abblack@xxx.com,
To: "Liz Dodson Gray"
Sent: Monday, May 23, 2011 11:23 AM

I hope you won't mind my taking this unexpected opportunity to thank you, Elizabeth, for your many insights that have been pivotal for me. I was not at your Ware Lecture at the 1991 Unitarian Universalist General Assembly, but after reading and re-reading <u>Patriarchy As a Conceptual Trap</u> which had been highly recommended to me by my sister, I "really" wanted to hear your UUA lecture. So I order the audio tape from the UUA, listened to it many times, and transcribed it word for word on my typewriter from my tape player. I still have that transcript and just pulled it out yesterday to read again your cautions about referring to the earth or nature as Mother Earth or Mother Nature, which terms I'm hearing more, not less, these days. Yours are the only words of caution on that particular issue I have, and I wanted to weave them into our group presentation on August 7th.

Again, my appreciation and thanks for all your work.

22.

Seeing & Hearing the Living Earth

"Living Earth" issue
Woman of Power magazine

March 21, 1991

22.

Seeing & Hearing the Living Earth

"Living Earth" issue,
Woman of Power magazine
March 21, 1991

To pull the blinds of habit from the eyes,
to see the world without names for the first bright time,
to wander through its mystery, to wonder
at every age and stage, at one with it—
to be alive.[1]

We Are Like "Who's" in the Biosphere

When scientists are thinking about the Earth as a living reality, they call the eleven-mile-deep zone of life that covers the surface of our planet "the biosphere." Further out there is no life, and deeper down there is no life. All the processes that make life exist are here, in this surface membrane that, like the fuzz on a tennis ball, is found only on the outer surface.

Scientists identify ten distinct cycles in that membrane we call the biosphere. These are processes that pervade and enable all life, and that recur so reliably day after day, century after century, that they can be diagramed as circles, sequential patterns of enduring chemical, physical and biological relationships which together stabilize and enable all life.[2]

For example, there is the hydrological cycle—in which water evaporates, moving about then in weather, coming down in rain, swelling rivers and lakes, being drunk by birds and swum in by fish and becoming our drinking water, bath water, sweat and urine and then going on to the sea, only to be evaporated again. Water is an important solvent on our planet, and the hydrological cycle provides the basic transportation system that makes life possible. Water means sap can flow in plants and blood can flow in us. Oxygen, hydrogen, nitrogen and carbon as well as essential minerals move in us with the help of water, and they support life. And then they are excreted back to the biosphere.

These elements are highly reactive and combine readily into various complex energy-absorbing molecules. The chemistry of life is invisible to most of us, but it is totally basic to life. Nitrogen combines with oxygen and carbon and hydrogen to become the DNA blueprints by which growth and life in the various plant- species and animal-species get organized into cells, tissues, organs, individuals. These same elements also become enzymes (catalysts that facilitate various chemical reactions) and amino acids and proteins and soft tissue and muscles. Then over time all these gradually break down again into simpler energy-poor molecules. They give up much of their energy and are available for being used again, taken by green plants powered by the Sun from the random clutter of atoms and simple molecules, and they start out once again as what we call food and oxygen and clean water and life.

These processes need no human intervention to do their silent work. They require no tax subsidies, unlike many forms of human production. And they guide themselves; they need no one with an MBA to manage them! So from the perspective of capitalist industrial culture, the living Earth's biosphere and its life-processes are what economists call "externalities," the "free lunch" that they have always maintained never exists. Who "pays" for this entropic miracle of the biosphere? The tab is paid hour after hour and day after day by our star, our Sun, as it gradually decays toward becoming a future cinder at some point long after you and I are gone.

Like the tiny Who's in the Dr. Seuss story *Horton Hears A Who,* we humans are invisibly small in comparison to the vastness of scale of the planet's size and even more so in comparison to the enormous distances to our Sun and to the other stars in the rest of our Milky Way galaxy.

But though individually we are invisible from space, our collective impact upon this membrane of life, the biosphere, is becoming severe. Our human numbers doubled from 1850 to 1930 and redoubled by 1976 and will quadruple by early in the twenty-first century and octuple shortly thereafter. The earth seems to have a cancer, and our species is it!

Partnership and Cooperation

Where does the air we are constantly breathing, the oxygen, come from? Certainly it doesn't usually come from you or another human being—unless you have a cylinder of oxygen gotten by putting large amounts of energy into some chemical or mechanical process. Usually the oxygen we breathe in was "breathed out" by green plants. The trees, the shrubs, the grass, even the phytoplankton in the oceans, all "*ex*pire" oxygen so that we may "*in*spire" it and live. Oxygen is a waste product of photosynthesis that all forms of non-plant life need (except the chemobacters). And photosynthesis in turn absolutely requires the carbon dioxide we along with other animals, fish, reptiles, birds and insects are constantly breathing out. They and we have coevolved together and so we are all radically dependent upon this mutual exchange, this "pneuma" of life-spirit, as it cycles through the atmosphere.

"How silently, how silently the wondrous gift is given." The silent earthwide inspiration and expiration of oxygen and carbon dioxide is quiet but it enfolds us all and it holds us in being together.

We don't usually think much about this extraordinary and essential partnership and cooperation between plants and us. We also do not think about how the life-processes of the biosphere are passing continuously through our lungs, our blood, our bladders, and through the pores of our skin. And we do not think much about the carbon cycle, the oxygen cycle, the nitrogen cycle and the other biospheral cycles of our planet which make possible the nourishment of food and water even as the silently moving cycles absorb and try to carry away our human and industrial wastes. Like Dr. Seuss' tiny "Who's," we humans live on our planet blissfully unaware that we might be inside the fuzz of one of Dr. Seuss' cosmic tennis balls. We are *that* unaware of the silent energy moving through these biospheral cycles and maintaining us in life.

Learning to Hear What Is Silent

Having eyes, do you not see?
Having ears, do you not hear?[3]

If biospheral cycles sang as they worked, would we hear their melodies?

The humpback whale sings as it moves through the waters, singing long ballads comparable in length and complexity to Homer's *Iliad* and *Odyssey*. Dolphins speak to their researchers and even try to teach them their dolphin language.

I ask myself, What language can I borrow to tune in to all this? How can I attune my listening ear to understand these mysteries?

The cetacean order (whales, dolphins, porpoises) all use sonar echos to echolocate. In this way they "read" other cetacean's body-states and emotions. They are able to discover if another cetacean is sick or well, happy or sad, or even sexually aroused. So much for humans assuming that ours is the most extraordinary species! In a rare moment of seeing ourselves as others might see us, a cartoon depicts one dolphin saying to another, "Although humans make sounds with their mouths and occasionally look at each other, there is no solid evidence that they actually communicate among themselves"[4]

And what of the silent language of the majestic mountain peaks clothed in snow like the ermine of a king's robe? "Time, like an ever-rolling stream, bears all of us away." But the mountains endure, created by geologic energies that move vast tectonic plates shaping continents and oceans into different configurations as ages roll on. What language do mountains speak to tell of the grandeurs of time so vast we can scarcely imagine it?

Do you begin to sense the *nonverbal language* of the earth as a living organism?

It is a symphony of diversity, a great chorale of life-energy. It is an intricate fugue of interconnection. Within it everything has its functions and nothing is ranked as above or better than another, for such a system lives and develops *through* its celebration of diversity. Large and small, tangible and intangible, physical, chemical and biological, solid and liquid and vapor—like the individual notes in a complex musical piece, each and all have a special place and an equal creation-based value.[5]

In diversely luminous ways each and all manifest the life-energy which brought them into being and which flows through them, ceaselessly transforming one manifestation into another. The themes of this grand chorale are creation, transformation and illumination, articulated by diversity exquisitely inter-connected, and based upon a deep nonverbal covenant between the creating and sustaining energy and the entire dynamic system.

The birds understand, and sing as the sun rises. "Every day is a renewal, every morning the daily miracle. This joy you feel is life."[6]

The Eastern Greater Sandhill crane—with its trachea curled like a French horn beneath its breastbone—calls out in ten different calls as it dances. Subatomic particles dance to music-like pulses of energy, some particles dying and some being born in these continually moving probability patterns of energy, energy which has the tensile strength to hold in being all that is.

The Throbbing Rhythms

O this awesome Reality in which we live and move and have our being! Can we open our ears to hear it? Can we in our mind's eye see those fiery angels of Genesis with their flaming swords guarding the limits of our fragile planet, ready to cast into outer darkness those unable to live within the bounds of this sturdy yet fragile life-system? Surely this is the only Eden we shall ever know. Those who claim to be superior, a master race, sow the seeds of their own destruction as they board, this time, a *sinking* ark for the flood that is to come.

Whether we are angels of death or cherishers of life, we are all caught up in a symbiotic dance of cosmic energy and sensual beauty, throbbed by a rhythm that is greater than our own, which births us into being and decays us into dying, yet whose gifts of life are incredibly good though mortal and fleeting.[7]

We are indeed surrounded by species other than our own, and we don't know what they are saying. But the throbbing rhythm of other life-forms calls to us, if we can but shed our self-serving illusion of being "at the top" of creation, can stop playing our childish game of King of the Mountain, and finally can pause to listen, and to look, and to attune ourselves. The call is clear:

So dear humans,
come inside the circle of creation, the community of life.
Find your unique place among your life-neighbors,
but give up your arrogance.
Join hands with insects, animals, and dancing light .
Find your place, and at last be "at home" upon the earth.[8]

NOTES

1. *To Be Alive,* a film produced by Francis Thompson, Inc., for Johnson Wax (text and pictures published New York: Macmillan Co., 1966), p. 1.

2. See *The Biosphere* (San Francisco: W. H. Freeman, Scientific American Books, 1970) for details. Also Paul R. Ehrlich, Anne H. Ehrlich, and John P. Holdren, *Ecoscience: Population, Resources, Environment* (San Francisco: W. H. Freeman, 1977).

3. Mark 8:18; also Jer 5:21, Ezk 12:2.

4. The cartoon by Sidney Harris (1976) appears on p. 90 of *Patriarchy as a Conceptual Trap* by Elizabeth Dodson Gray (Wellesley, Mass.: Roundtable Press, 1982).

5. See *Green Paradise Lost* (Wellesley, Mass.: Roundtable Press, 1979), p. 148 and *Patriarchy as a Conceptual Trap* (1982), pp. 132–134.

6. Gertrude Stein.

7. *Green Paradise Lost,* p. 158.

8. Adapted from Elizabeth Dodson Gray, *The Energy Oratorio* (New York: National Council of Churches, Energy Study Project, 1978), p. 18.

A COMMITMENT TO WALK LIGHTLY ON THE EARTH
by Elizabeth Dodson Gray, 1990

I commit myself, for this day and hereafter, **to attune myself** to the wondrous natural process of creation within which the Creator God has placed us.

I commit myself **to pay attention** to the sun and the wind and the rain, all of which nourish my body in its physical being, and make possible the food and water and air which in turn make my life possible.

I commit myself **to respect** the natural cycles of nitrogen, carbon, oxygen, hydrogen, phosphorous and the rest, which circulate so quietly and invisibly, making human life on this earth possible: "How silently, how silently, the wondrous gift is given."

I commit myself **to honor** the diversity of plant and animal species, evolved through thousands of ages, and forming the complex communities of life we participate in.

I commit myself **to examine** my own ways and those of my culture, so I can recognize—and avoid—what invades and destroys this web of life.

I commit myself **to be faithful and persistent** in amending and updating my personal lifestyle and that of my family.

I commit myself **to turn away from** anything which tramples upon these delicate webs of life-support. I will turn away from all the ways of destruction, domination, control and exploitation.

I pledge myself **to work** within my part of human culture to change all these destructive patterns.

I commit myself **to meditate** on these things in my prayer life, as an aid to attuning myself to the mystery and wonder of creation.

My goal is **to be a gentle and grateful participant in God's creation,** to "walk more lightly upon the earth."

To Be Religious
Today Is to Act on
Behalf of the Planet;

Such Action
Articulates the True
Dimensions of the
Holy Life in Our
Time.

Elizabeth/David Dodson Gray

23.

Power—
That
"Hot Potato"!

TOP Talk, March 30, 2006

23.

Power—
That "Hot Potato!"

TOP Talk, March 30, 2006

Power as a Problem for Women

I think power is a difficult thing for women. Power is subtle and real but very problematic for women. We treat power like a "hot potato"—You take it!—No, you take it!

And I think I know why. We live in a culture that declares power *natural* for men—power enhances men! But our culture declares power is *unnatural* for women. The culture says that power contaminates women and makes them unfeminine, and therefore unlovable and possibly evil. Think of the television portrayal of powerful women, such as Alexis in *Dynasty* and the matriarch in *Falconcrest*.

It is no wonder that women fear power and feel uncomfortable with it. Let me tell you some of my own experiences with power.

My First Discovery of Power

There was a city-wide public speaking contest my sophomore or junior year of high school. I can't imagine why I wanted to enter it but I did.

We were to write a three- or five-minute talk on some idealistic subject ("The world would be a better place if—"), next we were to memorize the talk we had written—and then we were to orate it, declaim it!

The first elimination round for me was in a classroom with about twenty other students and a teacher. When my turn came, I went forward to do my memorized talk—and I left at my desk the cards with my speech on them. I looked out at the other twenty students, and I went blank. I forgot everything—including what my

219

talk was about. If I had been able to remember that, I would have ad-libbed it! I was like the proverbial "deer in the headlights."

The teacher took pity on me and said, "We'll do the other students, and then come back to you. But this next time, bring your cards up to the front of the room with you!" So I got a second chance to do it again, and I can't imagine why—but I won that round.

The next thing I remember was being on the stage in front of my entire high-school student body for the final elimination to find one person from our school to go to the city-wide final of the contest.

Now I need to explain to you about the high schools in Baltimore when I was growing up in the 1940s. There were two girls' high schools, Eastern and Western, each with 2,000 girls. I went to Eastern, my mother had gone to Western. There were two boys' high schools, City College for 2,000 college-bound boys, and Polytechnic for 2,000 boys who were not college-bound.

Facing 2,000 Boys
At my own high school I was up on the stage in front of 2,000 girls. I don't remember speaking but I won and went on to the finals.

What I still do remember is being up on the stage at the city-wide final, which took place at Polytechnic before 2,000 adolescent boys. I can remember looking out and thinking, "This could be the worst experience of your life!"

But it also occurred to me that if I could get through this speech, I would never have to be afraid of speaking anywhere!

I was the next-to-last to speak, and that gave me some time to settle down. I did the speech, and *I didn't win!* A boy won. (Why am I now not surprised by that?) But the experience was for me like breaking the sound barrier.

I had experienced the gift of power. I had discovered I could hold listeners in the palm of my hand. I could do this with my voice, my words, my ideas, the passion of my convictions. It was a huge gift. *And because no one expected me to discover this gift of power—and certainly not so young*—it came to me with no warning labels which proclaimed "This power will hurt you."

So it was *my* gift, part of the gift of my unique genetic heritage. I did not experience this power as a "hot potato"; I could hold it in my hand and I did not fear it.

The Power of My Own Money
My second story is about money. We have heard that "Money is power." And we have observed that men have that money and that power. But conventional wisdom has it that women should not have that power of their own money because it will threaten the fragile male ego of their man. I believed that.

When I was born, my parents were much older than most parents of their day. My mother was forty when I was born, my father was forty-six. My father died my senior year in college. My father had been an investment banker and when he died I inherited some money (stocks). I am not sure why my mother did not inherit it all when he died. But I did inherit a clump of money in the form of stocks.

I put the fact of my money away in the hip pocket of my psyche and tried to forget that I had it. I went through Yale Divinity School and then came to Cambridge as Associate to the Baptist minister to students in Harvard Square. Then I married. And I couldn't wait to give my money away to David—not to him actually but to the legal entity of "us"—lest it threaten the fragile male ego of my new husband. As a new bride I did not know yet that David has the most *un*fragile male ego ever! It has been one of the great gifts of my life.

So I dragged us both to a lawyer's office. But our lawyer-friend told us that it was best if you leave money with the person who brings it into the marriage. "Why?" we asked. He said, "Because it makes it easier in a divorce." We said in unison, "But we're never going to divorce." His response was, "That's what they all say!"

So we left his office with my money still uneasily in my hip pocket. We used some of it to pay for private schools for our children, which we could never have afforded on David's clergy salary.

My House

We also knew that when we retired at the end of David's ministry, we would face a housing crisis because at that time churches *provided* housing for their clergy. And when you retired, you were supposed to move out of the rectory and get out of town so as not to threaten the minister who was coming after you. And you had no house and no equity.

To anticipate this crisis we bought with some of my family money a house on the Connecticut shore of Long Island Sound, a house we could use for vacations and eventually retire to. And because it was bought with my money, it *was*—and *is*—*my* house.

We occupied the shore house in the summer, and we rented it during the academic year. One year we rented it to a man who was CEO of his own company and he was building his own retirement home at Truro on Cape Cod. His house was going to be completed sooner than he had expected and he wanted to move to Truro and sublet our house.

But our lease with him said that before he could sublet *we* must approve the new tenant. So one afternoon we all met in the living room of the shore house—David and I, the CEO, and a very lovely mid-life couple. Both the CEO and the new couple were busy explaining their suitability to David, trying to convince him.

Then David said, "You know, it's really Liz who owns this house. It's really *her* decision."

Suddenly there was a large sucking sound in the room. It was like the moment when, in the Julia Roberts film *Pretty Woman,* Richard Gere's character is with her in a posh Rodeo Drive boutique in Los Angeles, and he tells the manager, "Suck up to her—she has the credit card."

Once again I knew I had power in the palm of my hand. And now the power of money did not frighten me.

Like the power to speak passionately and move people, this power of money was a gift, a part of the legacy of my family to me, and I could now be comfortable with it "in my hands." I did not any longer have to keep it hidden away in my hip pocket.

Power As Gendered

Power is very gendered in our culture. Let me tell you how I discovered some of the male/female dimensions of power. It was during our many speaking engagements together.

Once we were introduced late, and we knew we would have to stop precisely at noon because lunch would be served then. We started our presentation without our being able to consult together about how we would best shrink our presentation by about five minutes to meet that lunchtime deadline.

Now I need to explain just how David and I lecture together. This did not mean that one of us did Part 1. of a lecture and the other did Part 2. David created these large poster-board visuals—graphs and diagrams and key words about concepts. We were the forerunners of the *Powerpoint* software program, and we were still in an era when everyone else just lectured by reading from their lecture notes or their typescript.

We had these large brightly-colored visuals which accompanied our interactive and spontaneous "spiel," which was provided by both of us about each visual. We began with a pile of 30 to 40 posterboards on a table in front of us, and as we spoke David would pick up the next visual from the large pile, and we would both speak interactively about that visual.

Then while I was putting that visual down into the empty space beside the large pile, David was picking up the next visual from the other pile. It was fast-paced, it was easy to listen to and learn from, and we enjoyed a lot of rapport with our audiences.

This particular day when we are introduced late, we both know we are going to have a problem and we haven't decided how we will deal with it. So when David in the middle of our presentation picks up the next visual and he decides this was one we could skip, he says, "We don't have to talk about this one today." And I say, "Oh yes, we do!" And he says, "We have to eliminate something, and this is a good one to cut." And I say, "No, no, this is important!"

Slowly the audience realizes that their speakers standing before them are really disagreeing—yes, actually having a little fight in front of them, each tugging on their side of this one visual which David wants to skip over. Our audience is electrified. Here are two seemingly equal powers fighting, and they sense that no one knows who will win—least of all us! I don't remember if we used that visual or not. I do remember that our audience was dumb-struck with this suddenly-erupting power struggle.

Who Interrupts Who?

Social permission is given to men to interrupt women. Social permission is *not* given to women to interrupt men. Bear in mind that when we were lecturing together, we were doing it spontaneously. Sometimes we would finish each other's sentences. We would often interrupt each other with ideas or numbers the other had forgotten this time through, because it was all ad-libbed.

Gradually we noticed that when David interrupted me there was no resulting emotional ripple moving through the room, as there was when I interrupted him. People would shift their body positions or make a comment to their neighbor—definitely a ripple.

After a few years of observing this ripple-effect, we decided to incorporate into our introduction a comment about how, when we lecture spontaneously, we interrupt each other; and how we have noticed that when David interrupts me, no one notices. But when I interrupt him, people do notice. So we told audiences we wanted them to know that, yes, we would both be interrupting each other, and it doesn't bother us and we hope it won't bother them.

ELIZABETH DODSON GRAY

An Introduction Becomes a Model

We were asked once to speak to a national gathering of some 700 Roman Catholic women religious. The Leadership Conference of Women Religious (LCWR) were 700 mother superiors, each leading their own order of "nuns" or women religious.

We were the first couple ever to speak to them, and the first non-Catholics. And they had invited us to speak to them all day, in the morning on "Limits to Growth"—our visuals about the future. Then after lunch I was asked to do my eco-feminist critique of hierarchical theology, including my critique of our own Christian tradition (which is what I write about in my books).

Because we were something of an anomaly for them, we were asked to describe and identify ourselves *after* we were introduced by them.

We pondered about how best to describe ourselves. We finally came up with **"radically equal"** as a descriptive phrase. But sometimes couples who feel radically equal nonetheless have patterns in which the male initiates and the female responds. So we felt we needed something in addition. We finally came up with the phrase **"equally active."** We were not totally thrilled with it but we decided to use it.

Then we decided to have some fun. David would say we are **"radically equal"**—and pause. And then I would say **"and equally active."** That's what we would do.

So when we stood up to identify ourselves, David said (as we had agreed), **"We are radically equal"**—and paused. We were both amazed to be engulfed suddenly in a resounding room-filling spontaneous applause!

When this quieted down, I was feeling very much like a useless P.S. but per our agreement, I said, **"—And equally active!"** Much to our amazement we again experienced spontaneous and lasting applause.

These Roman Catholic women religious were very sensitive to hierarchy and to our critique of hierarchy. They knew about imbalances in power!

A Radical Act

We came to realize that our acting out in public our ***being radically equal and equally active*** was, in itself, a radical act. Just how radical we discovered sometime later in a much smaller meeting in a local church.

There were about twenty people gathered to listen to our Limits to Growth talk, and we were not up on a stage but on the same level with our listeners, standing behind a table which held our piles of visuals.

When we finish our talk, there is usually a pause in which people are collecting their thoughts, and then usually a torrent of questions. "This is terrible! We are destroying the earth! This is urgent! Have you told the president? Does the Congress know?" and so on. Remember, this was thirty years ago and our news of future problems with global warming and energy shortages and global population trends and food needs were exactly that, NEWS!

So this night there was the usual thoughtful pause before the questions. Then a man in the middle of the first row raised his hand and asked us, "Who is the *boss* in your house?" I was so astonished at his question that I said, "I beg your pardon?"—and he repeated, "Who's the *boss* in your house?" David and I, almost in unison, said, "There isn't any!" He responded, "There's got to be!"

The significant thing about his comment is where this man perceived the threat to his life. The threat he saw was not in destroying the earth, or running out of energy. The threat which frightened him was the lack of male dominance he saw in the equality of power which David and I were enacting before him.

What Is the Point of These Stories?

Power is given to us at birth as a part of our human talents and our personal uniqueness.

We are given the power of our minds, our bodies, our intentions, our purposes, our passions. This is our human package—our genetic heritage.

This is God's gift to us at birth, equally to female and to male. This is life's gift to us at birth, equally to female and to male.

Ours will never be the world we want until half of the human population, *our women half,* is able joyfully to claim our rightful power, to be unafraid of it, to be comfortable with it, and to use it for good purposes.

I had finished planning my talk when I found this quotation. I will close with it. It is from Nelson Mandela's 1994 Inaugural Speech:

Our deepest fear is not that we are inadequate. Our deepest fear is that we are powerful beyond measure. It is our light, not our darkness, that frightens us. We ask ourselves, who am I to be brilliant, gorgeous, talented and fabulous? Actually, who are you not to be? You are a child of God. Your playing small doesn't serve the world. There's nothing enlightened about shrinking so that other people won't feel insecure around you. We were born to make manifest the glory of God that is within us. It's not just in some of us; it's in everyone. And as we let our own light shine, we unconsciously give other people permission to do the same. As we are liberated from our own fear, our presence automatically liberates others.

24.

Looking for God

Sermon
First Baptist Church in Newton

—August 15,1996—

24.

Looking for God

A Sermon, First Baptist Church in Newton, August 15, 1996

I think we all want and seek the presence of God in our lives. The question is, how do we *find* it?

Or perhaps the question is a different one—how would we know the presence of God if we really did find it? How would we *recognize* the presence of God?

Or perhaps the question is whether we are not like the disciples on the road to Emmaus (Lk 24:13–35). Are we prepared to recognize God *in our midst?*

Capsized

There is a wonderful story of a very religious man who went out sailing one summer afternoon. His sailboat was capsized by a thunder squall and promptly sank, and this man was suddenly bobbing along in the water a long distance from shore.

Another man came by in his power boat and offered to rescue him. But the drowning man waved him away: "No," he said, "God will rescue me." Then a helicopter came, and he waved that away also, saying, "No, God will rescue me."

Finally the man heard a voice coming to him out of a cloud, or perhaps it was a clap of thunder, asking: "What are you waiting for?" The man answered: "I'm waiting for you to save me, God."

And the man then heard God say: "But I sent you a boat and then a helicopter. What do you want?"

I am suggesting that our problem may not be the absence of God's presence in our lives, but actually our failure to *recognize* that presence.

A New Thing

In Isaiah 43:19 God is portrayed as saying: "Behold, I am doing a *new* thing. Do you not see it?" In the Old Testament biblical tradition religious people felt the presence of God with them as they journeyed from bondage to freedom. In next Sunday's lesson from the Book of Exodus we will remember how Moses said, "LOOK—there is God in the bush that burns and is not consumed!" (Ex3:3)

I hope we will later hear Moses' sister Miriam's voice and her exultant song, saying, "LOOK—God has rescued us from Pharaoh's army in our passing unscathed through the Red Sea waters!" (Ex 15)

And later when they remembered that difficult passage and how their journey with Moses had seemed interminable before they finally got to the Promised

Land, they said: "LOOK—we saw God's presence guiding and protecting us. It was as though God provided us with a cloud for shade by day in that desert heat, and a pillar of fire so that we could see at night." (Ex 13:22)

"To Have Lived in a Time of a Council"

I remember teaching at Boston College through the 1980s in a summer program with a wonderful Roman Catholic woman religious, Sr. Clare Fitzgerald. She would tell our students, "Have you realized that we live in a time of miracles? We have lived in the time of a council!" [meaning the Second Vatican Council]. "Do you know," she would say, "how few Christians in the entire history of Christianity, have been privileged to live in a time of a council of the church?" For Clare, that Council was a spirit-filled miracle which had transformed her own life, and was transforming the church she loved.

I think that we too live in a time of miracles.

Look at what has happened in our time in South Africa. Nelson Mandela and the country's white prime minister, F.W. LeKlerk, led that country up to and through a peaceable transition out of Apartheid. What could have been a bloody and violent race-war of independence was averted. It was a miracle which is still happening.

Growing Up Amid People in Bondage

Now I grew up in the South of the 1930s and 1940s, when it was still dominated by Jim Crow laws and very segregated. For people, both black and white, segregation infiltrated even our life at home and dominated our awareness. For example, when I was growing up, the practice in my house was that our black cook ate by the kitchen stove while we ate at the family dinner table seven feet away.

It all made me deeply uncomfortable, and from an early age I knew it was terribly wrong. Everything my Southern Baptist church taught me of the Bible and God and Jesus reinforced my gut sense that these patterns of relations between the races was wrong, a great injustice that God hated and despised much more even than I did.

I was thrown out of my high-school lunch group following a classroom debate in which I had taken an anti-segregation stand. And this was Baltimore, Maryland. It was not the deep South of that day.

My University Baptist Church in Baltimore in that day was segregated, as was every other institution in the city. These were the World War II years, and I as a teenager was agitating, both at home and at church, over "the race question." My mother (who did not appreciate my views) finally pointed out to me that I would soon be going off to college—and she would really like me to tone down what I was saying about race, so she might be able to continue attending this church which she and my father had helped found!

Becoming an Outsider in One's Own Place

I did go to a college in the North, and I knew I would be in deep trouble if I ever returned to the South of that day. The people of the South then were keeping people like me "in line" in a variety of ways. There was name-calling. I was a "nigger-lover." There was social exclusion or ostracism. "We won't eat with you any longer, or come to your house any more." And the name-calling and the ostracism were backed up by the threat of violence. You knew of the Klan and about crosses being burned on people's lawns, and about lynchings of black young men who were regarded as "out of line."

I left the South in September 1947, almost exactly 49 years ago. I went to Smith College and to divinity school at Yale with the awareness that I could never go back to the South of my youth because I could not keep my mouth and my heart shut about the injustice of racial oppression. I would stay away because I did not want to die.

That era was brought back to me forcibly by the television dramatic series on PBS, *I'll Fly Away*. I could hardly watch this marvelous drama because it gave me that same old anxiety in the pit of my stomach. I have not yet been able to summon the spiritual energy to see the current film, *A Time to Kill*. But I know I must as a part of my continuing commitment to God's presence in the issues of justice and fairness today.

"Killers of the Dream"

When I read Lillian Smith's book *Killers of the Dream[1]*, I understood what she was saying. She as a white woman in the South saw that one effect of segregation on whites was to kill the dreams of their children. We are told we lived in a democracy. Yet our eyes and ears told us *we lived in a terrible caste system of race.*

Our churches and parents preached to us a gospel of love. "God loves you, Jesus loves you, love one another," we were told. *Yet we lived in a terrible system of racial hatred, hovering violence, and systemic oppression.*

For me, the result was what Harvard New Testament scholar Elisabeth Schüssler Fiorenza calls "a hermeneutic of suspicion." My basic stance was to be skeptical of religious claims that "God this . . ." or "God that . . ." As an adolescent I knew too many religious adults who could tell me the day and hour when they had "met Jesus"—but if they approved of segregation (and most of them did), then I was personally certain they had never met Jesus!

Why am I telling you this? Multiply my childhood experience a thousand or ten-thousand fold, and you have South Africa under the Apartheid caste system.

I could only imagine, based upon my own experience, the psychic trauma of living, white *or* black, in that South Africa. I have known personally what a tortured existence it is to be white in a deeply segregated society in which your supposedly privileged life as a white young person is poisoned by the corrosion of the daily denigration of another group of fellow human beings. You are also poisoned by that process. Your own white guilt, your deep sense of the betrayal of your own best ideals, and the hovering violence necessary to keep that system of oppression in place—all take their toll. And I knew that if this is the white experience of segregation in the U.S. South, then I could not possibly imagine all that it meant to be either white or black in South Africa.

An Historic "Miracle"

But in our lifetime—in our newspapers and across our television screens—we have seen a peaceful end to Aparthid.

In the early 1960s I personally knew a white family that had already emigrated from South Africa, fleeing what they were sure was going to be the future blood bath in their country. So this peaceful transition was something that not they, nor I, even in our wildest dreams, could imagine! Yet a few years ago a peaceful election was negotiated and, despite sporadic violent attempts to stop it, finally happened. Legal apartheid has ended, and a new constitution for the new government has been negotiated.

Richard Stengel, writing in *Time* magazine (May 8, 1995) had this to say.

> One year after the election of Nelson Mandela, blacks and whites live in proud, hopeful peace. . . . Anyone who knew it then and sees it now knows the country is utterly altered. A year of freedom has filled blacks and whites alike with pride, with a sense of renewal and, most important, hope. . . . [It is a] psychological sea change that this long-troubled land has undergone. (p. 80)

Don't you call that a miracle?—I do. Can't you just imagine God saying to us: "I sent you the Berlin Wall coming down. Didn't you get that?"

"I sent you the extraordinary person of Nelson Mandela to guide my people out of slavery into a new kind of possibility."

In our newspapers Nelson Mandela has been characterized as his nation's George Washington, and more than one writer has said that without the unique personal character of Nelson Mandela, a peaceful transition could not have been accomplished.

God might also say to us, "I sent you Martin Luther King, Jr. with a message of love and peaceful resistence to racial oppression here in the U.S." Again, God might ask, "What else really do you want?—Carry on this work, it is not finished. Do not look back only to Moses and to Jesus and to Luther and to Calvin—but also look to Rosa Parks and Martin Luther King, Jr., to Mikhail Gorbachev and Nelson Mandela."

Discerning the Presence of God in the Struggle

Now I did not promise you a sermon about racism but one about discerning the presence of God. But the truth is, you can always discern the presence of God in the struggle against injustice and oppression. Wherever and whenever that struggle is going on, count on it, God is in the midst of it. In countless burning bushes God says, "I have seen the suffering of my people, and I have come down to save."

When I grew up in the segregated South I could not have imagined today's sports fans cheering black athletes on integrated teams (which are predominantly black), or an ovation and presidential hopes for Colin Powell.

But the bush still burns in the South's arsoned black churches and the ruined lives of our inner cities.

God may well be saying to us today, "Do you not perceive my activity today, now, in your midst? Always I am leading my people from bondage to freedom, from unfairness and injustice to justice and peace."

"Do you see my hand in leading women through the ages into new possibilities and new choices? Do you see my hand now, leading women from bondage to freedom, out of a gender-caste system which is global in scope, and based on gender rather than skin-color?"

When women tell the story of the United Nations conference which took place in Beijing in September 1995, we might do worse than phrase the accounts in Exodus terms. To do this is to suggest that God has provided us with 20th century equivalents of the Exodus cloud by day and pillar of fire by night to protect and guide us on the still-long march to a gender-equal world.

Ask yourself: Do you only have eyes for what God has done in the past? The justice issues of our day, including straight and gay issues, present us with the challenge to respond to and work with God's righteous determination to overturn bondage and injustice and to raise people up into freedom, up into what Jesus in the Fourth Gospel characterized as "the fullness of life." We can be sure that the God who created the immense diversity of natural and human life is not pleased when that God-created diversity is put down, denigrated and oppressed.

Do we have eyes to see, do we really have ears to hear, what God is doing today, doing (yes, right here) in our midst?

I am convinced Sister Clare Fitzgerald is right: we do live in a time of miracles. The life of our times does not consist of just political events and what you see on television news. As in the past this is a time of birth: new children like Moses are being born and with them new possibilities. New leaders are coming of age and being brought forth upon the stage of history, bringing with them new possibilities for God and for us to reach toward the fulfillment of justice. And the biblical God of justice is always present in the cloud that shields us by day and in the pillar of fire that helps us see our way even in the darkest times. *God is always leading Exodus people toward justice.*

God's Presence in "the Still Small Voice"

But God's presence is not just to be seen and felt in the large justice movements of our era. God's presence is also available to us in what Elijah (1 Kg 19:12) characterized as the silence or "the still small voice" of life's every moment. *God's presence is here because every moment of life is a gift, a gift which (whether we perceive it or not) potentially reveals to us its giver, God.*

First, there is the gift of time. Sometimes we only really appreciate the gift of time when it seems to be running out, as when we are living with imminent death, as in cancer or AIDS or in wartime.

But even our personal gift of time is dwarfed by the immense gift of God's time in creation. We sing of such an expanse of time when we sing: "Before the hills in order stood . . ." This summer David and I traveled to the Grand Canyon. Here is truly the Creator God revealed in time and space. It took two *billion* years—two thousand million years—to lay down the layers of sedimentary rock under ancient continent-long seas. And then for the last 6 *million* years what we now call the Colorado River has cut a mile deep into those layers of rock, and then the rain and snow and wind have shaped the Grand Canyon to be the revelation of the grandeur of God which we can now glimpse in this way only at this spot. "Truly awesome."

As our traveling companion said, we were able to "see, comprehend, and revel" in that glory of God, as revealed in this one-of-a-kind window into the time and space of God's creation.

Richard Cartwright Austin writes of just such an experience in the Grand Canyon:

Today I noticed how pale the rock is when newly exposed by a break, and how complex the colors become as the rocks weather and age.

I realized that the colors around me were alive. That is, they expressed energetic chemical and biological interactions as rock met sun, rain, and wind, as leaching metals interacted with the atmosphere, as lichen and plant life took hold, and as the whole system was caressed by cycles of sun, shadow, and darkness and challenged by heat, freezing, and thawing. The rock forms seemed stolid, but their colors were alive and active, products of an ever-changing array of hues to delight the eye.

Cartwright continues:

Reading John Muir prepared me for the notion that rocks speak their history, so a knowing eye can read an exciting story. . . .
[But] what I saw was the life of today—the colors rejoicing.
In the Grand Canyon water and wind have rescued rocks from the dark depths of the earth and given them new birth in the light of day. They dress themselves in rich colors and give praise.[2]

We too can see the handwork of God and give praise.

Mary Southard, the wonderful creation-spirituality artist and poet-writer who is also a Roman Catholic woman religious, writes: *"I stand still until I wear the colors of the sunrise in my soul."*

There is this whole overwhelming gift of nature—the sea, the sky, the wind, the sunshine, the rain, the flowers, the trees, the animals, the sunrise and the sunset, all of it. What a rich heritage this is, steady but also constantly changing and evolving. In Hebrew Scripture, Job 38 and Psalm 136 are similar recitals of God's gifts to us in this world, a world which is such an incredible context for human life.

All of creation is trying to break through the closed doors of our senses, to reveal to us the presence of the Spirit-God who dwells within the gift.

The Question

Sometimes I have this fantasy about life after death. It is that when we come into the presence of God, the still small voice will say expectantly, "Well, did you enjoy it?" And we will say: Enjoy what? And God will say: "My gift to you—life—did you enjoy it?" And most of us will say incredulously: "Is that what we were supposed to do with it, *enjoy* it?" And God will say: "Yes! Time, life, beauty—it was a one-time gift from me to you. And I hoped you would enjoy it."

So ask yourself this question: *Do we receive the gift of life but fail to see in this gift the hand and the heart of God as the giver of life?*

The April 10, 1995 issue of *Time* magazine ran a major feature under the headline, "Can we believe in miracles?" The article had a quote from the great American poet and lover of life, Walt Whitman, who wrote: "To me every hour of the light and dark is a miracle. Every cubic inch of space is a miracle." Yes, I say, Precisely! Yes!

Do you remember Elizabeth Barrett Browning's lines:

Earth's crammed with heaven,
and every common bush afire with God;
But only he who sees, takes off his shoes,
The rest sit round it and pluck blackberries.

(Aurora Leigh, Book 7)

Or listen to e.e. cummings:

I thank you God for most this amazing day:
for the leaping greenly spirits of trees
and a blue true dream of sky;
and for everything which is natural
which is infinite
which is yes.[3]

ELIZABETH DODSON GRAY

So when you open your eyes tomorrow morning to the incredible gift of light and life, do not forget to perceive the miracle. And when you read the morning newspapers, do not forget to read between the lines of the Exodus God on the long march to justice. And when you move into your day, do not forget to be aware of the presence of God *within* your day, in God offering to you moment by moment the amazing gift of yet another day, a gift given to you daily by the God of all life.

NOTES

1. Lillian Smith, *Killers of the Dream: An Autobiography of a Southerner and an Analysis of the South* (Garden City, NY: Anchor Books, Doubleday & Co.).

2. Richard Cartwright Austin, *Beauty of the Lord: Awakening the Senses* (Atlanta: John Knox Press, 1988), pp. 43–44.

3. E.E. Cummings, *Complete Poems 1904–1962*, ed. George J. Firmage (New York: Liveright Publishing Co., 1991).

25.

Interpreting the Furor Over the RE-imagining Conference

Minneapolis, MN—November 4–7, 1993

Elizabeth Dodson Gray

—article—

—Presbyterian Outlook, April 11, 1994
—National Catholic Reporter, March 1994
—Witherspoon Society. May newsletter
—Resource Ctr for Women & Religion in the South,
May newsletter

25.

Interpreting the Furor over the RE-imagining Conference

Elizabeth Dodson Gray

The Furor

The feminist Christian RE-imagining Conference (held in the Minneapolis Convention Center November 4–7, 1993) has provoked a large controversy in some Christian circles (see *Christian Century,* Feb. 16, 1994). For example, Robert Bullock, editor of *Presbyterian Outlook,* in an editorial (Jan. 24, 1994) urged upon his Presbyterian Church USA a full General Assembly Council inquiry and council action. Bullock cited the strong support of the *Presbyterian Outlook* in the past for the "inclusion of women in the life and ministry of the Presbyterian Church" and expressed concern that the controversy over the conference "could damage the highly legitimate cause of justice for women" (p. 8).

As charges and responses fly back and forth, and inquiries and whatever else develop, it is important to clarify the real issue which is at stake in this conference. Attended by 2200 women and 83 men from all over the world, participants were intent on doing just what the conference title invited them to do.

The conference embodied the reality of women finally standing up in the Christian tradition as equal participants in the "naming game."

What Is This "Naming Game"?

Throughout recorded time men have "named the sacred" from the standing point of their male body and male life-experience. It is not accidental that the Genesis 2 account of the creation in Hebrew scriptures has Adam "naming" all the animals. Naming is power, the power to shape a culture's ways of perceiving and thinking about reality so that they serve the interests and goals of those doing the naming. Thus patriarchal Christian theology, as well as culture and history in general, has been male-reflective, truly "created in the image of him."

To stand on this power base of being the "namer" in the culture is to see oneself as "fully a subject" in the historical process—one who is acting out of one's own initiatives, and never acted upon as "object." One is a doer rather than the done-to.

The male of the human species has, in a grandiose way, always tried to claim such full "subject power" for himself (including sole possession of the power of naming). And almost invariably he has desired for his female partner in the species to be not the "namer" but the "named," not the "norm-maker" but the "normed-upon," not the active "subject" of history but the passive "object" of male naming. She is to be done-to, not the doer, in their relationship.

Within the social construction of reality done from the point of view of the male life-experience, woman is named as "Other" (as Simone de Beauvoir pointed out in *The Second Sex* [1949]), and defined as non-namer as well as non-equal.

Within our own Christian tradition, women were named from that male standing point to be inferior, evil, unclean, and grotesque. (For "chapter and verse," see Margaret R. Miles, *Carnal Knowing: Female Nakedness and Religious Meaning in the Christian West* [1989], and Uta Ranke-Heinemann, *Eunuchs for the Kingdom of Heaven: Women, Sexuality and the Catholic Church* [1990].)

Throughout the centuries of Christian theology, men have misused that power of naming to denigrate women in a kind of theological violence which many feminists feel has been the essential backdrop legitimating the violence against women. (See Rosemary R. Ruether, "The Western Tradition and Violence Against Women," in *Christianity, Patriarchy and Abuse,* ed. Joanne Carlson Brown and Carole R. Bohn [1989].)

A Fight Over the Power to "Name"

So the issue raised by the RE-imagining Conference is *not* whether some male-defined boundaries of orthodoxy, heresy and blasphemy have been transgressed.

This is really a fight over the power to name. It is a fight about who is to keep watch over the boundaries of orthodoxy and heresy, and who has the "naming" right to define those boundaries and make those definitions authoritative.

So fundamentally, the question is whether Christianity will go on for another millennium within its old rigid confines of being male-defined, male-reflective, and female-denigrating.

The Christians protesting the RE-imagining Conference are not repenting for those long centuries of the misuse of male naming-power in which the male shapers of our Christian tradition chose to denigrate women. The full extent of this denigration is only now being fully documented by Christian feminist scholars. Instead, these Christians are resisting sharing with women that power to name.

Most men today seem willing (magnanimously) to include women as full participants into most of their own male-clergy clubs and into their very male social construction of Christian reality. But more than a few apparently are not willing to move over and share with women that great and decisive power of naming.

The "Washington Monument" Syndrome

There is perturbation in some denominational circles about the use in the conference of the biblical metaphor of God as "Sophia," including some sensuous references in the closing worship to female bodily incarnation of Sophia.

But the sensuous bodily dimensions of the Godhead have never bothered male Christians when portrayed in their own male terms, as in the super-active and super-ethereal male sperm (Lk 1:35, 37) which impregnated Mary to "beget" Jesus. That sperm image resonated well with male sensibilities!

Likewise, the bodily dimensions of the Godhead were not considered heretical *or* blasphemous when, on the ceiling of the Sistine Chapel, Michelangelo portrayed the Great "I AM" Creator of the Universe as a very bodily-male patriarch with long beard and bulging muscles. No, there was no cry of heresy about this, then or now. Instead, this imagining by Michelangelo became for centuries a visual icon for the theological axiom that "God created man in *his* own image."

Why was there no great furor over this imagining by Michelangelo? —Because imagining God as male not only resonates with male sensibilities, but it also reflects a long tradition of human males in their imaginings creating God in their own (male) image.

Our language, as well as our theology, reflects our life in what I have called Adam's World (see *Patriarchy as a Conceptual Trap* [1982]). Our language is like a Rorschach test, imaging back to us reflections of uniquely male genital experiences. Recall such statements as "the *thrust* of his thinking" and "a *penetrating* statement." Recall also: "a *seminal* book" and even the word *seminar.* Yet male consciousness, like the Washington Monument to "the father of our country," has left us blissfully unaware of the frequently phallic nature of the sculpting of its monuments as well as of its words and doctrines.

A Problem of Keeping Control

But now here come these upstart women, thinking that *they* as female Christians can possess equally with men this "power to name." We women want the power to name and sculpt the idea of God in *our* own image, as men have done for millennia.

"How dare they," say their critics. "Who do they think they are? Do they really imagine that they as female Christians have an equal power with us to name the sacred, to see God in their own image?"

Pat Rumer, general director of Church Women United, rightly names the controversy as a problem of control. She is quoted in *Christian Century* as saying, "Men need to silence this kind of thing in order to be in control."

But this is a struggle over the most significant control of all, which is control over the "naming" function in the Christian tradition: Who gets to define what is "right" doctrine or unblasphemous worship?

Will the male always be presumed to be the one to decide these things? Is he to be the only "subject" in the Christian tradition, just as in Michelangelo's painting the male lies unabashedly male-conscious, his flaccid penis totally revealed?

In Adam the males of the Christian tradition have named the prototypical and normative human. Adam is the one around whom that so-called generic language of "man" and "mankind" has been fashioned in a male-reflective consciousness that *never* perceived its own form of political correctness but instead saw only what it called "truth."

What do these men think feminist Christian leaders will do now? Do they expect them to creep quietly into the male-defined Christian tradition, pacified finally by being able to be ordained, happy to join this male club at last, willing to settle for any diminution of the rhetoric of their own denigration, dutifully taking their named place within the defining and boundary-making of males in the millennia-old male-reflective Christian tradition?

Always the decisive question is one of power: "Who controls the myth system?" Who is in charge of the social and religious construction of reality? Who has the power to name something as Truth and thus orthodox, and something else as being "political correctness" and "male-bashing"—or in religious terms, "heresy" and "blasphemy"?

Woman as Namer Is Being Born

I have on my wall a poster which reads: "Woman is as common as a loaf of bread, and like a loaf of bread will rise." We are living today at truly a turning point in relationships between the genders. The power to name is being claimed by the man's ancient silent partner in the human species, the woman. Women for too long have been quiet and submissive helpmates to the "naming" male, content to love and nurture, support and assist, to give birth and care, endlessly to feed and remove dirt, always going where he led. For generations women have seemed content at home and in church to live within the male naming of sacred reality. But no more!

Women at last recognize that male "naming" always fosters male power, privilege and status—and denigrates women.

As if awakening from a long sleep, we women are slowly prying the film of male concepts and theology from our eyeballs, and we are looking at life as if for the first bright time. Unfamiliar as we are with doing this, we feel more and more compelled to find within ourselves the power of naming the sacred, to call it forth from within.

It is an awesome thing to find a voice within oneself to express one's own uniquely female life-experience, and then to shape that voice into words that utter one's truth a first tentative time—and then to come to believe that one has the right and indeed the power to do this.

The large numbers of us who participated in the RE-imagining Conference (as well as the 1300 women who were turned away) signified by our presence there (and by our desire to come even when we could not be accommodated), that there is a ground-swell of feminist Christians (women and men) who are ready and indeed eager for women to re-name the sacred. We expressed and embodied at that conference our intention to be fully "subject" in a Christian tradition we as women are now going to help define, shape and direct. We have begun as feminist Christians to claim and use our power to name the sacred for ourselves and to draw our own conclusions.

ELIZABETH DODSON GRAY

Do not expect this women's naming of the sacred to be like men's. The Spirit flows freely as always, and I would advise denominations not to guard the bastions of control and tighten up the boundaries of heresy-naming, because you will be blown away as the Spirit moves now across a broader landscape of human experience.

A new naming of the sacred is being born in the community of women. To be a part of this new community is like being with the women to whom the resurrected Jesus appeared on Easter morn, or like being present at Pentecost. We are speaking in tongues not yet understood. A new and alternative world of Christian meaning is being re-imagined today by a diversity of women around the globe. It will change everything for Christians, both women and men, and not a moment too soon.

26.

The Ancient Call to Newness:

Venturing Forth from an Old Land

Elizabeth Dodson Gray

—article—
The Presbyterian Layman magazine
Creative Transformation: The Journal of Process and Faith
May 18, 1994

26.

The Ancient Call to Newness:

Venturing Forth from an Old Land

Elizabeth Dodson Gray

May 18, 1994

The controversy about the RE-imagining Conference[3] has brought into bold contrast all of our attitudes about the conflict between being faithful to the past and also being open to God's action in the present.

The appropriate biblical metaphor here is the possibility of journeying from an old religious land into a new religious land. If you think God does not approve of such journeys into new religious lands, read your Bible again.

Do you remember the call to Abraham, then living in Ur of the Chaldees, to go out and venture forth into a new land promised by God? (Gen. 12)

---

[3] Minneapolis, MN, November 4–7, 1993.

Do you also remember the call to Moses to leave behind the land of slavery and to journey through the wilderness to a new land, a promised land, flowing with (of all things!) milk and honey? (Ex. 3:1–8b)

Our biblical heritage is full of stories such as the young Samuel's (1 Sam. 3:1–10), in which someone hears the divine calling in the middle of the night of one's own life. (In the new hymnal, see #525, "Here I am, Lord.") Everything is forever changed by that silent calling and one's own response to it.

Responding to that call has often meant leaving behind the familiar, the old land, the old ways, to venture forth into a new experience with that great I AM who calls.

I ask you, Do we dare to think this eternally calling-out-to-a-new-land God has stopped calling?

"Behold, I Am Doing a New Thing"

Remember the God who says, "Behold, I am doing a new thing; now it springs forth, do you not perceive it?" (Isa. 43:19) Remember the God glimpsed by Second Isaiah who says, "From this time forth I make you hear new things, hidden things which you have not known" (Isa. 48:6b).

These are not scattered proof-texts but a pervasive theme running throughout Hebrew Scripture and the New Testament. Jeremiah talks of a new covenant (Jer. 1:31), Ezekiel of a new spirit within (Ezk. 11:19).

Psalm 96 opens with an invitation to worshipers to "Sing to the Lord a new song," and Psalms 144 and 149 echo those words of invitation.

The three synoptic gospels portray Jesus teaching about the need to not put new wine into old wine skins (Mark 2:22; Matt. 9:17; Luke 5:37–38): "New wine is for fresh skins." Finally there is the resounding summary in Rev. 21:5, where God is portrayed as saying, "Behold, I make all things new!"

Re-imagining What God Is Doing

Now I ask you, do we dare to think that the God who is eternally creating newness has now suddenly stopped doing it? How can we not perceive the continuing activity of that God in today's "stillness of the night," calling *us* from the old places and out into new and fresh ventures of the spirit?

Those contemporaries of Jesus who in his day could not venture out of their Jewishness, could not become followers of Jesus. Those who could not "re-imagine" being Jewish, could never have made the incredible post-Easter shift from keeping a Saturday and seventh-day-of-the-week Sabbath to a celebration of the radically new first-day-of-the-week Sunday of resurrection.

Without this ability to "re-imagine" they could not have followed Jesus into the Jesus movement, which then developed later into what we call Christianity

Do we need reminding that those who were unable to "re-imagine" the medieval Catholic Church could never have created the Protestant Reformation? Prior to Martin Luther the superior way, the holy life, was celibate. It was Luther who "re-imagined" what a holy life could be—that the married state could be as holy as the celibate state. That was perceived in his day as being as truly radical as today re-imagining that homosexual lifestyles can be truly holy. Luther and Calvin had no Reformed Tradition to appeal to; they were creating it as they went along. And if everyone had been like those who shunned their re-imagining in *that* historical moment, then there would *be* no Reformed Tradition today.

ELIZABETH DODSON GRAY

Is Our Generation To Be Spared?

How ironic it is that today the descendants of those re-imagining Protestant Reformers are boggled by the thought of again re-imagining!

Do we think the life and the Dynamic Call to Newness stands still? That this Call to Newness somehow called *previous* generations into strenuous new journeys of faith, but now that Calling Presence has gone to sleep or is "out to lunch"—and surely cannot be calling *us* to such a journey, to such a newness?

If that is not it, then what really is the problem today?

When Abraham received his call to leave Ur and to venture forth on a great new journey of faith, his wife Sarah went along with him, sharing his call— *even though the call did not come to her.* Today's men, today's sons of Abraham, are being asked to accompany *their* women (the daughters of Sarah) on women's call out of an old past.

The question is, Can today's men have "the faith of accompanying" which Sarah had? Can today's men of fidelity and trustworthiness share the women's call?

Women's Liberating Call to a Promised Land

Cannot men understand how the male-reflective, male-dominated, and female-denigrating Christian past has been for many women a land of slavery and spiritual bondage? These Christian women are experiencing today a liberating call of truly biblical proportions.

Women today are discovering we are being called into a new place, a new life. In biblical terminology, we are being called to "a Promised Land flowing with milk and honey" which God has promised.

Now, with this present-day women's calling still ringing in your ears, hear once again the Good News of liberation given by God to God's people through Moses:

> I have seen the affliction of my people who are in Egypt, and have heard their cry because of their taskmasters; I know their sufferings, and I have come down to deliver them out of the hand of the Egyptians, and to bring them up out of that land to a good and broad land, a land flowing with milk and honey. (Ex. 3:7–8a)

Is There Offense That God Is in Solidarity with Women?

Many Christian women today are experiencing those biblical words deep in their beings. We are being called into a new land and into a liberation, and we know it. We are claiming the Promised Land, a land flowing with milk and honey, as a biblical symbol for us of a promised justice and abundance.

The Liberator God, the great I AM who is forever rescuing those who are oppressed, has no problem being in solidarity with women. God is *always* in solidarity with women and with the poor and with whoever dwells in a land of bondage, just as the pillar of cloud by day and the pillar of fire by night led the Israelites out of Egypt (Ex. 13–14).

That same God is calling and leading into newness today, as of old. The only question you have to answer is—**Are you ready for the journey?**

27.

Toward a Theology of Diversity:
A Way Out of the Culture War over Homosexuality

—May 2000—

27.

Toward a Theology of Diversity: A Way Out of the Culture War over Homosexuality

May 2000

The Battle Over Multiple Sexual Orientations

Our culture, and especially our religious culture, is having a difficult time dealing with the presence of multiple sexual orientations within our human species.

Gay men, lesbians, bisexuals and the transgendered proclaim their "gay pride" even as religious organizations across the spectrum, from the Catholic Church to the Mennonites, struggle in huge intramural battles over knowingly ordaining gays, extending hospitality and welcome to gays, and the nuances between "welcoming" and "affirming" gays.

In secular settings it is the courts and state legislatures and our city and town governments which are the settings where gay rights, gay "marriages" or "civil unions," and hate-crime legislation are considered and contested.

In the midst of all this we never ask ourselves the most basic and relevant theological question: **Is there perhaps a theological insight underlying all this which we have not yet perceived?**

Sorting Out Religious Assumptions

Much of the religious opposition to the gay sexual orientation is based upon the religious assumption that God has created only one way to be sexual. Anything other than that one Creator-sanctioned way to be sexual (male/female) must be wrong, unnatural, and therefore an abomination.

But look at the created natural world, and you find DIVERSITY writ everywhere and very large. Various people are different, species are different, snowflakes, leaves, flowers are different. **Nowhere in the natural world does a principle of "only one way" prevail.**

Consider what happens *after* conception in different species. Marsupials such as the kangaroo gestate their young without a placenta, and after birth they carry their young about in a chest pouch. Other mammals—such as whales and dolphins and humans and dogs and cows—gestate in a different, placenta-in-uterus mode, and after birth they all breast-feed their offspring in quite a different way from all the marsupial mammals. Birds, of course, are gestated in shells which mature in nests, totally outside the female birds' bodies–and they <u>never</u> breast-feed their young. Diversity, diversity, diversity!

When we have thought of our human diversity in terms of tall and short, thin and fat, right-handed and left-handed, brown hair and black and blond and red and gray hair, eyes that are blue, brown, gray, hazel, green, and of all the ranges of skin color, we may think we have comprehended our human diversity.

But the medical experience with modern pharmaceuticals suggests a much more pervasive human diversity. When a new drug goes from clinical trials with a few thousand patients and is quickly prescribed for millions, totally unforeseen "side effects" (a euphemism for "surprises") occur in some people. Viagra was prescribed 30 million times in the first nine months after it was approved by the FDA—and in that nine months 60 men died using Viagra.

Prescription pharmaceuticals now come with a standard "insert" which specifies all the *known* possible side effects. No one person will experience all these side effects, and many will experience none at all. But such is the diversity of our human bodies that *some* people have already experienced *some* of these side effects (or those possible side effects would not be required by the Food and Drug Administration to be listed on the pharmaceutical insert—and to be broadcast with the drug's TV ads).

Although each person's organs, blood, liver, heart, brain, and so on are almost identical, it is clear that pharmaceutical companies and modern medicine cannot *predict* which of us nearly alike people will be vulnerable enough to this medication to produce one or more undesirable "side effects." Our human diversity is so great that all they can report is what diversity of consequences they have learned of after they have occurred; no precise prediction about side effects for you or for me is possible.

What does this vast panoply of diversity suggest to us who are religious, about the will and the intention of the Creator? It says to me that the more you look into the ecology and the biology of the natural world, the more you are confronted by **the *intention* of the Creator to create difference, and the Creator's *affirmation* of that difference, that diversity.**

Difference As A Gift, Not a Curse
So now let's talk sex. If you look at a created world simply brimming with difference, why would you ever *imagine* that there would be only *one* way for the human species to do sex?

The truth is that *for there to be only one way* would be profoundly unnatural. It would be like a dropped stitch in an otherwise seamless garment of diversity.

So do we not as religious people have to ask ourselves if we have not totally *missed the point* in God's creation of human sexuality? If difference is so deeply embedded in God's gift to us of the natural world, have we not *totally misunderstood* that gift of difference when it comes to human sexuality?

Phyllis McGinley puts it best in her poem "In Praise of Diversity," written for a Phi Beta Kappa dinner:

> Since this ingenious earth began
> To shape itself from fire and rubble;
> Since God invented man, and man
> At once fell to, inventing trouble,
> One virtue, one subversive grace
> Has chiefly vexed the human race.
>
> One whimsical beatitude,
> Concocted for his gain and glory,
> Has man most stoutly misconstrued
> Of all the primal category—
> Counting no blessing, but a flaw,
> That Difference is the mortal law.
>
> Adam, perhaps, while toiling late,
> With life a book still strange to read in,
> Saw his new world, how variegate,
> And mourned, "It was not so in Eden,"
> Confusing thus from the beginning
> Unlikeness with original sinning.
>
> And still the sons of Adam's clay
> Labor in person or by proxy
> At altering to a common way
> The planet's holy heterodoxy.
> Till now, so dogged is the breed,
> Almost it seems that they succeed
>
>   *   *   *
> . . . Yet who would dare
> Deny that nature planned it other,
> When every freckled thrush can wear
> A dapple various from his brother,
> When each pale snowflake in the storm
> Is false to some imagined norm.
>
> Recalling then what surely was
> The earliest bounty of Creation:
> That not a blade among the grass
> But flaunts its difference with elation,
> Let us devoutly take no blame
> If similar does not mean the same.

ELIZABETH DODSON GRAY

And grateful for the wit to see
　Prospects through doors we cannot enter,
Ah! Let us praise Diversity
　Which holds the world upon its center.[1]

We as religious people welcome the natural world as the gift of the Creator God. Should we not take another look at the ecology and biology of its diversity?

And then should we not, finally and at long last, perceive and articulate a theology of diversity which encompasses the obvious intention for and blessing of the Creator God upon diversity, including our human sexual diversity?

So far we have not understood, we have *mis*understood. **It is now time to place the controversies about multiple sexual orientations into the context of a better theology of creation, and for those who see God's hand in the stars and in the snowflakes also to acknowledge the intention of the Creator for diversity not only there but also in our human sexuality.**

NOTES

1. Phyllis McGinley, "In Praise of Diversity," in *The Love Letters of Phyllis McGinley* (New York: Viking Press, Compass Books, 1954), pp. 12–14, selections.

28.

Beauty and the Beast:

A Feminist Parable

•

*A chapter from **Women Respond to the Men's Movement***

—1992—

28.

Beauty and the Beast: A Feminist Parable

*A chapter from **Women Respond to the Men's Movement***
(San Francisco: Pandora, 1992)

January 1992

Robert Bly and the Men's Movement in its mythopoetic form is totally focused on myth and story as meaning. So it seems appropriate to focus on a story as a lens through which to examine the Men's Movement.

A Mythopoetic Tale

"Beauty and the Beast" is an old fairy tale which has recently been powerfully recast by Disney in animated-movie form. Beauty in the movie is a daringly different girl. She is full of life and energy and in love with reading (she has a mind!). She dreams of a wider world not seen by the villagers and yet disparaged by them. In the movie Beauty magically has no mother but is totally devoted to her father. Beauty is also easily able to discern that the arrogant but handsome Gaston is a macho fluffhead.

The village where Beauty and her father live is fully populated with typical patriarchal values, and the center of attention in the movie is the Beast. The Beast, living in isolation in his castle, is really a male under a spell.

The Beast is not himself but is ugly on the surface. And he has a terrible temper. Does the Beast's psychological profile in the film remind you of a violence-prone wife batterer? Hmm!

And the story line? Beauty sacrifices herself to save her father's life. She then feels called upon to sacrifice herself again, this time to save or redeem the Beast. The spell that is upon the Beast is broken "by the love of a good woman," and Beauty frees him finally to become his concealed wondrous self.

The movie retells the story behind the tee-shirt caption, "To find Prince Charming you have to kiss a lot of toads."

All this is a typical patriarchal tale about what is required of the good woman. She is to sacrifice herself for a man. What is exceptional about the "Beauty and the Beast" story is the additional condition of the Beast's release, that he is to "genuinely love another."

Common Themes in the Movie and the Men's Movement

What reminded me of the Men's Movement was that, while Beauty gets co-billing in the title of both the story and movie, the whole focus is really upon the Beast.

The central question is, "Will the Beast be delivered from his enchantment? Will he be returned to his true identity?" This focus on the Beast, the male, is shared by the Robert Bly contingent of the Men's Movement. The central question for them is the redemption of the *male* from his enchantment, by a journey that is the man's perennial quest for his true identity.

In the movie and in the Men's Movement, the old macho hero is dead. Robert Bly and Sam Keen and others are clear that the true male self is *not* the Gaston of the movie. Gaston in the movie is clearly the outdated male stereotype: handsome, arrogant, athletic, conceited, macho, and attracted to Beauty only by her physical appearance.

The old macho hero may be dead but the Beast is still with us. In "Beauty and the Beast" there is the clear mythopoetic representation of the man who is totally preoccupied with his own situation, who is prone to violence, and who is still very much "under the spell" of an enchantment. While he was living his life and occupying his own niche or slot within the patriarchal system, he was overcome, captured, transformed in his being, "enchanted."

What is unsaid (and unseen) is that it is actually the patriarchal system of relationships itself which has done this to him, and which has transformed his life, making him into the Beast.

We glimpse this man also in the men caught up by the Robert Bly portion of the men's movement, men who are the audience for his best-selling book *Iron John.*[1] They are men desperately searching for the salvation of their male souls. Their quest is for the Holy Grail of a "primal" masculinity.

But sadly what these men (and Bly) do not yet perceive is the true cause of their enchantment. They do not yet grasp what it *is* that holds them captive, namely the patriarchal system itself.

According to the mythopoetic Men's Movement, each man seeks—and Robert Bly offers—an individual journey of salvation. They do not yet understand that this is impossible unless they break the spell that holds them captive. The spell is not individual and personal but instead organizational and cultural, comprising the entire system of male power and privilege and violence, to which feminists have given the name "Patriarchy."

Bly himself does not understand this. While he says he eschews the macho male of the past, Bly's foundational myth of "Iron John" is taken from the Brothers Grimm's collection of fairy tales which arose out of our patriarchal past.

Honoring Men's Sacred Spaces

Like everyone else I laughed when I saw on the television comedy *Designing Women* their parody of Robert Bly and his men's circles, with their rituals of passing the talking stick as men share their stories.

But I also felt sad. I do perceive grievous flaws in Robert Bly's mythology and I also bemoan his lack of any feminist analysis of male power in the culture. But I feel I must also honor what happens in a talking-stick circle.

As a woman and a feminist I know it to be a sacred space when women gather to tell their own stories. I can light a candle to celebrate this as a sacred space. So when men gather in a circle not to talk of football or how many notches they have on their shooter but to talk instead of their own interior life, so long concealed and coerced by a John Wayne model of manhood, then I think I must also honor as sacred these spaces being created by men.

I want us all to honor whatever spaces men find helpful, where they can finally tell their own stories of childhood, tell of their wounds and dreams. I know it to be a healing miracle when women touch their deep feelings of hurt. So I think it must be even more of a miracle when men, so long walled off from their feelings by patriarchy, can touch their deep hurts and begin to heal them.

Muriel Rukeyser is quoted as saying, "What would happen if one woman told the truth about her life? The world would split open." The same may be true of men.

What I want for men is that they be able to find again their interior lives which for so long have been largely inaccessible to them.

It is true that only men are going to be able to redefine masculinity, and shape it into new personal and cultural formulations which are *not* woman-hating. Robert Bly does not do it. Sam Keen begins it. And as men do it, it is sacred work.

The Place of Repentance in Men's Sacred Work

Men's healing themselves must be done *within* a fundamental repentance for the essential male-centeredness of the past. Gus Kaufman is right in his critique of the Bly movement: "It's defect is that it never challenges, never even sees, *the most fundamental problem of the construction of manhood: the assumption of male centrality.* It therefore reproduces patriarchy."[2]

All of us, both male and female, have been socialized into "Adam's World,"[3] into a social construction of reality done from the standing point of male life-experience. The biblical account of Adam naming the world and everything in it (Gen. 2:19–20a) is a mythological account of a profoundly important truth in the sociology of our contemporary knowledge.

Within that "Adam's World" there is a major conceptual trap that confuses being human with being male. Men must discover that they are not the center and fullness of the human world, but rather *they are not identical-twin partners within this human species. They are but half the human race.*

Therefore, while men work out their own salvation with fear and trembling, it must *not* be done at the expense of women. They must see, understand, and change what they have done to their mothers, wives, sisters, daughters.

Even while they are grieving the wounds they carry as sons of absent and nonfeeling or deriding fathers, they must face up to the present task of being very different fathers for their own sons and daughters.

Rewriting Patriarchal Scripts

Both Bly and Keen assume men can only find themselves by "leaving their mother's household." *This is the old patriarchal script of masculinity being named only in opposition to anything female.* If women are soft, then men must be hard. If women are nurturing, then men must not nurture. And on and on.

All this continues the old patriarchal sense that boys are somehow deeply contaminated by their mother's child rearing. What is missing here is a grasp of how it is patriarchy which forces women to do most of that child rearing, even as patriarchy is coercing most men to avoid it.

Bly also never examines patriarchy's role in scripting men to overwork. This pattern of overworking causes men to neglect their children and to wound their daughters as well as their sons. Nor is Bly clear about the role of patriarchy as a systemic repressive phenomenon, causing boys and men to bury their feelings and become remote father-figures who cannot express love.

Bly apparently does not see how, generation after generation, patriarchy has coerced us all, so that men are reared by women, ignored by fathers, and then want to flee women in order to "discover their true masculinity." *These social roles, which patriarchy designs, coerces and perpetuates, cause the inner wounds Bly describes so eloquently and seeks to heal.*

Bly tries nobly to lance men's inner wounds. But he does not perceive their root cause in the power system of patriarchy. So he is helpless to interrupt this process as the generations roll on.

Women's Part in Breaking the Enchantment of Patriarchy

There is a further aspect of "Beauty and the Beast" which delights me. In the story, the release of the Beast from his enchantment can only be accomplished by Beauty, "by the love of a good woman."

I find I can read this role for women in either of two ways. If I think of Beauty sacrificing herself for the Beast (as she did for her father), it seems like a nasty replay of patriarchal scripts which exploit women into endless self-denial and self-sacrifice.

But on the other hand, if I imagine that this Savior role gives to women—and *only* to women—the power to "break the enchantment" of patriarchy, then that appeals to me.

In Hindu tradition there is a wonderful story about the Savior role of a goddess named Durga. She is a young and beautiful woman at the height of her sexual powers. Durga comes riding into a world of chaos on the back of a tiger. She saves the day by slaying with her powerful sword the wild boar who is threatening everything with disaster.

Durga is a female Savior who is sexual, powerful and virtuous all at once. Now that is a role for women which I think many of us can identify with. *The Durga myth suggests it is only feminism which has the power to lift the spell of patriarchy.*

ELIZABETH DODSON GRAY

Patriarchy As A New Jericho

I often visualize patriarchy as a castle (much like the one in "Beauty and the Beast") standing high on a forbidding hill, an entrenched system of male power and privilege protecting fragile men living inside its defended walls and wide moats.

I also visualize the work of feminist women as being like Joshua in the Hebrew Scriptures, marching around those defended walls (Joshua 6:1–21). We are blowing our trumpets of the feminist critique of male culture, marching and blowing, marching and blowing, seven times around, even seventy times around, until the walls of this Jericho come tumbling down.

To dissolve the enchantment of patriarchy requires a feminist analysis of culture, something the pro-feminist wing of the Men's Movement understands very well. These pro-feminist men understand that *a men's movement that is centered only upon men and is only pro-male, and only looks at the costs of masculinity (i.e., the costs of patriarchy to men), can never break out of its own enchantment.*

To free ourselves from patriarchy, we must all—both women and men—become pro-female and look at the costs *to women* of male power, male privilege and male violence. It is also equally true that to free ourselves of racism, we can never just look at the cost to whites, but we must identify with the true costs to African-Americans of white power, white privilege and white violence.

So I see feminism as leading the way in a cultural procession of conceptual Aha's—the breaking of evil enchantments, as in "The Emperor has no clothes."

I would invite into our procession around the walled city of patriarchy all those whose lives are emerging out of the cultural myths of the past and coming into new and liberating identities which are expressions of their own uniqueness.

I invite to join us all women who are increasingly claiming their power to name themselves, and are finding in their re-naming that they change their world. Patriarchy has been a prison for women that none of us—women or men—any longer need.

I would also open our ranks to all those women who suddenly understood while watching in 1991 the Anita Hill-Clarence Thomas hearings, that sexual harassment, rape, date rape, pornography, battering, and violent death for women, are part-and-parcel of patriarchal male power. I would welcome also all those women who that week learned anew that within patriarchy "A woman will not be believed."

Feminism—recognition of the imbalance of power between men and women, combined with an explicit commitment to correct that imbalance—is the only solvent which will dissolve patriarchy and release all of us, women and men, from its power. It is like the water thrown upon the evil witch in *The Wizard of Oz,* which dissolves the witch down into a puddle—releasing from those being liberated the triumphant shout, "The wicked witch is *dead!"*

But I also want to open our ranks to all the children who care about their future on this endangered planet. Patriarchy is a root cause of "ranking diversity." It is the conceptual basis for male dominion over—and exploitation of—"lesser" genders, peoples, races, species, and of nature and the planet itself. Patriarchy is thus a conceptual cancer which is simply not compatible with the health of our interconnected Earth-system.[4]

And finally I open the ranks of our marchers to men. We can welcome every man who can finally touch his feelings, name his wounds, and look in new places for the core of his positive male energy, as Sam Keen does in his book *Fire in the Belly*.[5]

Men Challenging Men to End Violence Against Women

I like Sam Keen's book very much because Keen says that male identity and virility in *this* historical time is found in a new vocation to save the planet.

But it is distressing to me that neither Sam Keen's book nor Robert Bly's book *mentions* the epidemic of male violence against women. That omission seems to me like building a boat (a new sense of male identity) in a thunder storm and never mentioning the thunder storm! Or it is like focusing on the feelings of S.S. guards while the ovens of genocide burn a few feet away. It is like pondering the feelings of white people while black people are being lynched just over the hill.

For men challenging men to end violence against women, we must look to the pro-feminist men within the men's movement. These are the men who have focused upon trying *as men* to stop the male violence against women. The White Ribbon Campaign in Canada was organized by such men. The campaign focused around the second anniversary of the Montreal massacre of women when 25-year-old Marc Lepine denounced "feminists" as he shot fourteen women dead in a rampage at the École Polytechnique.

The campaign was thought up by three men (Ron Sluser, Jack Layton and another) but joined by other prominent Canadian men including Senator Trevor Eyton, environmentalist David Suzuki, and actor Bruno Gerussi.

They were very clear about the need **for men** to accept the responsibility both for the violence of men toward women and for trying as men to get that violence to cease.

This is the text of their 1991 "White Ribbon" Statement:

> If it were between countries, we'd call it a war. If it were a disease, we'd call it an epidemic.... But it's happening to women, and it's just an everyday affair. It is violence against women. It is rape at home and on dates. It is the beating or the blow that one out of every four Canadian women receive in their lifetime. It is sexual harassment at work and sexual abuse of the young. It is murder
>
> There's no secret enemy pulling the trigger. No unseen virus that leads to death. It's just men. Men from all social backgrounds and of all colors and ages. Men in business suits and men in blue collars. Men who plant the fields and men who sell furniture. Not weirdos. Just regular guys.
>
> * * *
>
> Men have been defined as part of the problem. But we are writing this statement because we think men can also be part of the solution. Confronting men's violence requires nothing less than a commitment to full equality for women and a redefinition of what it means to be men, to discover a meaning to manhood that doesn't require blood to be spilled.[6]

I find the White Ribbon Campaign encouraging because it reassures me that it is possible for men to take responsibility for the actions of their own gender. Because men commit the violence, it is men who can and must stop it.

ELIZABETH DODSON GRAY

At the end of Robert Bly's book *Iron John*, the newly revealed baronial king says, "I am Iron John, who through an enchantment became turned into a Wild Man."

Any Wild Man who wishes to be free of the evil enchantment must turn away from himself and from a male-centered world and life, and become pro-feminist enough to care about what is happening to women, to care as much as the men who started The White Ribbon Campaign in Canada.

The truth is, you cannot affirm life without affirming women, because women's bodies are the only gateway to life for *all* of the human species.

The Men's Movement, unless it is embracing women—their health, their safety, and their equality—will never be a way *to* life for men. Remember—the Beast, to free himself, had truly to love another.

NOTES

1. Robert Bly, *Iron John: A Book about Men* (Reading, Mass. : Addison-Wesley, 1990.

2. Gus Kaufman, Jr., "Healing the Pain by Misplacing Blame: Some Thoughts on the Men's Movement." *Working Together* (newsletter of the Center for the Prevention of Sexual and Domestic Violence, 1914 North 34th, Suite 105, Seattle, WA 98103) 2:3 (Spring/Summer 1991), p. 8. Emphasis added.

3. Elizabeth Dodson Gray, *Patriarchy as a Conceptual Trap* (Wellesley, Mass.: Roundtable Press, 1982), pp. 48–49. See also the 18-minute film "Adam's World" (1989) by National Film Board of Canada, about Elizabeth Dodson Gray and her feminist thinking and work.

4. See Elizabeth Dodson Gray, *Green Paradise Lost* (Wellesley, Mass.: Roundtable Press, 1979).

5. Sam Keen, *Fire in the Belly: On Being a Man* (New York: Bantam, 1991).

6. The White Ribbon Campaign: Breaking Men's Silence To End Men's Violence (December 1–6, 1991), 253 College Street, Box 231, Toronto, Ontario M5T 1R5. The action program statement follows.

With all our love, respect and support for the women in our lives:

• We urge men across Canada to hang a white ribbon from their house, their car, or their work-place and to wear a white ribbon or armband from Sunday December 1 through Friday, December 6, the second anniversary of the Montreal massacre. *The white ribbon symbolizes a call for all men to lay down their arms in the war against our sisters.* (Italics added.)

A FEMINIST MOMENT REMEMBERED
Liz wows the E. F. Schumacher Society of America.

In the fall of 1986 (perhaps late October) John McKnight and I each delivered the Annual Lecture of the E. F. Schumacher Society of America, in New Haven, Connecticut. Two people are invited each year, and each delivers "The Annual Lecture." My talk was later published as *The Spiritual Dimension of Green Politics* (Rochester, VT: Bear & Co., 1986). John McKnight's talk was on "John Deere and the Bereavement Counselor." The invited respondents that year were Elizabeth Dodson Gray, Thomas Berry, Patricia Mische, and Nancy Jack Todd.

John McKnight began his lecture with a mocking depiction of a young woman recently graduated from a state university with professional training to serve as a grievance counselor. She arrived in a small community, presumably working for a non-profit organization or a governmental agency, and is attempting to enact her new role.

McKnight described these efforts with dripping sarcasm. How stupid the young woman was to think that professional caregivers could—or should—attempt to replace the age-old structures of community that traditionally have comforted and assisted bereaved families. I was somewhat offended by how moronic he made the (fictitious) well-meaning young woman appear.

As we were soon to find out, however, one of the invited respondents in the audience—Elizabeth Dodson Gray—was annoyed by a very different aspect of McKnight's vision. When Liz was asked to make her response to McKnight's lecture, she walked to the microphone, squared off behind it, and faced the audience. Speaking in stentorian tones, she asked, "How many men . . . in this hall . . . have ever made a casserole . . . and taken it . . . to a grieving family?" There was dead silence in the hall. Everyone knew she had succinctly and authoritatively nailed the implicit patriarchal assumption.

Sitting in the front row, I experienced her response as a revelation: "Ah, so *that's* how it's done—a feminist critique that's incisive, irrefutable, and powerfully grounded . . . even witty."

It was a moment I have always remembered with delight and admiration.

Instantly, Liz had touched the audience's own experience to make the point that the informal helping system prior to the professionalized grief counselors was one in which the women in the community were expected to do the extra work.

Why, as McKnight suggested, should we go back to that traditional model? Liz then presented a fuller, wiser vision of community caring when a family is grieving: a caring community in which both sexes would share the work.

Charlene Spretnak, 12 October 2011

ONE MUST CARE ABOUT A WORLD ONE WILL NEVER SEE.

—Bertrand Russell

Elizabeth/David Dodson Gray

29.

Hidden Life Metaphors

TOP Talk, May 3, 2001

29.

Hidden Life Metaphors
TOP Talk, May 3, 2001

The Hiddenness of a Hidden Life-Metaphor
A "hidden life-metaphor" is a deeply hidden and totally unacknowledged bargain with the universe.

Because it is deeply hidden, I did not know I had such a thing at work deep in my life until late October 1983. Then, at age fifty-three, I had the first of what would be five surgeries for breast cancer in three-and-a-half years.

In the aftermath of my first "modified radical mastectomy," the entire upper right quadrant of my body was assaulted, first by a clogged lymph system in my arm, and then—because I stopped moving that arm and shoulder very much (because it hurt to move it)—I got an extremely painful and immobilizing (and I now know, life-threatening) "frozen shoulder."

It would take me more than eleven years of intensive physical therapy—and heroic and painful effort—finally to get my arm and shoulder and entire upper right quadrant back to full use and totally without pain. It was a terribly difficult time.

The Discovery
It was in these circumstances that I discovered that I had been living with what I came to call my hidden life-metaphor. It was a deeply hidden and totally unacknowledged bargain with the universe, to the effect that I was really "lucky"—and that truly terrible things really did not happen to me.

I had been born in Baltimore, Maryland on July *thirteenth,* 1929, and I think some friend of my parents had expressed concern about the possible effect upon me of being born on the 13th, since the number thirteen was considered to be an unlucky number. There were no 13th floors on buildings or houses numbered 13 on their street, and so on.

That was also not an unreasonable concern because of another incident from my early childhood. When I was very small we went summers to visit my father's relatives in tidewater Virginia. The relatives always took one look at me and said to my father, "She looks just like your sister did when she was small." Then they usually went on to comment about the little curl at the nape of my neck, which was clearly visible because my mother liked to do my hair into pigtails.

"Yep," they would say, "she's the spitting image of your sister, even to that curl. Died when she was seven." Their final memory was always the same, "She died when she was seven."

I don't guess I had any real sense in those young years of what death involved, because I don't remember any fear or dread of my own dying. But what I do remember is how surprised I was when I got to celebrate my eighth birthday and I was no longer seven. Somewhere deep in my consciousness I really had been expecting that I too would die when I was seven, because I "looked just like her."

My parents really did not "do" psychology, but they apparently took very seriously a friend's comment about my possible reactions to having been born on July 13th. And, to counter the "unlucky" nuances surrounding the number thirteen, they told me from as early as I can remember that 13 is a *lucky* number, and that 13 was *my lucky number,* and that July 13th was *a very lucky day for them,* because that was the day I had been born.

And either they said it or I concluded out of all of this, that *"I am lucky!"* But having told you all this by way of background, I must also add that I never thought too much about it. It did not seem like a big thing in my life.

A Sudden Glimpse of That Hidden Life-Metaphor

Now fast-forward to many years later. David is driving me to the airport to depart for a weekend speaking engagement in some other part of the country. Our aging red Volvo chose that moment to die on the Massachusetts Turnpike.

We did not know exactly where we were when we came to a halt. But David helped push me over a six-foot chain-link fence, threw my luggage over after me, and then, as luck would have it, we found we were at the lower end of Parsons Street in Brighton. Our daughter Lisa, right out of college, lived at the *other* end of Parsons Street, and we prevailed upon a nearby house to let us phone our daughter, wake her up, drag her from her bed where she was sick with a cold, and insist she drive me to the airport.

It was a small airline (I was flying, as I recall, to Syracuse, NY), and when I ran in to the check-in counter, breathless and almost late for the plane, the nice young woman behind the counter said, "You look like you have had a bad morning." I said, "You better believe it—our car died on the Mass Turnpike, I've climbed a six-foot chain-link fence, I've rousted my sick daughter out of her bed, and I've nearly missed my plane. It definitely has been a bad morning!" And she said, "But what can you expect—it's Friday, the 13th!"

And I drew myself up, looked at her and said, "I am lucky and the number 13 is my lucky number, and bad things certainly don't happen to *me* on Friday-the-13th!"

I remember being mildly surprised by my own outburst. But I really did not think much about it at the time.

When Reality Breaks Through

Now fast-forward again to that terrible moment in October 1983 when I was told by my surgeon that he had found cancer in my right breast.

I was in disbelief.

I could NOT have breast cancer.

Beyond the usual reaction of disbelief and denial that all of us would have, my reaction was qualitatively different. *I felt totally betrayed.* It was as though some deep "contract" in my life had been broken, shattered, violated—a contract between myself and the universe.

Then later, when my lymph system clogged after my first mastectomy, I was told by my surgeon that this happened to 2 percent of women who had this operation. I said to myself, "Now I'm in the negative 2%—how *unlucky* can you get?"

Facing Into a Kind of Identity Crisis

Finally, when I pondered all this over several weeks and perhaps months, I realized that my parents' words to me—and the emotional meaning I had made of them so early on in my life—had given me what in 1983 I came to call "a hidden life-metaphor"—That I was LUCKY.

And now it seemed to me that life-metaphor was wrong, because lucky people don't get breast cancer. And they are *not* in the negative 2% of a health problem. *I felt deeply betrayed.*

Discovering the Unexpected Usefulness of Fantasy

Finally someone said to me, "Well, your life-metaphor *was* wrong, but your feeling that you were really very lucky must have done *something* for you."

I tried over the next months to think about that. Had my hidden life-metaphor really done something for me even though I now saw it was not true?

Slowly I came to image that hidden life-metaphor as being for me a small flame alive and burning in the center of my identity, hidden but very real and powerful in supporting the way I thought about my life.

I came to realize that this small flame—"I am lucky"—had been for me a talisman always magically protecting me, a mantra I must have been repeating silently deep inside myself. It had worked remarkably well for me, *because if you believe the universe smiles at you, it is easy to smile back.*

Let me repeat that because I think it is very important: IF YOU BELIEVE THE UNIVERSE SMILES AT YOU, IT IS EASY TO SMILE BACK.

That belief system—the belief that I was truly lucky—had helped me believe in myself, to move out into my life with confidence, to expect the best in any situation—to expect to succeed.

Looking back I could see how the hidden life-metaphor of "lucky" was probably the seed-bed of a lot of self-affirmation in my life. And now, as an adult, I know how important that sense of self-affirmation is, in anybody's life.

When a Life-Metaphor Dies

As I was thinking all this to myself, I wanted to cup my hands over that little flame, to protect it from being blown out by disasters like breast cancer. But as I reluctantly came to the conclusion that my "lucky" life-metaphor had been an inappropriate fantasy, that flame slowly did go out. I experienced it as happening gradually, the way helium leaks out of a dying balloon.

My "being lucky" was not realistic in the light of the "bad things that happen to good people," as Rabbi Harold Kushner put it in the title of one of his books. I realized I needed to search for another, different life-metaphor—this time not a hidden one, but hopefully one which would still be affirming and uplifting. But one more congruent with the realities of illness, accidents, misfortunes, aging.

A Cautionary Word

What is my conclusion about all this?

We should be very careful what we say to our children or grandchildren, BECAUSE THEY WILL BELIEVE US! And it can affect their lives, for good or ill.

30.

Breast Cancer:
Choosing Aesthetics, Identity, Survival?

TOP Panel Presentation
November 16, 2001

30.

Breast Cancer:
Choosing Aesthetics, Identity, Survival?

TOP Panel Presentation, November 16, 2001

Making the Choice

Was I choosing aesthetics, identity, or survival? I must confess that the aesthetic component of my breast cancer choices felt unimportant to me because I had never perceived myself as beautiful. Therefore it never occurred to me to try either to maintain my beauty or to maximize a beauty I did not think I had. But I have always liked my breasts. I felt they were not too big and not too small and I really liked them.

Identity was also not a factor in my decision because I have felt totally sure of my womanhood, and it doesn't rest in my breasts at all. It's inside—who I am.

Survival was the category for me. I knew survival was what I cared about. Perhaps my sense of that was maximized because one of my very closest friends had died very quickly of metastacized breast cancer six years before. So the possible reality of dying of breast cancer was very real to me.

I am very happily married and I'd like that never to end! At the time I had a son in college and a daughter who was twenty-four. I wanted to have more of my children's lives. (I have lived to see my children marry and to enjoy my grandchildren.)

So because I knew I cared the most about survival, I chose a modified radical mastectomy. Despite the statistics it felt safer to me. I know the statistics about lumpectomies are that they are equally effective. But I have intuitively felt that it is better to get rid of the entire breast. I have always said that for me, the worst thing would be the first five years of the waiting period. I knew that a mastectomy would make this time of anxiety easier for me.

I also knew that I wouldn't have to worry about my husband David, that he would always be erotically attracted to my body no matter what. So I felt totally free to make my own decision.

My Story

My first brush with breast cancer happened in 1968, our children were ten and seven, and our family was vacationing in California. We were spending the night camping at the top of Mount Tamelpais outside San Francisco. All of a sudden my left breast was very full and hard as though it had become one entire lump. I spent all that night worrying about having breast cancer and David and I decided the best thing to do was to put in a phone call at 5:00AM California time and 8:00AM East Coast time, to his college roommate who by now was a pathologist at Johns Hopkins Medical School

You can imagine the scene. I am describing the condition of my breast and the only pay phone is three feet away from the only water spigot—where the early risers are brushing their teeth and getting ready to go to breakfast!

David's friend Sumner said, "I don't think that's the way breast cancer works. But let me give you a referral to one of my favorite teachers, who is a surgeon now on the faculty of San Francisco Medical School half an hour away from where you are. I'll call him and he'll see you immediately."

Encountering the Medical System

I went in, he examined my breasts, and then he came at me with this simply enormously long hypodermic needle. I said, "You're going to put *that* into my breast?" He said, "Yes"—and he did, and through the needle came this blue liquid. "It's *blue?*" I said incredulously. "Yes," he said. "When you menstruate, your breasts fill with fluid." And it actually is blue. "What happens is that when you finish menstruating, there is a little valve which opens and this fluid leaves your breast. And that little valve in your left breast is not working this time."

He finished removing the blue fluid and said that this would take care of my problems now. In two weeks when I was back in Boston and my body was more at the midpoint of my cycle, a surgeon in the East should examine surgically what was happening in there.

With difficulty I repressed my anxiety for two weeks, got back to Boston and had Sumner's list of four top Boston surgeons. I called the first two, and they were on vacation (this was August). I called the third surgeon, Kenneth Warren, and he said, "I will do this for Sumner. I am going on vacation tomorrow morning but I will see you at the end of my office hours today."

Feeling Like The Fish Who Escapes the Net

He examined me and he said, "I can't tell. I will have to look at this with exploratory surgery. But I know this is anxiety-producing for you so I will meet you at 7:00AM on the operating table and I will do it for you before I leave for vacation. And by the way, would you like a sleeping p\ill for tonight?" (You can see why I adore him!)

He went in and, whatever it was, it was not breast cancer and I was out of that entire experience and could go on with my life.

But it left me with three holdover things. First, it found me my fantastic surgeon and put me within his care (and it was considerable care).

It also furnished us with a trial run with David, who became quite withdrawn during the whole experience, including just dropping me off at the hospital for the surgical exploratory procedure.

When I really got in touch with my feelings about that, I was very upset. And when we talked about it, he admitted he was totally withdrawn because he was actually totally emotionally engrossed with his own fears about what would happen to him if something happened to me, and how could he rear our children (who were then ten and seven).

I said to him, "Look darling, you have got to do better if there is a next time. You're my best friend and I need to have your companionship. I need you to be really present for me. And please remember that I'm the one going through the trauma, you're just along for the ride, for God's sake! If you can't deal with your own feelings better than that, I really need you to!" That conversation was really helpful later, believe me.

The third thing it left me with was the illusion that I would always escape breast cancer. I always felt like a fish, with a net always trying to capture you. I always was trying to slither out of the net and I felt as though I had found a little hole and I had slithered away again, and—you know what—they always captured *other* people (which is not true).

Checking for Changes

Now fast-forward to 1983. (That earlier experience was 1968—this is 1983 and my son is in college, my daughter is twenty-four.) For all these years I have been checked every six months by this surgeon. He is aware that I have cystic stuff in my breasts and surgeons are always questioning whether cystic stuff becomes cancerous.

I was in between checkups. One night when I was bathing, I realized that there was a little lump in my navel. I rushed in to see him.

He examined me and said, "Yes, there is a lump. But I have no idea what it is. Come back in a month." And being the kind of careful doctor he is, he also examined my breasts.

I came back in a month and he said, "The lump is exactly the same."

Naively I said, "Would it have changed?"

He said, "You better believe it would have changed in a month, if it were cancer." So he said, "Come back in three months," and he checked my breasts again.

I came back in three months and he said "The lump is exactly the same, and I'm not going to biopsy it because you wouldn't have a navel if I did. But I'm sure that, whatever it is, it's not cancerous." He examined my breasts again.

"Something has changed," he said, "between last time and this time."

Looking at the Cellular Level for Cancer

So he sent me across the street to get a mammogram immediately. I had been getting regular mammograms but he said I want one *now*.

Literally before I changed back into my street clothes and was out of the hospital, he had someone at the door saying to each woman who was leaving, "Are you Mrs. Gray?" I was told I needed to go back to his office and see Dr. Warren.

He said, "The mammogram is suspicious. I just think I need to go in and look at it at the cellular level, and I can't do that without an exploratory. I want you on the operating table tomorrow morning."

Now I was going to give a speech that night, which somehow I did, repressing all this. I took the sleeping pill I had from him for such occasions, and I met him on the operating table the next morning, thinking, "Ough—I'm going to get through this one again."

And indeed apparently I did.

He went in and removed a lot of the breast, approximately a third, in a pie-shaped wedge. And while I was still on the operating table a pathologist did a quick frozen section; my surgeon and I were clear that, if there was any cancer there, I wanted a mastectomy, I wanted the breast off. The frozen section revealed no cancer. (They don't use frozen sections now because they have concluded they are not reliable as they are just one little slice. One cross-section does not show anything definitive.)

They and I thought I was home free again, and three days later I went to his office and had the drains removed. Twenty minutes after I left his office the pathologist called; they had sliced up the entire pie-shaped wedge and there, in the corner of it, was a small cancer.

CANCER!

But David and I had already left on a professional trip and we had not left any phone numbers where we could be reached because our children were grown. My doctor had to wait five days to contact me. He said, "There is cancer there," and I said, "Then I want the mastectomy."

He did the mastectomy. And because we had already cut into the cancer, we were both fearful of the cancer cells being released into the blood stream. It was important to see if there were any cancer cells in the lymph nodes in my armpit. So he took *all* of my lymph nodes.

That is not usually done; most surgeons "sample" them. Frankly, I was very happy to have every lymph node gone. I am the kind of person that, if they told me there were five lymph nodes and they sampled 2 and 3 and there was no cancer, I would be sure it was in 4 and 5—and how the hell did they know otherwise? So I said, "Take them all—with my blessing!"

Because the pathology revealed that my lymph nodes were clear and my cancer was found to be *not* estrogen-sensitive, it was not suggested that I have either chemo or radiation.

Immediately after the operation I was in terrific shape. When my doctor came to see me, I could pull my arm way up. He said, "You have fantastic movement; you're going to make a great recovery."

The Arrival of the Pain
Then three days later I went into a lot of pain and my entire chest began to turn brown, the color of a brown paper bag, and be dry and scaly. I asked Dr. Warren what was going on. He said, "A-ha, your lymph system has clogged. It only happens to two percent of the women who have a modified radical mastectomy." It was two percent, a bad two percent—and I was in it!

The Clogged Lymphatic System
I could not believe that!

I had had difficulty believing I had cancer. My getting cancer was a huge shock to my system because I was sure I would never get cancer.

Suddenly I have cancer and then you tell me that I'm in a bad two-percent category of all the women with breast cancer? It was hard for me to believe.

My arm never became bloated and swollen, because I used it very little—David was doing all the housework. I never raised my arms except while I was giving a speech occasionally. I did do the "walking up the wall" exercises they prescribe after a mastectomy, but I didn't do them properly. It is easy to twist your body so that you don't actually stretch the muscles. Unfortunately I did that.

Adhesions
Because I did not use my muscles enough, I developed incredible adhesions, which are like glue, and they gave me a "frozen shoulder." The adhesions "glued" every muscle to every nerve to every bone from my breast bone to my right elbow—my entire upper right quadrant. It was painful even to dial a touch-tone telephone.

I now know what I ought to have had with my clogged lymph system was *passive* physical therapy. With passive physical therapy the physical therapist will move your muscles so that you will *not* get the adhesions and the frozen shoulder that I got.

If you do go ahead and use your own muscles when your lymph system is clogged, those muscles will give off lactic acid—which has no place to go—and your arm will swell. And once swollen it may never go down; you live with a swollen arm. But if a physical therapist moves your muscles until your lymph system regenerates, your arm will *not* swell <u>and</u> you will *not* get adhesions. But I didn't know all that!

So after my mastectomy surgery, I went into a terrible period in which for six months I was in pain from the clogged lymph system, and then for two years after that I was in constant pain from the frozen shoulder.

It is the worst thing I have ever experienced. By constant pain I mean pain all the time except when I was asleep. In the midst of this I had two months of not clinical depression but situational depression, because of the post-trauma stress.

The Frozen Shoulder

What people need when they are in a period like this is friends to walk with you, and that is what TOP did. Hurting people don't need cheering up, they don't need lectures, they don't need suggestions from you about what they should be doing to heal themselves. They just need you to *listen* and *listen* and *listen* and care about them.

I need to say that David was wonderful at this point. He had learned, he had taken a vow to do it differently and he did. He became my personal daily physical therapist that all of my professional physical therapists taught how to do the physical therapy. He worked on my body in such a way that my muscles did not tighten up in between my three-times-a-week physical therapy.

He even mastered the extraordinary thing of allowing me to get angry at him and not get defensive. I would get angry at him because I was in pain and he was never in pain, and it really annoyed me. I don't know what I would have done if I had not found an absolutely fantastic young physical therapist, Scott Cushing, who probably saved my life emotionally. I remember sitting on his table crying and being in despair, saying I will never get out of pain.

I can't believe a young man could have the empathy to do this: he would hold my hand and look in my eyes and say, "If you can't believe yourself you will get out of pain, *believe in me*—because I know I can help you find your way out of this maze."

Scott got me off of all pain killers because, he told me, "the pain tells us the path" which was to be the way out. After about a year-and-a-half I could get my hands and arms all the way up above my head. For many years I was still in pain because I was pulling on adhesions that were still there. But Scott had started me on a way to becoming totally pain-free now, some fourteen years of physical therapy later.

The Cancer Watch

Meanwhile, "back at the ranch," I was seeing my surgeon for checkups every 90 days to make sure my other breast stayed cancer-free.

Nine months after my mastectomy my surgeon decided he really needed to do another exploratory because there was so much "cystic stuff" in my other breast and he was nervous about it. He went in, removed one-third of my breast, entirely rebuilt my breast so you even couldn't tell there was any change in the shape, and left me total feeling in my nipple. The pathology was fine and we thought he had removed fifty-five-year's accumulation of cystic stuff.

I thought, "I'm home free again!"

A year later *all* that cystic stuff was back. We couldn't believe it. I had surgery again to remove it, and this time the cell pathology was worse. There was now microcalcification and hypoplasia (distorted cells). Both are *possible* pre-cancer signs. That was of concern, both to Dr. Warren and to me.

Deciding on a Preemptive Strike

My surgeon said to me, "You can't go on doing this. Four surgeries in three years is more anesthesia than you should have."

I said, "Well, what do you propose?"

"A scoop."

"Yes—and put what inside, silicone?" I did not think it needed a brain surgeon to realize that silicone was not a good thing to put in your body. I was never tempted by that.

He said, "I don't know. All I can tell you is we can't go on doing this."

So I asked my gynecologist, whom I trusted a lot. He said, "I know I have never had any breasts, and I don't know how I would feel about a breast. But I do know, Mrs. Gray, that if that deteriorating cell pathology were happening in your pelvis, I would want to remove your pelvic organs. You don't sit there and wait for that cell deterioration to produce cancer."

So I said, "Okay. . . "

What Did I Fear the Most?

I then asked myself, "What did I fear the most?"

I would suggest to you that you do that at *any* point in whatever is bothering you! Ask yourself, "What do I fear the most?"—-and get straight with yourself about that.

My answer was at that point that I not only feared dying of cancer. I feared losing my lymph system in my other arm, and even the *possibility* of another frozen shoulder! And therefore I wanted to get there *before* the cancer.

Therefore I made a decision to have a *simple* mastectomy. No lymph nodes would be removed. The pathology on the breast they removed was clear of cancer cells, so I could keep my lymph system—and I had accomplished my mission by these five surgeries in three-and-a-half years.

Aftercare

I want to tell you about my aftercare. Most women don't get the aftercare I got, and I know that they should. I know a lot of women who have mastectomies never go back to their surgeons again.

For the first five years I was checked every ninety days by my surgeon. By check-up I mean he felt the tissue over my rib cage, to make sure nothing had developed there. He felt all of the lymph nodes throughout my body, and he explored manually deep in my abdomen to check all the organs to be sure no tumors were growing there.

I found very this reassuring. He was still on watch for the metastatic spread of any breast cancer to other organs, particularly to my liver, lungs or bones. Every March his office arranged for me to have a bone scan (for bone cancer) and lung X-ray (for lung cancer).

Twice a year I also saw my gynecologist forty-five days after I had seen my surgeon, and he was checking me in his ways.

We continued to have our annual July physical checkups with our primary care physician, with blood work including the CEA (carcinoembryonic antigen) test, an inexpensive non-specific test indicating whether there is cancer *anywhere* in your body.

Alarm Bells

Yes, there were some subsequent alarm bells. Two years after my second mastectomy, when I had just passed my five-year mark, my surgeon at my six-month checkup found a lump in the chest tissue between my skin and my ribs. He scheduled surgery to remove it. It was a fibroid and not cancer. Home free again, but I went back to checkups every ninety days.

Two more years later he again found something at one of these now-routine quarterly checkups. This time it was so small it involved only local anesthesia and it turned out to be a fat globule the size of a pea. But it wasn't there three months before—and it could have been cancer!

I want to tell you I found all of this extremely wearing emotionally. I really felt, as a cancer survivor, that the possibility of my cancer metastasizing was *not* something I could deny or repress. I felt as though there was always a sword of Damocles hanging in the corner of my psychic universe, which would always come and sit on top of me every time I had one of these exams.

I complained to Scott, my first physical therapist, that I felt as though I was always in anxiety. He said, "You will be the last of us to die of cancer because they are watching you so closely!" And so far that has proved to be true.

My Tale of Improbable Possibilities

My story is one of problems with complications after surgery—my clogged lymph system that only two percent of women get after mastectomies, which led to a frozen shoulder because I didn't do the exercise in the right way.

But if I had moved more (without passive physical therapy), I would have ended up with a possibly permanently swollen arm, which I am glad now that I do not have.

These are improbable possibilities, things which *can* happen but usually do not.

Did I resent that they happened to me? Absolutely!

Did they make me regret my decision with my surgeon to have him remove all of my lymph nodes so there was no chance of missing any cancer? No, I would do that again too!

Did I feel my surgeon had caused my frozen shoulder? No, I appreciated his reputation and his practice of being meticulously thorough. He came in after my first mastectomy and said rather proudly, "I did it for you in two hours."

And I said, "Take three hours—I don't care. Why rush?" I did not understand until later that he had spared me an extra hour of anesthesia! I was really dumb!

Improbable Possibilities Which Went in My Favor

Did I reflect with gratitude upon all the improbable possibilities which had gone "for me" rather than "against me"? No, not until much later.

Only later did it occur to me that my five operations in three-and-a-half years (late 1983 through January 1987) had occurred at a time when all of the blood supply was potentially contaminated by HIV—and I had not received a drop of transfused blood or blood products. It had never even occurred to me to be grateful for that. Certainly a very big improbable possibility had quietly gone "for me" rather than "against me."

Only looking back did I appreciate how fortunate I had been that in none of those five operations in three-and-a-half years did I have any problems with anesthesia. There were also no emergencies in the operating room. And I came away from the hospitalizations without a staphylococcus infection.

Looking back I could finally feel I had been extremely lucky.

What Conclusions (Not) to Draw from This

At this moment I must tell you I do have a fear right in the pit of my stomach, that someone will say, "All those terrible things which happened to Liz and she chose a mastectomy; I'd be afraid to choose a mastectomy because all of those things might happen to me."

I hope you will not draw that conclusion because it is not a good conclusion.

Improbable possibilities *do* exist, and they do occasionally happen to some people. You should know about them. But you should also know that they are not frequent. So I urge you to go ahead and make your own best decision. But know also about these dark edges of possibility.

Back to My Choice

It would be nice to be able to tell you that, having rejected aesthetics and identity as decisive factors in my decision-making, I then never had to deal with them at all, which would not be true!

About aesthetics, I still do not *like* my lack of breasts. My upper torso disappoints me! It still does.

About identity, I never doubted my womanhood, but I did stop identifying with full-bosomed nude goddess statues! (I do not identify with them at all!)

I searched for an image of the female that had no breasts and found one in the female dolphin who is erotic, fertile, and nurturing to her young, but has no breasts that are discernible to me!

Lovemaking without Familiar Landmarks

But there *was* a long-term impact to my decision for survival—which I had not expected although I probably should have. It had to do with our love-making as a couple. My personal pathway to my orgasm had always been through my breasts. As long as I had one breast, this continued to work for me. But when I lost the second breast, I had no way to go.

When I tried to make love I would burst into tears every time, because these familiar landmarks on my love-making path were gone.

You need to understand that I knew on a very deep level that my love for David did not depend upon our making love. And I knew—*absolutely* knew—that on that same deep level, that his love for me did not depend upon our making love. He is very capable of meeting his own sexual needs himself.

So I did not feel the pressure of his needs, nor did I fear he would love me less. Nor did I fear he would turn away from me when it was too emotionally painful for me to want to make love. That gave me a real freedom just to feel my own feelings and not worry about his.

Together we realized that I needed time to grieve the loss of my two breasts, the grieving I had not done after the first mastectomy because I was too engrossed in getting out of the pain of my clogged lymph system and then my pain-filled frozen shoulder.

I needed time to grieve the loss of my familiar and much loved pathway to my orgasm. And we both needed time to slowly and creatively imagine our way into another, alternative pathway to my orgasm. It took time, and tears, and creativity. But finally it did happen.

Life Is the Prize

You might well ask again, given all that I have told you, "Have I ever regretted my original choice for survival and for peace of mind?" My answer is, "Never!"

I did understand my own needs quite well. I do understand that I chose what I felt would give me the most "peace of mind" as a cancer survivor. And it has.

And I really do understand that all the rest of the things that happened to me—many were "by-chance fall-out"—might *never* have happened to me. But they did!

I suffered through them, emoting as I went. But I never for a minute doubted that *if* I survived for what has now been seventeen years, I would have snatched the golden ring from a deadly ride on the Carousel of Cancer. *For me, life is the prize!*

Every day is a renewal,
every morning
the daily miracle,
This joy you feel is life.

GERTRUDE STEIN

Liz/David Dodson Gray

1987

31.

Glimmer:
A Meditation on
Death & Living

—September 1982—

31.

Glimmer: A Meditation on Death & Living

September 1982

Presence
The light is out there, glimmering on the teal-blue water like a silvery glaze on a cake's icing. Except that it is dancing and moving as it spreads its silvery patterns with shining tentacles further and further out from the point.

But the light is also there on the shore, like a silver edging, illuminating every wave that gently cascades along the brown sand. And sometimes there is glimmer there too, patches of luminescence that make the whole area sparkle with presence.

That's it, you know. The presence of the Ultimate in our present. The way the water and sun and air combine in wondrous alchemy to create the Presence in our midst, so powerful yet so elusive, so trustworthy in maintaining the universe in existence moment by moment, yet so hard to trust in life and in death.

Terror
I find my being pervaded with the conviction that when that Ultimate Presence affirms my being, I am given life and health and mission. What then do I make of the logical human necessity of death?

I have written about the naturalness of death for us mortals, that it is not strange or alien, or a punishment for sin. I have many times been able to trust that Ultimate with the ups and downs of my life. How come, then, when I for a brief moment allow my consciousness to imagine myself coming to an end as a live human being, I am filled with terror?

My reverie is interrupted by a gull flying low over my position on our deck. They seldom venture so far over the beach in summer, but this is autumn and I am wrapped in robe and serape to protect myself against the brisk fall wind which blows the dry leaves scuttling across the deck, as I drink in the glitter on the water. It is a brilliant autumn day and even as I watch and meditate, the glimmer spreads further and further down the horizon, past the few rocks jutting up their black outlines, further and further the silvery sheen goes, as though it will encompass all the teal-blue water and transform it into sparkling wonder.

Why is it so hard to trust that sparkling wonder with our lives? We have heard the testimonials of those who have come back from clinical death and they witness to the beneficent presence which is light, to the warmth which evokes their desire to stay forever and to not return to this mixed blessing of mortalness.

So why do I cling to this "mixed blessing" so much? Is it just the fear of the unknown? Is it true, as Jesus said in the story of Dives and Lazarus (Lk 16:19–31), that no one will believe even if people do come back from the dead?

But how curious that this biblical story was a story about hell, and all the experiences of life-after-life recorded so far have testified to the "heaven" of coming into the presence of that which is light and warmth and beneficent Being.

Flow
It is clear now as I look out on the glimmer that it is indeed a flow from left to right (or is it east to west?), from a solid pool of glimmer to separated streaks of silver which ray out to the right. It is moving, flowing, proceeding even as it sparkles and dances.

Is this part of the answer? Is there a flow in the divine, a process of becoming which encompasses the whole universe from galaxy to electron and quark, which flows through the spinning electrons and slowly-revolving planet Earth to the whirling balls of hot chemical stars, evolving them moment by moment and year by year and eon by eon from non-being into being, from one process into the next, from water into snow and ice and then into vapor.

Nothing stands still.

We look at a waterfall and see an entity we can name *waterfall*. But the endlessly flowing waters through that waterfall know themselves to be constantly moving. We look at a candle-flame, and again we see an entity, a something to which we give a name. But the carbon atoms which are changed as they burn in that flame know all too well they are not that constant "candle-flame" which we name.

Perhaps humans are around too long with the average human life span. We misunderstand the flow and the process. We feel too fixed, too static, about ourselves, and we look for what remains the same in the process. We tend to name ourselves as static "I-am-I," and not even understand our own lives and personhoods as the flow of changing consciousness we surely are.

ELIZABETH DODSON GRAY

The Presence Moving Here

So we panic at the thought of death and the coming of death, and we clutch at the human condition as it is dropping away from us, not understanding that *all* is flow and change and process and growth, and that the glimmer, the sparkle, the energy with its beauty and its dynamism pervade all the flow and the process and the change, even in our departing.

That old hymn I love, despite its patriarchal overtones, conveys this sense of the Presence moving through eons of time:

A thousand ages in thy sight
are like an evening gone . . .

Time moves on, and we too must go with that flow. Everything comes into being for a time, and then is changed into another being. Perhaps the best we can do with our faint hearts that quail before the mystery of such change, is to remind ourselves that we did not plan for ourselves the mystery and wonder of this universe. As God says to Job in Job 38 and 39

Where were you when I laid the foundation of the earth?
says the Lord.
Tell me if you have understanding.

Who determined its measurements? Surely you know!
Or who stretched the line upon it?
On what were its bases sunk,
or who laid its cornerstone,
when the morning stars sang together
and all the children of God shouted for joy? . . .

Have you commanded the morning since your days began,
and caused the dawn to know its place? . . .
Have you entered into the springs of the seas? . . .
Have you entered the storehouses of the snow? . . .

Where were you when I laid the foundations of the earth?
says the Lord.
Tell me, if you have understanding.

Or who shut in the sea with doors,
when it burst forth from the womb,
when I made clouds its garment,
and thick darkness its swaddling band.

From whose womb did the ice come forth,
and who has given birth to the hoarfrost of heaven? . . .
Do you give the horse his might? . . .
Is it by your wisdom that the hawk soars? . . .

291

The Transforming Universe

We did not plan our first creation into the wonder and mixed blessings of planet Earth. Can we trust our birth into the next creation?

Perhaps yes, perhaps no. But we shall be born into the next creation, whether we like it or not, because all that streaming gleaming glimmer is not *"for"* us. Here our tendency to measure and to value everything by what significance and benefit it has for us, simply bumps up against the creation process which is profoundly *"for itself"* and not *"for"* us.

The glimmer is fading. The sun has been obscured by a cloud, and the glimmer has retreated to the far horizon near the outer islands. I feel desolate and abandoned. I want to shout "Come back." I want to reach out and possess it to keep it always as my own.

Now again the cloud is gone and the sun returns to warm me and the glimmer to companion me. But as the sky fills again with clouds, I am powerfully reminded that the sky moves on, the weather moves on. I do not possess the glimmer. It dances to me, comes to "presence" my life and meditation, comes to pierce my consciousness with intimations of the Ultimate, comes to remind me of my mortality and also to warm my heart with glimpses of the reality of life itself. But it does not belong to me.

With gay insouciance and sparkling verve it gives itself to me, witnesses and testifies to true Being in my midst, and then it dances lightly off to rejoin the flow which ceaselessly flows onward through the transforming universe.

So it is, yes, so it is.

32.

Sometimes The Mystery Speaks

32.

Sometimes The Mystery Speaks

July 7, 2007

Experiencing the "Dark Night of the Soul"

It was during the terrible time of my breast-cancer surgeries (between November 1983 and January 1987, five surgeries in three-and-a-half years). This included two mastectomies, and by June 1984 a huge "frozen shoulder" in which every muscle and muscle fiber from my breast bone to my right elbow was glued together with adhesions.

The slippery stuff we see on a chicken-breast—under the skin and over the chicken-flesh—is called facia. When our muscles and skin do not move, this slippery facia layer becomes solid. It heals solid in the same way a cut (or a surgical incision) heals, and it is called by physical therapists an adhesion. These adhesions were a "lock" on the muscle-fibers of my right chest and arm, which produced pain every time I moved, even to dial a touch-tone phone.

I know some people speak of the comforting presence of God in such terrible times. But that has not been my own experience.

My father died after a long illness in October of my senior year in college. I felt guilty about my going away to college while he was ill—every time I left he told me I was killing him! After his death I could not sleep for months—and I was haunted by the fear that I was having a nervous breakdown. I was a good Southern Baptist and I believed in the power of prayer. And I prayed devoutly and desperately for God to deliver me. And I experienced what the mystics have called "the silence" or "absence" of God and "the dark night of the soul."

So when my cancer-surgeries aftermath involved constant pain in my right chest and arm, I was not surprised that nothing happened when I prayed. I had been comforted after my college experience by Davie Napier, my Old Testament professor at Yale Divinity School. He very sharply contrasted our praying to the biblical God Yahweh as very different from someone's rubbing an oil lamp to produce a genie. Rubbing the lamp to evoke the genie was magic and it was guaranteed to work every time. But praying to the great I AM of the universe was not magic, and it was not guaranteed to produce our desired result.

Going On with My Life As Best I Could

During the time of my frozen shoulder, I was coping as best I could with the constant pain and with my own fear of dying of cancer. And I was going on as best I could with my life of lecturing at various places around the country. I was also still leading the Theological Opportunities Program at Harvard Divinity School.

I told people then that my living with this pain was like trying to relate to people while peering over and around a huge "burning bush" which was in the forefront of my consciousness.

I was scheduled to lecture at Pendle Hill, a Quaker conference center near Philadelphia. When David and I appeared, we were greeted by several lovely young women who were working at the conference center. They had read my book *Green Paradise Lost* and they had decorated our room with flowers to welcome me. I was touched by their thoughtfulness.

So when one of them told me that she and a friend had been working with "healing touch," and would I like them to use it with me and with the pain of my frozen shoulder, I said yes.

That night, after the program, we assembled in a darkened room. I had asked if David could be with me and they said yes. (He immediately went to sleep but fortunately did not distract us by any snoring!)

They said I should sit comfortably in a chair with my eyes shut—and they would stroke their hands *over* my body *without touching me.* I was told to relax my mind, and to just wait for what might "come to me."

So I sat, and waited and waited, and nothing came, which again, did not surprise me.

But then suddenly and quietly there appeared what seemed to be big capital letters in my mind's eye, and the letters said, "THIS IS NOT YOUR ENEMY."

"THIS IS NOT YOUR ENEMY!"

Now you might wonder if I knew what "this" meant. But I knew instantly. If you remember the movie *Field of Dreams,* Kevin Costner's character gets the message "BUILD IT AND THEY WILL COME." He too understood immediately, and so did I.

"This" was my pain, the constant burning bush that tormented me every moment I was not asleep. (I was sleeping then only with the help of sleeping pills.)

"This (pain) was *not* my enemy"?—how could it *not* be? It was destroying my life or was trying to. It stood with its burning sensations between me and every relationship, between me and every thought, between me and every project or lecture. How could it *not* be my enemy?

"The time is up," I was finally told, and I am sure that I was asked if anything "came to me." I don't remember what I said. I only know that, like the legendary cow chewing on her cud, I "chewed" on those words. Like the biblical Mary who "pondered all these things in her heart," I ruminated on these words.

What gave me pause and made me think was that I could not imagine that it was *my* own mind which had produced those words. *My* mind and heart were convinced very differently, and it seemed to me that it was this very pain which *was destroying* my life.

How then could some deeply subterranean portion of my mind produce such a startling reversal as "THIS IS NOT YOUR ENEMY"?

The more I pondered, the less it seemed possible that any part of ME could have plastered those words across my mind's eye. Okay, if not me, then who or what?

Reaching Out for the Ultimate

I have always liked for God the name MYSTERY.

Feminists often have a big difficulty even with the word *God* because it feels male, and it conjures up visions of what Alice Walker in *The Color Purple* called "that man on your eyeball."

I have moved on to names like the Ultimate, divine Presence, Creator of the Universe, Paul Tillich's "Ground of Being," and the great I AM of the Old Testament, and the Blessing One.

But in and around all these names for God, the simple word *Mystery* (with a capital *M)* appeals to me, for we truly are confronting a mystery when we seek to *know* the unknowable, when we seek to *relate* to the creator of the entire universe, when we seek to *draw energy* from the source of all the energy of Being for all time. It *is* rather presumptuous, don't you think? Yet we persist in trying to capture the ocean in a thimble, because *we* need it.

Re-Understanding My Pain

So as I pondered, I came to feel that somehow, some-way, for a brief moment the curtains hiding that Mystery had parted for me, and the Mystery had spoken.

But still, I did not understand or comprehend the meaning of what had been said.

As the months of my physical therapy for my frozen shoulder went by Scott, my extremely talented first physical therapist, told me at one point that *"Your pain is like the markings of the trail on the trees in a maze of the forest. It is your pain which is helping us see, you and I, how to travel in order to break your next adhesions and finally free you from your pain."*

I could hardly believe what he was saying.

My pain was the path. It was the way *out* of my pain. It marked the path of deliverance which my skilled physical therapist was following. My pain was *not* my enemy!

Railing against the Universe

My second "epiphany" came months later. David and I had driven from Boston to New York City, to stay with a friend and attend a conference where we truly wanted to hear the speakers. So even though I was still hurting, we made the effort and we traveled with my physical therapy supplies so as to be able to warm and relax my shoulder-muscles deep within and then stretch my muscles and their adhesions. and so each day to find another small release from pain.

It had been a bad day for us. It was the first day of the conference. The subway was a disaster of heat and crowding. There was a long way to walk, and my pain got worse until, about 3:00 PM, I told David, "I give up, let's go back to Janet's apartment and to the comfort of my hot pack!"

So here I was in a back bedroom of Janet's huge penthouse apartment, resting in bed while David and Janet chatted in the kitchen, way down a long hall. David was boiling the hydrocolators—8-inch by 12-inch sand-filled canvas bags which, when boiled, absorbed a lot of heat. He would then with tongs take them out of the special pot we had brought to boil them in, and wrap them in layer after layer of heavy towels, and finally he would bring them to me to warm and relax my painful muscles.

I was sitting up in bed, cursing myself for ever having thought I could travel or enjoy the conference, making mental lists of all the things that had gone wrong in my life recently. Wasn't cancer enough? Weren't the surgeries enough? Wasn't losing both my breasts enough? Wasn't the frozen shoulder enough? Wasn't the pain in my muscle fibers enough? Then tell me why, at fifty-five, on top of everything else I had to go into menopause right now?

It was truly a rhetorical question, flung out to the universe. Tell me why!

"I DID THE BEST I COULD FOR YOU!"

Then, to my amazement, there appeared another message, only this time it was more heard than seen.

"I DID THE BEST I COULD FOR YOU!"

Given the mood I was in, that really made me indignant. If this was the best, I'd hate to see the worst!

But what stopped me cold in the midst of my indignation was the pronoun "I." Was the Mystery truly speaking, truly revealing the Mystery at the heart of the universe?

"I DID THE BEST I COULD FOR YOU." So this was a limited and not an all-powerful divine—limited by chance and by illness and by misfortune but trying to bring healing in the midst of other factors in the strange intertwining of life.

That was, as a matter of fact, the kind of Mystery I believed in—a divine which was limited by human freedom (and probably also by germ freedom), intending good for all the created world at the moment of creation, and struggling to bring good out of all the evil and the pain which develops in "human time."

How from My Litany of Misfortunes . . .
But once again, those incredible words seemed impossible for my angry mind and soul and heart to produce. I was raging, I was railing at life for my litany of misfortunes, and now suddenly some audio experience says to me, "I DID THE BEST I COULD FOR YOU!" When did you do that? And how did you do that?

Once again I ruminated and pondered. And only perhaps years later could I ennumerate those "best things."

Only much later did I realize how fortunate I was that I had had *no* chemotherapy or radiation treatments. My cancer had happened *not* to be an aggressive one. And it was *not* estrogen-sensitive. My skillful surgeon had located my cancer very early. I had five surgeries in three-and-a-half years, at a time when the blood supply was sometimes contaminated with HIV, and I never needed a blood transfusion! And I did not get a staph infection from my multiple hospital stays.

I had a devoted and care-giving husband, I had caring young-adult children and my circle of caring friends at TOP.

And briefly I had a incredibly skilled physical therapist, Scott, who started me on the pain-marked path to total freedom of movement and flexibility for my right shoulder, chest and arm.

In all these ways I was very fortunate.

Once again the deliverance pointed to by the epiphany was not a vivid and sudden "parting of the Red Sea's waters." Instead it was an "intertwined" deliverance, one which was deeply woven into the complexities of human interactions. It was a deliverance which was slow in time, not immediately accomplished or immediately visible. It was partial at many points, not complete, and it was made possible by the flawed human actors at work in my life.

But its full meaning was obscured to me for many years and it was more fully realized by me only much later.

Saved from Drowning in My Own Life
My third epiphany came some years later. It had taken me more years to subdue the pain of my frozen shoulder, and I was just beginning to feel I was returning to health and a semblance of well-being.

One morning I woke up slowly from my sleep, with the sensation that a giant bird was carrying me in its talons, carrying me over water, until the bird finally landed me on the shore and released its grip on me. It seemed to sigh with relief at a job well-done, but now "over," and it then flew away.

Was I wakening from a dream? Perhaps. God imaged as a bird is biblical.

"Like birds hovering, so the LORD of hosts will protect Jerusalem. He will protect and deliver it, he will spare and rescue it" (Isa. 51:5).

"The LORD said to Moses, 'You have seen . . . how I bore you on eagles' wings and brought you to myself'" (Ex. 19:4).

"Hide me in the shadows of thy wings" (Psa. 17:8).

"The children of men take refuge in the shadow of thy wings" (Psa. 36:7).

" . . . safe under the shelter of thy wings!" (Psa. 61:4).

"In the shadow of thy wings I sing for joy" (Psa. 63:7).

You need to know that water is for me a dangerous, frightening image. I don't swim and I come from a family of non-swimmers. Left to my own devices I would drown.

So this epiphany was that the Mystery had carried me over a dangerous and threatening time, when I could not carry myself, and during which I felt as though I was drowning.

"Footprints in the Sand"
I later resonated to Mary Stevenson's famous poem about "Footprints in the Sand":

> One night a man had a dream. He dreamed he was walking along the beach with the LORD.
> Across the sky flashed scenes from his life.
> For each scene he noticed two sets of footprints in the sand: one belonging to him, and the other to the LORD.
> When the last scene of his life flashed before him, he looked back at the footprints in the sand.
> He noticed that many times along the path of his life there was only one set of footprints. He also noticed it happened at the very lowest and saddest times in his life.
> This really bothered him and he questioned the LORD about it:

"Lord, you said that once I decided to follow you, you'd walk with me all the way. But I have noticed that during the most troublesome times in my life, there is only one set of footprints. I don't understand why, when I needed you most, you would leave me."

The LORD replied:

"My son, my precious child, I love you and I would never leave you. During your times of trial and suffering when you see only one set of footprints, it was then that I carried you."

Does The Mystery sometimes reveal itself to us? For me, in those three epiphanies, I feel it did.

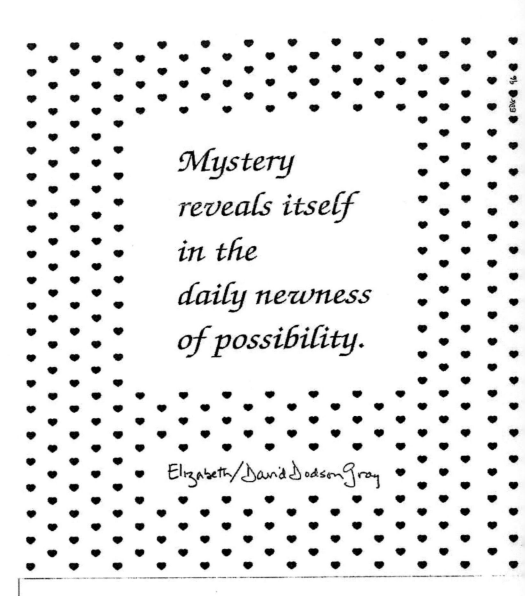

Mystery
reveals itself
in the
daily newness
of possibility.

Elizabeth/David Dodson Gray

33.

Why Do the Birds Sing?: *Healing after Trauma*

from *Sacred Dimensions of Women's Experience*

—1978—

33.

Why Do the Birds Sing?
Healing after Trauma

from *Sacred Dimensions of
Women's Experience*
1978

Awakening

This morning is an extraordinary morning for me. But in order to understand that, you have to understand my last two-and-a-half years.

I came awake slowly, aware of how cool the summer air was and how good it felt to snuggle my body close up against my husband/lover/colleague. How purringly lovely it was to be so close and so contented as I stirred from sleep on a morning cool enough to subdue my hot flashes. My skin, smooth now from too many showers and therapeutic hot baths, luxuriated in touching our skins from toe to shoulder. We moved and turned together in our bed, resting like nesting spoons.

This was the first morning in two-and-a-half years that, when I came awake, I was not in pain. I was reveling in my newly regained abilities to feel totally sensual and be without pain, when I noticed the birds singing. I glanced at the digital clock; it was 8:30, yet they were singing as though it were dawn.

You need to understand that here in New England in recent years we have heard very few birds, what with the ravages of DDT and more recently the spraying to control the ravages of the gypsy moth. So until this morning the only such outpouring of birdsong I could recall ever hearing had been from a remarkable phonograph recording that consisted of an LP-length recording of midday sounds in an August rural meadow.

ELIZABETH DODSON GRAY

Another Time, Another Place

But today I heard again. The birds really were singing. And as I lay there listening, I remembered another time, another place. I was near the Delaware Water Gap atop a mountain in eastern Pennsylvania. It was the time of morning meditation at Kirkridge, an ecumenical retreat center, and as a sun-lover I chose to do my quiet time outside on the deck of the lodge with a 240-degree unobstructed view of the horizons all around me.

As I was settling into a comfortable position in the sun, I noticed that there was a bird perched on the very top of each of four tall trees whose tips were near the deck of the lodge. And those birds were all singing.

As I "centered in" to meditate, I suddenly came to the strangest feeling, that I was coming late to prayers and that the birds were already deep into their morning praise and I was being privileged to join them, except that I did not know how to sing.

So today, listening to the birds through my open bedroom window, I again felt as though I were somehow slipping late into a pew and joining a celebration already in progress.

The Flow of Being in the Universe

But this time I asked myself a new question—"Why do the birds sing?" The answer came to me strong and clear from someplace deep in me or deep within the universe—"Birds sing because rejoicing is the center of the universe."

It was a deep-gut feeling embodied in a new set of words. I had known that feeling before. I had felt that deeply in some non-verbal interior way. But I had never formulated it into those particular words.

And then suddenly I knew why I had felt so alienated from the center of my life and from the center of the universe by my last two-and-a-half years of pain. Before my pain I had rejoiced, and I had felt deeply centered and connected. But then the pain, the anxiety, and the despair had been like some terrible filters which had distorted everything and had made it impossible for me to rejoice in creation.

I could not look up at the stars and marvel in simple amazement. I could not look at a sunset in a winter sky and lose myself in pure joy. I could not feel the sensual luxury of my woman's body. Always there was intervening, like a nightmare filter, the distraction of physical pain, the diminishment of my feeling tortured, and the threat of my own not-being in death.

I hope that someday I can discover the secret, if there is one, of rejoicing in creation while in pain, and while dying. I don't know how to do that yet. But my bird-filled reentry into wonder this morning allowed me to put into words something I have always known, that *rejoicing is the flow of Being in the universe.*

ELIZABETH DODSON GRAY

Stepping into the Flow

This rejoicing, this flow of being, is the intention of creation. This is the intention of the overflowing and bubbling up energy of creativity which has brought everything in this 193-billion-galaxy universe into being. It is rejoicing, it is wonder, it is beauty, it is flow, it is energy, it is creativity, and it is good.

And when we step into that flow of rejoicing, alone or in the company of other celebrants, we are connected, we are home.

I have always felt this. It goes back with me at least to my early teenage years. But I could seldom put it into words. So imagine my delight and surprise a few years ago when I heard theologian Margaret Miles put this into her words in talking about "The Courage to Be Alone, In and Out of Marriage." She was pondering Augustine's statement about "loving the other in God." "Augustine speaks," she said, "from a world view which assumes a center of being, of value, and of reality that the individual has access to only through her personal center."[1]

I was awestruck. She had said what I had long felt. You connect to the center of reality when you deeply connect to yourself, so being alone is coming home.

The Perfect Place

I remembered now my earliest childhood recollection. I was sitting underneath my grandfather's hydrangea bush in my backyard. I was about three and I was alone, "playing house." I was bathed in warm sunshine, and I felt very happy and deeply companioned in my aloneness by the sun, the air, the bush and the flowers. I was deeply, blissfully, contentedly at home.

Suddenly there is another memory, this one a recent one, from this spring's recuperation. This was in a time of diminishing pain as I would exercise and stretch and break adhesions. It was time of daily struggle but with each broken adhesion I was becoming a little more free of pain, a little more free to use the muscles of my shoulder and to move. I was getting well. This particular day was Memorial Day weekend and we were taking a three-hour cruise on an inland lake in New Hampshire, Lake Winnipesaukee, aboard a large ferryboat.

I was prowling the decks looking for the perfect spot to feel the wind and sun on my body and to contemplate the wonder of the very blue sky and the sun-dancing glimmer on the water. I finally found it, and I put my face up to the sun, feeling its warmth bathe my face while the strong breeze caressed my whole body. I gave a big shuddering sigh, and I knew I was back home. Back to the sun and wind, back home to wonder and celebration, back home to my deeply integrating connection to my own center and to that center of reality which grounds my life in Being itself.

ELIZABETH DODSON GRAY

The Constancy of Change

Suddenly the ferry's direction had changed. We had left Center Harbor and were heading for Wolfeboro about an hour's ride away. My old perfect spot was no longer perfect. The sun was coming upon the boat from a totally different angle, and I had to put sun and wind and location together in a totally different way to approximate the previous hour's contentment.

The sun-glimmer on the water was different now. We were no longer moving closely through passes and islands and my perfect place for sun and shielding from too much wind gave me suddenly a vastness of view and horizons. I settled in again.

It was only after letting off passengers at Wolfeboro and the ferry's heading off in still another direction to complete its triangle–like course—and my having to find a third perfect place on the same boat and on the same day with the same weather and wind and sun—that I began to think about the perfect places in my life and how they were constantly changing. As the journey goes on, I thought, even with much staying the same, I have to stay in touch with myself and my center in order also to stay in touch with the equivalent of that sun and wind and sun-glimmer on water and shelter that made for a perfect place on our ferryboat ride.

To stay the same in the rush of change, I had to adapt. The ferryboat ride was a metaphor for my life. It had perfect places but I had to seek them out and enjoy them and make use of them. Then like the birds and their nests, I had to sense changes and know I'd seek other perfect places, other places to sing and to be.

Recognizing Home

But amid the change I knew the center, the grounding, the pulse, is rejoicing. To be rejoicing, to be able to rejoice, is to be home. And all the famine in Africa, all the suffering of the Holocaust, all the pain humans cause one another—that is aberration. That is not the norm, not the pulse of creation. Suddenly I am remembering George Burns in the movie *O God* saying, as God, "It's all here. It all works."

Life is brought into being in joy, in rejoicing. The pain of childbirth is not the theme of the melody, rejoicing is. Celebration is. The energy that creates the atoms and that flows through the chemical processes of the burning stars and galaxies, flows in rejoicing.

Suddenly I heard the words and song of an old hymn:

> The spacious firmament on high
> with all the blue ethereal sky
> And spangled heavens, a shining frame . . .
>
> What though in solemn silence all
> move 'round the dark terrestrial ball,
> What though no voice nor sound

> amidst their radiant orbs be found,
> In reason's ear, they all rejoice
>   and utter forth a glorious voice,
> singing as they shine . . . [2]

I thought to myself, someone else besides me has had ears to hear that silent but profound rejoicing. Then my memory suddenly caught up another fragment of melody and words:

> Mortals, join the happy chorus
>   which the morning stars began.
> Stars and angels sing around thee,
>   field and forest, vale and mountain,
> Flowering meadow, flashing sea,
>   chanting bird and flowing fountain,
> Call us to rejoice in Thee.[3]

A Microsecond Out of Phase?

It is clear to me that the pulse of rejoicing is there in the whole of creation. It awaits only our joining in.

George Leonard, in *The Silent Pulse: A Search for the Perfect Rhythm Which Exists in Each of Us,* suggests that "perhaps, after all, perfect rhythm is always present in our every action and relationship, and it is only our awareness of it that is a microsecond out of phase. Could it be that we miss the experience not because it is so distant but because it is so close?"[4]

What if the rhythm we sense is the rhythm of rejoicing? Perhaps that is what holds the stars and planets on their course and centers the animals and birds. Perhaps we have only to step one microsecond to the side, into our own centeredness, to find that deep connectedness to the whole chorus, and to come home again to ourselves.

NOTES

1. Margaret Miles, "The Courage to Be Alone—In and Out of Marriage," in *The Feminist Mystic and Other Essays on Women and Spirituality,* ed. Mary E. Gibbs (New York: Crossroad Publishing, 1982), pp. 96–97.

2. "The Spacious Firmament on High," words by Joseph Addison (1672–1719), based on Psalm 19.

3. "Joyful, Joyful We Adore Thee," words by Henry Van Dyke (1852–1933).

4. George Leonard, *The Silent Pulse: A Search for the Perfect Rhythm Which Exists in Each of Us* (New York: E. P. Dutton, 1978), p. 134.

34.

Scattered Families:

Maintaining Intimacy & Connection in the Long-distance Relationship

TOP Talk
November 20, 1997

34.

Scattered Families:
Maintaining Intimacy & Connection in the Long-distance Relationship

TOP Talk, November 20, 1997

Following Their Hearts

When our children graduated from college, it seemed both Lisa and her younger brother Hunter wanted to settle in the Boston area. They had never, to our knowledge, even thought about living out their adult lives in other parts of the country.

After graduating from Smith College, Lisa went to work as the Area Manager of The Sandpiper, a women's clothing boutique with stores in Chestnut Hill, Manchester-by-the-Sea and Faneuil Hall Market. Then after a few years she fell in love with a young man from Pasadena who was managing a nearby store at Faneuil Hall. When he chose to return to *his* native California after going to college in New England and working here for a few years, Lisa elected to go with him in order to explore the unfolding potential in that relationship. But, doing that, she knew she would terribly miss her family and close friends.

To assuage Lisa's homesick feelings when they left here after Thanksgiving in 1986, Rob took Lisa on a month-long cross-country journey to California by way of all the best ski resorts. Our son Hunter had graduated from the University of Vermont that spring, and he was going to work that winter on the ski patrol at Killington, Vermont, at the largest ski resort in New England. Hunter arranged a weekend off from Killington to fly out to Park City, Utah, to ski with Lisa and Rob and have his first experience "skiing powder" in the light and fluffy Western snow, so different from our usually heavier and wetter Eastern snows.

A Fateful Crossing

For both our children this was a fateful crossing! Hunter fell in love with skiing powder and decided to move to Park City, Utah, for that skiing. He met his future wife that winter at Killington, and two winters later they were married and had moved to Park City.

ELIZABETH DODSON GRAY

Lisa's relationship with Rob did *not* work out. But she had done her grieving about leaving family and friends, and she fell deeply in love with the almost daily sunshine of California, and now she is married and settled in a wonderful marriage in Scottsdale, Arizona, with a two-year-old son, Jake, and a twenty-year-old step-daughter, Marie. Arizona also majors big-time in daily sunnyness.

Friends told me, "Don't worry, they'll be back. They are just trying on other locales and climates!" I always told them, "No, I don't think so." Lisa has had a life-long love affair with the sun. Her professional life in retail in Boston made her hate waking up on a day-off to an overcast or rainy day—actually, to wake up on *any* day when the sun didn't shine! She is now married, and she and her husband are solidly settled in the golf world which is centered, "big-time," in the marvelously mild winter weather of Arizona.

Likewise Hunter has had a long-term love affair with powder snow and gorgeous mountain vistas! Utah "feels right" to him, and he has become very appreciative of the child-and-family-centered values and society of Mormon-dominated Utah.

"Living Emotionally Alongside, at a Distance"

So today both our adult children are "happily settled," one in Arizona and the other in Utah. We are very proud of the energetic, competent, honorable ways they are living their lives. It is "happily settled" for them, but not for us. David and I now think about our lives (as we wrote in this year's Christmas letter) as "our now-adult children's lives *and our life lived emotionally alongside them* but now separated by nearly a continent's distance."

I am talking here about sharing our adult lives with each other, not on a daily basis but on a constant, steady basis. We would like as parents to live life "emotionally alongside them." But we find that is not easy, given the geographical separation *and* the pace of our modern lives.

We are truly grateful for the modern technology of the telephone, which allows us to bridge the miles (and two and three time zones) with voice lines which really do convey feelings—joy, sadness, anxiety, frustration. Phones are so much more expressive than written letters, e-mail or faxes. I can tell in an instant from Lisa's voice how she is feeling, whether she is speaking in real time to us or she has left us a recorded message on our answering device.

Let me be clear about what I am saying. I am *not* saying adult children should not live in other parts of the country (and indeed the world). I am *not* saying we as parents would want them next door or down the street, if following their hearts leads them to other places.

What I *am* saying is that geographical distance, *even with* mod-ern technology, poses great problems for maintaining connection in relationships—problems which most relationships don't cope with very well. And the result is the "thinning" of the relationship—with consequences for all concerned.

It is not without irony that I now ponder my own mother's plaintive wail, "How come *my* children decide to move away from home when all my friends have children who stay in Baltimore?" Why, indeed? I did not feel her pain then; I *do* feel it now.

What We Have Lost—and Grieved

When Lisa first left, I did my own grieving. She and I are close, and her friendship lights up my life. When she was working in Boston, Lisa shared a condo in Charlestown with a best friend she has known since kindergarten. Every week Lisa would come to dinner some night, bringing with her all her dirty laundry. And we would hear all about her week over supper, in and around her run-ning up and down the stairs changing washer and dryer loads. It was wonderful connecting.

In those years David was looking forward to helping Lisa with her child-rearing when she married and had kids, so she could successfully juggle both a career and having a family. When Lisa moved to California, his hopes for that kind of role in her life were laid aside with regret.

Two Adult Children, Two Different Responses

Because Lisa did miss us a lot when she first moved, I was relieved to discover that she very much wanted still to keep in touch by a phone call every few days. It turned out that it was *important* to her, as well as to us, to "walk together" through our lives. Since we work at home and have a business with a toll-free 800 number, we invited her to use it. So the timing and frequency of the phone calls was totally up to her. And I discovered that the emotional closeness and connection I so much treasured in our relationship was still there, even across the miles.

With our son Hunter it was a different story. Hunter had *never* communicated to us his emotional ups and downs. Is this a gender difference?—I really do not know. I do know that when he moved to Utah, Hunter did not have a real pattern of on-going emotional connecting to continue. During the worst of my years of recovery after breast-cancer surgeries, Hunter really did "rally to the cause" very nobly when I asked him to call me every week.

But when my health and life began to stabilize again, Hunter relapsed into his more usual pattern of long intervals between his phone calls to us. By then he had added a wife, Sherry, and then two children, Tricia and Jon-Hunter. He is making a living for his family in addition to skiing, and he spends a lot of time with his children. The time pressures of that life put his phoning us well toward the bottom of his list of must-do's.

"Why, Then, Don't We Phone Him?"

We try to phone him. But they are seldom home, and when they are at home, they have the pattern of not answering the phone so they can have some uninterrupted time with one another and their children. He has needed to put a firewall between himself when he is at home and unnecessary calls from those he supervises who are still at work.

What about leaving messages for them on their answering device? Yes, we do that. But we have learned that in the press of other things, they often do not take the messages off for days at a time, and then they don't call back.

Write them letters? For the past ten years they have lived in Park City, Utah, where there is no home-delivery of mail. Everything goes into your mailbox down at the post office in the center of town. Hunter finally confessed that they only pick up their mail there about once a month. And then there is so much stuff that they haven't time to read it all, or even *our* part of it.

United Parcel Service does deliver to their front door, and I have used UPS to get an important letter or birthday card or gift to them. But Hunter and Sherry have finally told us that often they go for several weeks before they can find a "family time" to open the Valentine presents and cards, or Easter presents which I send them.

A Grand-Canyon of Distance to Span

I end up feeling as though I am on one side of the Grand Canyon, stretching out my hands to have a relationship over an incredible distance that is not just a matter of geography. With Lisa I feel her two hands stretching from her side out to meet me. But with Hunter I too often do not feel that.

Please do *not* tell me that my children must be turning away for a reason. I have too much written evidence in cards and letters from them both that I was, that we both were and still are, as they have experienced us, very loving and supportive parents.

I find I can celebrate our children's childhood experience of my very good mothering, even at the same time I have to grieve the sacrifice of my adult ministerial-self, my own professional "calling," which was the cost to me in those years of that good mothering. But perhaps because I feel I paid my full dues in the Mothering Club, I am very sure I have the right to expect my life as a mother and friend of adult children to be rich and full, not thin and attenuated.

I am reasonably sure that our children arrived at adulthood with a "clear" relationship between them and us. By "clear" I mean one unmarred and undistorted by lots of bad feelings, angers, traumas, etc. Because of my confidence in that clarity, I dare to expect clear, rich and sustaining relationships with my children in these years of my life.

Missing the Growing-Up Times of Grandchildren

Today our now-grown children have children of their own. I (and we) grieve the growing-up time of these wonderful children, which we are missing. I envy grandparents who have children and grandchildren close by, who can experience the delights of ages 2 and 3 and 4 and 5 on a weekly or monthly basis. We revel in the verbal pictures of our grandkids which Lisa and Hunter give to us over the phone. But we crave more!

Even our grandchildren crave more. Tricia at three would say on the phone, "Can't you come over and play with me? Why do you have to get on an airplane? I wish you guys lived down the street." And we would sing songs with each other over the telephone, which was the best we could do.

David and I are lucky if we get to see our children and grandchildren "in the flesh" every six months. And even that requires money we often don't have. For several years, it has been Lisa's generosity with the money she earns which has paid for our plane tickets at Christmas and at any other times we can go back and forth.

The Dilemma and Illusion of "Quality Time"

But even such occasional visits are both a joy and also a painful experience. I love seeing our youngest grandchildren (now ages 2, 3 and 5). But I must spend the majority of each visit "making friends," because to them I am essentially a stranger! What do they know of this strange couple who suddenly descends from an airplane, expecting (or hoping) to have a relationship with them?

And after all the months of our *not* being together, there is a terrible pressure on these few days when suddenly we *are* together for a visit.

Somehow, the few days must be wonderful—*super* wonderful. They can't be just ordinary days because they must *make up* for all the ordinary days which we did *not* spend together. They must be super *quality* time, because we don't have *quantity* time together.

This problem is summed up in a comment our son Hunter made when we were visiting for three days the summer of my sixty-fifth birthday (compliments of Lisa's plane fare). We were spending the day with Hunter who was giving us a guided tour of the Utah mountains he so loves. When we passed beyond the lunch hour without stopping to eat, Lisa (who was pregnant at the time) finally complained. And Hunter uttered these immortal words: "You come 3,000 miles to see my mountains, and you want to *eat!*" He was indignant; it was too precious a time to waste *eating*.

A Wasting of the Emotional Potential of Families

When I say I yearn to do more emotional living with my children and grandchildren than distance and busy schedules allow me to do, I am not saying this as a woman who has nothing else to do with my life. I have a full life. I write books, I am invited to lecture around the United States and Canada, I am happily married, I coordinate the Theological Opportunities Program.

But I yearn for my children and grandchildren to be more a part of this life of mine. **Being alive and being human means to me to dwell within a richly textured network of relationships.**

Why would I *ever* imagine my own network of such relationships *not* to include deeply and wonderfully my own children and grandchildren?

Didn't We Intend for Them to Be Independent?

But when I try to clarify and put into words the pain I feel as a parent in a "scattered family," I get told all the time that this state of affairs is "normal." After all, I am told, didn't we raise our children to be independent and to live without us?

The conversation then moves on to what may be the matter with me, that I have these bizarre expectations of my adult children. "You must want to *control* them," I am told.

Then others say, "Don't expect *anything* of your adult children. We don't want to 'overload' them with the need to relate to *us* when they are already living such busy and pressured lives. Don't expect anything—so then you won't be disappointed!"

My response is to want to cry out (and sometimes I do actually say this to people): Young-adult children being *related* to their parents has nothing to do with their *independence*.

And our *being related to* our adult children has nothing to with our *controlling* them.

This has to do with our continuing to love—and to be loved—as we did when our children were small and we as parents were young. When children are grown and parents are older, it is still loving and being loved, only different.

But "different" does not mean seldom, or minimal, or not much.

ELIZABETH DODSON GRAY

What My Heart Tells Me

Let me tell you what my heart tells me. Families were intended by their nature to be a supportive web and an emotional context for each other. Families are intended to enrich the texture of each others' lives by the excitement of differing perspectives, the comfort of loving arms, the companionship of people who know you very well over long periods of time.

Families scattered by geographical distance and harassed by the extraordinary time-pressures of our hurry-up culture, are *eroded, thinned-out, washed-out to a shadow or whisper of what they might be.* The lives of all of us are diminished when that happens to our family connections and day-by-day emotional ties.

Then both the parents and their adult-children are left to struggle alone and by themselves with *problems* which are better shared and borne together. Equally, both parents and children celebrate *joys* alone, and only "hear about" birthdays, Thanksgivings, anniversaries, Halloween, Christmas.

My heart tells me that the human life of the generations was meant for more companionship, more support, more joy, even more tension of perspectives and different experiences, than most of us have today in our so-called "scattered families." It will always seem sad to me, and so much a waste of our God-given relationships between us as parents and children.

May the love we share
keep us all afloat and buoyant
as the tide turns, and
the waves beat on all shores.

Elizabeth/David Dodson Gray

The Theological Opportunities Program (TOP)

What Is the "Theological Opportunity" at TOP?

Theology, by its Greek derivation, is "thinking about God" (*theos* [God] and *logos* [word]).

But in actual use the word *theology* has been extended—to cover thinking about humans, and then extended still more to cover thinking about our human place in the cosmos.

Theology, thus, is about "naming," and that naming has power—the power to shape the way people perceive their lives and their world.

Throughout many centuries male theologians have been unapologetic about making theological statements about "human" life based only upon their *male* life experience. And male theologians through the centuries have been unapologetic about projecting their own theological speculations upon females and female life ("Women as like Eve, evil," et al.).

Let us as women then not be reticent about our doing our own theological reflection about our own lives and women's life experience, and our women's search for purpose, spirituality and moral meaning.

Theology in the past, though it presumed to speak for the entire human experience, has been based upon only the life experience of one half—the male half—of the human species. It is our challenge and opportunity as women to explore the theological reflections of the other—silent or unrepresented—half of the human species.

We invite you to this "theological opportunity"!

35.

What TOP Has Meant to Me

From *Weaving Communion,*
25th anniversary of TOP

Fall 1998

35
What TOP Has
Meant to Me

TOP Coordinator (1978–1998)

Twenty-five Years Ago

I slipped into a chapel pew for the first TOP lecture (October 1973). I was forty-four, and my mid-life journey would have been so very different without all that TOP has brought into my life.

Since that day I have lived the issues of my life—personal, theological, spiritual—within the wider context of the dynamic questing and always profound woman-centered spirituality of TOP. Nothing was off-limits at TOP. We could ask any question, question any assumption, speak any truth, expose any bad secret, share any pain, celebrate any joy, dream any dream, empower any new life within us, forge any new identity. Having such a context in which to think and feel and live my life has affected everything I have experienced and done.

Discovering Feminism

These were the years in which I discovered feminism, and it changed my perspective on just about everything. At TOP we shared our feminist journeys, and we constantly pondered in what ways our emerging feminist spirituality was transforming our religious consciousness, moving us *away* from our roots or origins in our various religious traditions, transforming our identities, changing how we lived and understood our roles and our relationships, and finally empowering us to name the sacred for ourselves as women.

These were also the years in which I began writing my own eco-feminist books, lecturing at campuses and churches and conferences throughout the U.S. and then Canada.

Naming Myself As a Feminist Theologian

In 1978 I became the coordinator of TOP—and I became able to "name myself" as a feminist theologian. It was TOP which kept me honest when I talked and wrote about "women *this*. . . " or "women *that*. . . . "

It was TOP which grounded me in the shared lives of a diversity of women, TOP which gave me the privilege of being one woman among the many women who come here (and have come here), nearly 1700 of us just in the last ten years.

It has been TOP which increasingly gave me the passion to try to articulate the "voice" that together we were struggling to find, deep within our woman-beings.

Surviving Breast Cancer and a Severely Frozen Shoulder

These were also the years, starting in late 1983, in which I had breast cancer—diagnosis, surgical biopsy, mastectomy, painful post-surgical complications including finally a frozen shoulder locked in pain.

I had five surgeries in three-and-a-half years, including finally a second mastectomy and ultimately eleven-and-a-half years of physical therapy until finally I was out of pain. All this was concurrent with menopause, followed by post-trauma stress and depression.

Beyond my devoted husband David and my nurturing already-adult children, it was that "blessed context" at TOP which carried me from Thursday to Thursday, picking me up from my isolation and despair, in support groups endlessly hearing my pain, and always counting on me to keep on presiding Thursdays over our fall and spring program meetings, as if I were still my former self.

It was the women of TOP who were always there for me, sharing in my dream, supporting my guiding vision of finding my path out of my pain and back to health and to myself. I shall always be grateful for this blessed ministry to me of cards and phone calls, empathy, and the sharing of their own traumas.

Companions on My Journey of Life

The women I have met at TOP as companions on my journey of life and faith have enriched my emotional landscape in ways I did not even dream possible.

I have learned to *listen* as intently as I speak. I have learned humility and compassion in the presence of women whose lives have been touched and distorted by male violence, abusive parents or elitist educational systems.

I came to treasure the precious opportunity each Thursday to go through life *together,* bearing each other's burdens, weeping together, rejoicing together, laughing together. I came to appreciate deeply and value the different lenses through which we each viewed our lives.

I realized that, but for the many different women and standing points and life-experiences I met at TOP, I would have gone through these years from 44 to 68 **with *only my own* perspective upon reality—and how impoverished my life would have been.**

Redeeming my life from that narrow constriction of knowing only what I personally can see and feel as my own experience, has been TOP's greatest gift to me.

Life is short
and we
never have
enough time
for gladdening
the hearts
of those
who travel
the way
with us.
O, be swift to love!
Make haste to be kind.

— Henri F. Amiel

36.

Surfing at the TOP Planning Process

From *Weaving Communion*
25th Anniversary of TOP
Fall 1998

36.

Surfing at the TOP Planning Process

From Weaving Communion
25th Anniversary of TOP
Fall 1998

Coordinating the planning process is like riding a surfboard.

You've seen the image many times. It is of an athletic young man astride a moving surfboard, his feet planted firmly and his weight shifting this way and that as the surfboard "rides" a huge incoming Hawaiian surfing wave, followed by another wave, and still another. That is my mental and emotional image for how it feels to me to be coordinating the dynamics which are our TOP Advisory Committee.

It is like riding the waves of rising and falling energy as we mix together the best creative ideas and passions we all possess. Each week we always begin from no wave, no energy, and I as the facilitator of the process try to state as clearly and cogently as I can *where we are in the planning process,* and what is needed of us today to move ahead.

I ask questions. David writes the issue of the day onto newsprint. Slowly we begin to come up with reactions and to generate possibilities, thinking against each other, building on each other's suggestions, sometimes rejecting each other's ideas, but always reaching, reaching for the theme that will encompass everything for us this time, reaching for the nifty title which is just eluding us, reaching for the *integration* of all the possibilities we are playing with, reaching for the right turn of phrase which will properly describe what we are all feeling.

You can feel the energy building in the room, the voices getting more alive and excited, people speaking and interrupting each other, giving voice to creativity bubbling inside them. Then I know the energy is cresting and I only need to get out of its way and ride that wave in, only making sure that the more patient people, who don't interrupt but instead put up their hands, get recognized and have their voices heard even as the energy wave continues to run.

If we are lucky, the wave lands us all on the shore of consensus, and you can hear as well as feel the "YES!" that breaks out through the group as we finally can touch and are giving words to that passionately reached-for resolution. That *Yes!* is the resonance which happens when we hit an emotional golden nugget of possibility that resonates in the heart and mind of almost everyone.

I have a poster which says, "None of us is as smart as all of us." Exactly. In our consensus moments of Yes!, we know and experience the wisdom of that poster.

As coordinator and facilitator of this dynamic planning process, I try to nurture a collective free-flowing creative "brain" we are all a part of, and an atmosphere both demanding and affirming, where everyone puts out ideas without trying to "own" them but rather can enjoy tossing them into the collective consciousness. Some will be affirmed by other people, some will be ignored. Some of what is said will be disagreed with, some will be built upon. But all will be a part of the energy as it builds, and our building this emotional wave of shared creative energy requires the best of *all* of us.

I try as facilitator to let the energy of the group flow, sparking in others reactions by my questions and assignments, when we are beginning on "low." I notice when and where the group energy builds—because precisely *there* in that cluster of feelings or ideas is something we want to stay with and pay attention to. At times I step in, to synthesize, summarize, or lay out options (One, Two, Three). Other times I step back and rejoice in the building energy and simply ride that wave along with everyone else. At still other times I assume the leadership more directly, pointing us to the next step in our planning process, urging us, when I think the moment calls for it, to move on to the next conceptual task.

Before Thursday I try to get a good night's sleep so I can deal with equanimity and good humor with the emotional demands and frustrations of this creative process. And I try *never ever* to make up my own mind about *anything* before we meet, so I can lay out a level playing field of affirmation for *all* possibilities.

Finally, I try never to lose faith in this process, even when we are stuck in the muddy flats of muddling around in the third and fourth and even fifth sessions, searching for an overarching theme that just won't come into focus and continues to elude us. It is hard, as the facilitator, when we have ridden a wave of energy up and then again down, and there still is no consensus, no Yes! And it is late and we have been going at it for two hours and we are all getting tired and we are not there yet. It is hard then to *declare defeat* and go home. That is when I need to remind myself that there is fresh energy waiting in another day, and a new mix of people. But I still must *not* let myself pre-think!

The dynamism of this planning process is rooted in a radically open, *large* Advisory Committee. Soon after I took over as TOP coordinator in 1978, I determined to make the Advisory Committee open to everyone, instead of following my predecessors' pattern of a smaller, invited committee. I repeatedly issue invitations from the podium of the lecture series, inviting everyone who attends to join us in our afternoon sessions. I often liken it to a floating crap-game: Anybody who is there, gets to play!

As the numbers joining the committee started to increase, I resisted the conventional wisdom that effective committees could not be larger than a certain size. My thinking was that women's lives are continually intruded upon by children's illnesses, family crises, work demands, elderly parents' needs, travel vacations, and so on. I somehow intuited that it would be better to have such a "large" committee that it would be clear to everyone that the committee would *always* have a critical mass, even if some always had to be gone, even for weeks at a time.

I also realized that it would be an advantage, not a disadvantage, to have people rejoin us after an absence, or to have genuinely "new" people join us at any stage. These people would magically give us instant insight into how our new series theme, or any of the titles we were trying so hard to fine-tune—how these would "play" to someone sitting at home receiving our publicity brochure, someone who had not been with us through our committee's thinking-together process. So a blend of "new to the process" and "old to the process" became a valued recipe for any given week.

But the power, the deep emotional power of our planning process comes from our women's lives and the emotional gut, as we share our life issues during those first two sessions. This is our taproot, this is our living water.

When we are truly and deeply talking about our life issues, we are laying out the building blocks of our process, building blocks which will never betray us because they are true and honest and come from deep inside us as we struggle to live our lives as women.

All the rest of our process, as we reach for words and concepts, titles and speakers, is our attempt to do justice to those original emotional foundations. We are simply trying to work out the important details of finding for ourselves the integrative theme, the right topics, the nuanced titles, and the best speakers. All this is done in the service of enabling our TOP series a year hence to feel deeply and think well about these depths of our lives.

But it is our passionate commitment to our women's lives and to the validity of our women's issues which gives us the passion and the energy that "rolls the waves" in our planning process.

37.

Lifelines & Miracles

•

Elizabeth Dodson Gray

—essay—

May 27, 2007

37.

Lifelines & Miracles
May 27, 2007

Like Being Hit by a Tsunami

I have likened it to a tsunami in my life. I thought after my breast cancer surgeries in my mid-50s—five surgeries in three-and-a-half years, including two mastectomies and a "frozen shoulder" which would immobilize my right shoulder for three years and take a total of fourteen years of physical therapy for me to get totally pain-free—that nothing could again "shake my life."

But in August 2006, at the tender age of seventy-seven, I decided to have a right-hip replacement. I had severe tendonitis pain below that hip. Every time I put my weight on my right leg to walk, I winced. My surgeon informed me that my physical therapist and I would not be able to heal that tendonitis, despite years of trying, because of its proximity to my deteriorating hip. So I decided to have the hip replaced, which my surgeon told me would solve both my problems.

I had a very good hip-replacement surgeon and I am sure the operation went well, though I now do not remember anything about the days after that surgery. What I do remember is that nine days after that first surgery (several days of which were spent in a rehab hospital), I had to have emergency intestinal surgery in another hospital, to keep my intestine from "exploding," as the trauma surgeon put it.

That surgeon removed twelve inches of my small intestine, and also separated another portion of my intestine which, he said, had attached to yet another part of my intestine and was "strangling" it.

Two big operations nine days apart, with probably a total of at least two to four hours of anesthesia, put me into a psychological black hole of drugged obliviousness and pain. I had several blood transfusions, dozens of different medicines, IVs, nose tubes, a night in Intensive Care, and several days on a heart monitor. My hip surgeon told me later, *"Mrs. Gray, you were very sick!"* My articulation of it was what I told David, "I am in hell."

For a total of forty days and forty nights I was in two hospitals (one for each surgery) and two different rehab hospitals. That is five-and-a-half weeks. The Bible speaks of "forty days and forty nights" when it means "a long time."

Three days after my hip-replacement surgery, my husband David came down with shingles, and, because he was contagious, he could not visit me for at least ten days—which was three days *after* my second surgery.

My blessed friends from TOP, about five of them, scheduled time into their busy lives to stay with me in his place, for the entire visiting hours of every day. I am told I often slept through their visits. But I am sure that somewhere in my unconscious state their loving companionship registered with me.

Lifelines

But what I want to tell you about is my experience of that which I came to feel were "lifelines" in a time in my life when I felt myself to be drowning.

My first 'lineline" was a beautiful arrangement of two dozen blood-red roses. The roses were packed solidly with practically no stems into a low tight container, so that without any long stems they would not fall over as so many roses do after a few days. This arrangement, as well as the quality of the large partially-open deep red roses, had become a trademark of the Winston Florist in our Boston area. These glorious roses had another trademark; they lasted without any change for about two complete weeks.

They were sent to me by a dear and cherished younger friend who, two years before, had herself experienced a long illness, during which she knew I was "holding onto her" and waiting for her to return to her health. Her last message to me before she disappeared into illness was "You'll never lose me." She and I both held on to that promise like a mantra until she reemerged into health.

She knew how much I loved flowers, and how much I would feast my eyes (and soul) on the breath-taking beauty of the roses. She also knew how they would *last*.

Every time I looked at those roses, I felt her pulling on an emotional lifeline between us, holding on for dear life, holding me up as I felt myself disappearing down into the pain and darkness of trauma. Every time I looked at those roses I felt the lifeline of her concern holding onto me so that I could not disappear into the quagmire I felt myself to be in.

After two weeks, just when these roses were beginning to darken on the edges of their petals, a fresh new *duplicate* arrangement arrived to be yet another lifeline for the next two weeks! And I held on for dear life.

ELIZABETH DODSON GRAY

When I Thought I Could Be Dying

Another lifeline came to me with Joan. Hers was the first get-well card I had read before the darkness descended, and in it she wrote about the appreciation she had for the "ministry" I had had with many women, including those in TOP. Sometime after I had read her card, I experienced a very dark night alone in my second hospital, when I felt it was possible I was dying. I have no idea what my medical condition was at that point in time. I only know that I thought I could be dying and I was able to view that possibility with equanimity *because of her card.*

I have *never* felt good about dying, or hospitable to the idea of dying. I have felt a great craving to be alive, and very grateful to the good Creator who gave me, and all things, life and breath. But here I was, feeling that I could die in peace, knowing that I had made a difference in people's lives. Surely I knew that before. But the ministry of that card was that it "said it" at a critical moment for my consciousness, and thus that one night, when I contemplated the imminent possibility of my death, *it gave me great comfort.*

Again, it was like a lifeline, anchoring me with comfort and with the loving companionship of a friend in a time when I felt totally lost and adrift.

Joan also gave me a very soft and cuddly twin-size white acrylic blanket in Hudson Bay colors, to use when I was cold. I was cold a lot, and I found that at both hospitals their version of a blanket was simply a thin cotton bedspread! So I would ask the nurse or aide to cover me with Joan's blanket. Not only did it make me physically warmer but every time I snuggled down inside its warmth, I felt enveloped by Joan's concern for me, and, through Joan, by all of my TOP friends who were "pulling for me." Once again, it was a lifeline that several times a day comforted and sustained me—reminding me of all those who counted on me to come back to my life and health from wherever I was now.

The Importance of Saying "I Love You"

My next lifeline came from my daughter Lisa and her oldest son Jake. When Lisa, who lives in Scottsdale, Arizona, heard of my second operation, I am told that she was very concerned, knowing that the convergence of two serious operations in nine days portended trouble. I have always had a special bond with Jake, my grandson, and have long felt that my words "I love you"—which I have expressed often in words, and cards, and special small gifts—were a deep bond between us.

Lisa, in spite of her super-busy schedule—as mother of two boys, chauffeur to school, homemaker, and her own business as a manufacturer's representative for four companies—resolved to write, with Jake, a note to me *every day.* Jake was just learning to print. Those notes, with Jake's awkwardly-printed "I love you, please get well soon" were a lifeline to me every day when they arrived. And then one day my husband David brought me a large suit-box-size parcel and the news that Jake had insisted on his packing a box for Grandma, the one who was always sending packages to *him.*

In the box were a small photo album with photos of the family; a framed picture that said "I miss you"; a special small box packed by Jake himself with a jewelry pin, a Christmas pen, a votive candle to light for all the special Christmas times we'd had together; a votive holder saying "I love you"; and a keychain attached to a lucite photo-holder with his picture in it.

All this was another lifeline to me. Now, this time, it was Lisa and Jake who were tugging at the other end, reminding me of all the great love between us, expecting me to recover and to spend more time with them. It was as though Jake was saying to me, "You've always been telling me 'I love *you,*' and now I want to tell you that I love *you!*"

That refrain which I had repeated so many times through the years with Jake in my lap, has become a benediction of blessing between us, a true lifeline.

Miracles

Now we come to miracles—a different perception perhaps. It just so happened that during my entire five-and-a-half-weeks stay at two hospitals and two rehab facilities, I had never been able to answer the telephone in my room. When it rang (which was infrequently), it was always too far away for me to pick up and answer. I hated missing those calls!

One morning back in Scottsdale the day was beginning for Jake and Lisa at 7:00AM. Jake, who is extremely intuitive about emotional realities, took one look at his mother's face and said, "You are worried about Grandma. You need to call her *right now.*"

At that moment it was 9:00AM in Boston. I was already sitting in my wheelchair in my room at my second rehab hospital, trying to settle my stomach and my nausea after having been forced earlier—on an empty stomach—to take my morning's supply of nine pills and to receive into my bare abdomen an hypodermic injection of the blood thinner heparin! Soon I would be wheeled to my dreaded Hitler-like physical therapist who arrived at 10:00AM.

My head is down and I am breathing in slowly, as they teach you to do when you feel terrible and have to sit upright. Suddenly there is someone beside me, *dressed in street-clothes,* identifying herself saying, "Hello, I am (whatever name she used) and I am here to clean your room."

Just at that moment my phone rings. I realize I can get her to answer my phone, so I ask her to do that and to hand me the phone. It is Lisa and Jake on the other end of the line, and Lisa says, "Jake said I should call you *right now!*"

After we talk, I look around because I can't hang up the phone, and there is no one in my room. I honestly do not know if the lady actually

338

cleaned my room or not. What I did know, when I reflected on the incident, is that I have *never* had a cleaning person at any hospital or rehab appear in street-clothes and not in hospital garb, and they *never* introduce themselves to me using their real name. They usually move as quiet workers from mopping halls to mopping rooms, never introducing themselves.

She may have thought I was asleep and not wanted to startle me. All I know is that her appearing at the very moment Lisa and Jake phoned felt to me like a miracle— a moment out of time and out of the ordinary processes of hospital procedures because of the way she was dressed and the way she spoke.

In the Mysterious Intertwining of Human Lives

My experience of life leaves me aware that in the mysterious intertwining of human lives, we never know what casual gesture or word of ours will be a lifeline for another person, or perhaps even be perceived as a miracle.

I remember once, years ago, lecturing at a divinity school in Minneapolis. After my lecture a woman came up and asked me if I had read a certain book. I said that no, I had not. She took a copy of the thin paperback book from her purse and gave it to me "to read on the plane home to Boston."

I did read that book, and it became the inspiration (acknowledged to her) of my next book. I am sure that this woman had no idea it could mean that much to me. Nor did I when she gave it to me. But at that moment in my life and my feminist journey, the gift of that book was pivotal.

I remember another lecture when a young woman came up to me and put into my hand a small broach with an beautiful inlay of a cat done in marcasite. She said, "Here, I want you to have this, to thank you for your lecture." That is all she said, so I took the cat pin and brought it home and put it in my jewelry box. Now I am not a particular fan of marcasite and at that time we didn't have a cat. So there it sat month after month in my jewelry box.

Then after some period of time one of my friends at TOP experienced the loss of her very beloved cat, and she was grieving deeply. I thought of that cat pin and I sent it to her. She loved marcasite and it seemed to her like a lifeline of understanding, saying "I stand with you in your sorrow and your loss." It seemed like a lifeline of companioning—of walking with her on her journey of grieving.

A Letter to Me from a Stranger

Another time in my own life it was a letter. As I recount in "A Ministry by Inadvertence," I was ready *not* to press ahead with what became my first book. I was on a summer vacation, with my time broken up by teen-age children, guests, and for July a once-a-week teaching responsibility at a somewhat distant location.

ELIZABETH DODSON GRAY

Just when I had decided to *not* press ahead, I received a letter from a stranger—an English professor at my alma mater, Smith College—who had read an article I had written for the Alumnae Magazine. She took the time to write to a total stranger to say that I was a good writer and I should continue writing.

Do you know how often (or seldom) college professors do that? I know it is very seldom. And yet I can say without equivocation that without *that* letter on *that* day, I probably would never have started writing my first book.

That says to me—to repeat what I said earlier—that in the mysterious intertwinings of human interaction, we never know when a casual gesture, or a word, or a letter, or a gift, will be a lifeline *or* a miracle in someone else's life.

38.

Retirement Garden Party

—June 3, 2010—

38.

Retirement Garden Party

June 3, 2010

Invitation

We are inviting you to help celebrate a very important milestone in the life of TOP and the lives of Liz and David Dodson Gray.

As you know, the Theological Opportunities Program was inaugurated thirty-six years ago by Brita Stendahl and then-dean of the Harvard Divinity School Krister Stendahl. Our lecture series each fall and each spring has grown since then from four sessions to our present ten sessions. With series themes such as "What We Might Be: Coming Alive to Ourselves" and "Navigating with a Moral Compass in This Turbulent World," we have carved out a special niche between the personal and the wider culture. With fabulous pro bono speakers, our programs have moved from the subtle but intense dynamics of family relationships to the far-reaching effects of sexual trafficking and globalization.

It has been our pleasure and privilege to have Liz serving as our Coordinator for this vibrant group for thirty-two years, from September 1978 through May 2010. Liz will be retiring at the end of May 2010, along with David, who has handled our database and computer and financial needs with diligence and a deep commitment to women's voices.

TOP has just completed the process of hiring a new Coordinator. It would have been impossible to replace Liz and we made no attempt to! She is such a very special woman and leader. She has presided over the several configurations of our organization with wisdom, skill, patience, tact, humor and love. She is chock full of good ideas for lectures and speakers. She is a solicitous friend who maintains close personal relationships with so many of the TOP members. And she has raised to an art form the more traditional modes of communication—the telephone and the hand-written note!

Liz explains the "theological opportunity" at TOP in this very cogent and helpful way. "Theology is about naming. That naming has power—the power to shape the way people perceive their lives and their world." Through the years the Theological Opportunities Program as been a doorway into naming the world from a woman's perspective.

More than 4,300 different individuals from a multitude of faiths and backgrounds have walked through that doorway to find intellectual excitement, empowerment, and nurture in the unique community of TOP. Many of us are determined that TOP continue its important mission of women committed to justice and peace in our time. We the Advisory Committee of TOP, the active core group of women who plan the lecture series, would very much like to have our coming years with our new Coordinator be absolutely as exciting and rewarding as have been the past thirty-one years led by our esteemed and beloved Liz.

There is simply NO other gift that would please Liz as much as the financial assurance that TOP can continue to be strongly supported in its vital mission. Toward that end, we are asking you to please consider an inaugural gift to the Elizabeth Dodson Gray Fund to ensure TOP's successful future. This Fund will be administered by the Boston Foundation. Please see the enclosed pledge /remittance form for details re. your contribution.

In order for us to be able to make the announcement of a substantial dollar amount at the party for Liz and David on June 3rd, we request that you please return the enclosed donation form by May 30th.

We hope you will be able to be present to greet Liz and David in person, and to share stories and memories with them and with past and current TOP members.

With gratitude for your friendship and support in the past, and with hope for the same going into TOP's future,
Yours sincerely, for the TOP Advisory Committee,

Martha Nielsen, Kathy Jellison, Priscilla Donham, Nancy Hurlbut, Marcia Boehlke, Chris Farrow-Noble, and Joey DuBois

Tribute to Elizabeth Dodson Gray on the occasion of her retirement as TOP Coordinator for thirty-two years

How is it possible to pay tribute to Elizabeth Dodson Gray for thirty-two years of exceptional leadership as Coordinator of TOP without leaving something out that matters greatly to someone who might be in attendance today?

It is precisely why we dare to do so, know that the issues, opportunities and memories we share all stand out differently for each of us—the common denominator being that we each shared them with Liz. I might have had the ah-ha moment when listening to a speaker talk on the subject of life with her adult daughter; you might have been particularly challenged to learn how the environment was being compromised; another's growth moment was learning that she might be a victim in an abusive relationship. All private moments as we listened and learned—yet corporate and communal moments that we shared as women together in the safety of Liz' steady care and love. She knew well that what is personal is also communal—our particular Ya-Ya Sisterhood came from responding to each Thursday's Ya-Ya's as the speakers held up to the light the facets of our lives.

Liz was there in our moments of self-realization and personal growth. Liz knew on a cellular level that each woman's story is every woman's story. She knew that taking the pain and joy of the moment could and should be translated into the larger LEARNING for us all.

Here are her words on the subject as she described the process of coordinating the planning for upcoming series: "The deep emotional power of our planning process comes from our women's lives and emotional guts as we share our life issues; this is our taproot, this is our living water. When we are truly and deeply talking about our life issues, we are laying out the building blocks which will never betray us because they are true and honest and come from deep inside us as we struggle to live our lives as women.

"You can feel the energy building in the room, the voices getting more alive and excited, people speaking and interrupting each other, giving voice to the creativity bubbling inside them. Then I know the energy is cresting and I need only to get out of the way and ride the wave in, only making sure that the more patient people, who don't interrupt but instead put up their hand, get recognized and have their voices heard even as the energy wave continues to run.

"If we are lucky, the wave lands us all on the shore of consensus, and you can hear as well as feel the 'YES!' that breaks through the group as we finally can touch and give words to that passionately reached-for resolution. That 'YES!' is the resonance which happens when we hit an emotional golden nugget of possibility that resonates in the heart and mind of almost everyone."

ELIZABETH DODSON GRAY

This then is the legacy of the great and wonderful Elizabeth Dodson Gray, that we speak the truth and that we share that truth with each other and all those who join with us.

This is OUR Elizabeth Dodson Gray who has taken on with a passionate human cry and challenge to address the Institutional Church and its betrayal of women in her book *Sunday School Manifesto.*

This is OUR Elizabeth Dodson Gray who explores in her book *Green Paradise Lost* the mythic and psycho-sexual roots of our Western image of Nature that is about our "fall" into the illusion of human domination of the planet we inhabit.

This is OUR Elizabeth Dodson Gray who explores with us the "sacred dimensions of women's experience" that engage us in a new revelational encounter with the Divine in and through that very experience.

And she is OUR Elizabeth Dodson Gray who sends the most thoughtful and personal handwritten notes, who calls one on the telephone to share a thought or wish. This Elizabeth of the big thought and the big idea is the Elizabeth of the kind and loving gesture.

Never will there be another YOU, Liz. We know you, love you and thank you for all you are and all that you have brought to the work. Go in grace. Go in love. But don't go far.

—Written by Kathy Jellison and presented by Martha Nielsen, on behalf of the TOP community

---

Tribute to David Dodson Gray on the occasion of his retirement from responsibilities to TOP

David, your personal contribution toward these 32 years of TOP is immeasurable. Your close bond with Liz, within your extraordinary partnership, so ahead of its time, enabled you to give freely of your time, efforts, energy, wisdom, guidance, patience, and love.

You and Liz have lived and breathed TOP all these years. Your home has provided a welcoming meeting place for planning, mailings, supporting, storing, and envisioning TOP.

Your careful attention to detail—financial and other—helped keep TOP viable. Your ongoing bookkeeping, plus your dealing with income and expenses, attendance, annual funds, address lists, mail merges— all were constantly beckoning you. Your home was your office, TOP headquarters, your storage bin, and your sacred family space, all packaged into one.

Your constantly evolving use of the computer helped to bridge the gap between handwritten and emailed TOP communications. You absorbed the frustrations of technological resources, including postal regulations, for the greater good of TOP.

Yet as each Thursday drew closer, you were committed to the program. You knew that with each lecture came the packing up of the car. Then along with Mike Donham the picking up of the sound equipment, setting it up and later taking it down. And the parking. You were always an attentive, intelligent listener, and responder. You made sure that everything was in its place for the highest success of the program. Each week you made the Book Table a moveable feast of hard-to-resist books by speakers.

We so appreciate your honest, direct involvement with the content of the lectures and the process of the planning. You were the front man, hanging large sheets of paper, adding and subtracting suggestions as they came forth from the participating program planners. You remained nimble on your feet and flexible in your mind, yet acutely aware of the group process.

In the midst of this, Roundtable Press took form. From the core elements of outstanding talks you reproduced numerous affordable pamphlets, helping us to revisit these inspiring, motivating, challenging talks. Your expertise in the desktop publishing realm benefitted both us as individuals and TOP as an organization.

Many changes and health challenges have come your way during these 32 years. Your loving support and encouragement to Liz helped her heal and recover, and we feel certain the reverse has been true as well. May you two continue to be there for each other in whatever way is needed. Your 50-plus years together will be a strong footing for these next years ahead as you begin to have more time for yourselves.

In many ways you have graciously been behind the scenes, although you've remained visible, fully supportive yet not demanding attention, loving yet clear and direct. You have offered to many of us a glimpse of a true partnership, where each person expands and grows. You remained consistently engaged. Though the work you and Liz did for TOP blended seamlessly, you each held onto your unique, precious selves.

Thank you, David, for all that you have offered to Liz and the entire TOP community.

—Written by Christine Farrow-Noble, on behalf of the TOP community

USA\COR

David and Elizabeth Dodson Gray, recipients of the USA\Club of Rome Donella Meadows lifetime achievement award.

The Donella Meadows award of the USA\COR (USA Club of Rome) honors Donella Meadows as the author of the ground-breaking 1972 study about the future, based on system-dynamics computer modeling done by a group at MIT, which was done as the first report ever to the International Club of Rome. She died far too young at 59.

Limits to Growth is the best-selling non-fiction book of all time. That work and book were reassessed ten years later in *Limits to Growth Revisited* and two decades later in *Limits to Growth—30 years Out.*

Donella Meadows was never honored by the International Club of Rome, the group to which the books were reports, She was never asked to join the Club of Rome, while her husband Dennis was.

Although Donella Meadows had written *Limits to Growth* and was listed on the American earlier edition as the first author, when the books were translated into European languages, her name was downgraded to second place.

Elizabeth and David Dodson Gray were involved for many years in our group—USA\ COR—and we honor them with this award and medal for their usual profound effect on our moral and spiritual thinking about equity and the place of gender in our global paradigm.

Very early in the formation of USA\COR, the economist and author Hazel Henderson had said she would not join the new USA\COR unless 50% of those who were elected members were women. Over its history USA\COR has had 50% women and had three women elected as president. For half a decade three of the four officers have been women. Donella Meadows believed in equality and women's abilities. She admired Elizabeth and David greatly and would be delighted that they are receiving this award.

Elizabeth and David were the first husband-and-wife team to be brought into USA \COR. To say that this dynamic duo had an effect, would understate the situation. Both David and Elizabeth have strong positive personalities with their own talents and concepts to give to groups pondering the future. Women, professional ones particularly, were encouraged by Liz and David's philosophy of equality and their modeling of it in their marriage and work.

ELIZABETH DODSON GRAY

Their service to USA\COR was abundant and selfless. Elizabeth served as co-vice-chair with Dr. Donald Michael, she was an important board member for a series of terms, and was always making members aware of their moral compass as they made decisions.

David became secretary of the board under the first female president (Dr.Anitra Thorhaug, marine ecologist now at Yale School of Forestry and Environmental Studies) and continued under the first black president (Consul William B. Davis of US Information Service) and under a second female president (Lucia Bravo, Chair of the Board of Hobart Industries). The work David did as newsletter editor to inform all members of actions and news of members was spectacular and has never been duplicated.

David also was very central in editing and publishing with Dr. John Richardson of American University the first report of the USA|CoR, *Making it Happen: A Positive Guide to the Future* (1984).

Books by one or both of the Dodson Grays came out rapidly in the 1970s and 1980s, and were central to their message. These books were well received and they became the center focus of several USA\COR conferences. The books showed clearly how all human beings needed to have a fully functioning world, particularly the half that "slept with the master." The absurdity and distortions of the male-dominated-and-entitled patriarchal paradigm—and ways to change that paradigm.—were discussed repeatedly, particularly among the female members and those men who were sensitive to why changes should and could occur.

The other important point of Elizabeth and David's work and lives is that they walked their talk. They both could lead. They both could support, They could both think clearly. They could both play back-up. They seamlessly could change roles and formed a strong vibrant team. In many activities, each took the lead. During this time each were strong models for the prizes of their lives, their two marvelous children, Lisa and Hunter. The long, lingering death of David's mother from Alzheimer's disease was turned by David subsequently into a book for families about "the Alzheimer journey." Elizabeth's illnesses and eleven surgeries tested their strong bonds, and David became caretaker par excellence, and their roles were switched again.

We thank Elizabeth and thank David for years of service which was undersung and underpraised but kept the group going in the "rocky years" when support waned as well as in the plush years.

As role models showing to all of us how to live more clearly, more purely and with better moral clarity we award Elizabeth and David the USA\COR —Donella Meadows Award.

Anitra Thorhaug, President
on behalf of the USA\COR board and membership, June 3, 2010

June 4, 2010

Dear Friends:

David and I are overwhelmed with gratitude for the <u>fabulous</u> garden party we experienced yesterday afternoon. The balloons, the orchid leis FedEx'd from Hawaii, the flowers, the delicious home-made cakes and cookies and cucumber sandwiches and great breads and two kinds of punch, the tributes, the gifts, the singing of Carolyn McDade's songs, the written-for-the-occasion song, the TOP documentary on the big screen, the sound system and the projector (all of which worked)—what could be better??!!

We want to thank <u>everyone</u> who contributed to the festivities—the amazing committee nobly co-chaired by Martha Nielsen and Kathy Jellison (with Marcia Boehlke, Priscilla Donham, Joey DuBois, Chris Farrow-Noble and Nancy Hurlbut). We thank Priscilla Donham and Nancy Hurlbut and their wonderful committee, who hand-addressed all of the party invitations. And we thank Martha Nielsen, who wrote and arranged the printing of the invitations and the accompanying letter. And Kathy Jellison, who directed the fund-raising appeal.

We thank Priscilla for the gorgeous flower baskets and table flowers. We thank Chris for the amazing flown-by-FedEx-from-Hawaii rosebud lei and orchard lei. We thank Marcia and all of you who brought home-made goodies and contributed to the punch.

We are grateful for the many cards and gifts and words of appreciation that we have received. We thank all of you who have contributed to TOP's grand total of $11,000-plus for the EDG Endowment Fund, now residing at and managed by the Boston Foundation for investment in TOP's future.

It was a totally wonderful, mind-blowing, deep-feeling celebration in honor of us, and we thank each and every one of you for your part in it.

We depart for our vacation time in Connecticut with enormously happy hearts, and we look forward to sharing the future with all of you and our new coordinator, Muna Killingback.

Love, LIZ

39.

Looking Back: Who Am I As a Woman?

Class Presentation with Slides,
November 1972, revised April 1996,
shortened May 2008

39.

Looking Back:
Who Am I As a Woman?

Class Presentation with Slides, November 1972,
revised April 1996, shortened May 2008

The Emergence of Mind and Will

Who was I growing up as a young girl? Some felt I was clearly inferior. I was, after all, a girl.

Was I really free to reject that perception and concept of me? Did I not grow up in a culture which socialized that view into me, whether or not I wanted or liked that view of myself? I certainly experienced, as I am sure most women do, the great social pressures upon us as girls in our adolescence, lest we become too bright, not feminine, unpopular, and all the rest.

But many of us persist in spite of all this. We major in intellectual achievements. We mold our lives in that direction. And I was one of these.

I can hardly account for why this happens, except that within the personal dynamics of my family's life it seemed the obvious way to go. My mother was dealing with her feelings of oppression by being a martyr, and it was clear to me that you wanted to avoid the womanly martyr-model and instead model yourself upon men. Furthermore, I was competing with a favored older brother who was very bright, and boys were not exactly clamoring at my door seeking dates. There were no other alternative models which were attractive to me—so I moved toward the style of life characterized by vigor, and I aggressively pursued intellectual accomplishment and success. I found ego satisfaction for myself from things accomplished and offices held, from high marks and awards won.

By the sex-role stereotyping of that time, such a life-style as I had worked out for myself was masculine. But it formed the content of my self-identity for many years through countless achievements at school and college and a three-year graduate program in divinity. After I began my work-life, I further consolidated this sense of myself through sermons preached, organizations chaired, battles won.

What was my woman's understanding of my self in those years? I saw myself as mind and will, and I was both. I was active and dynamic. The world was my oyster, and I could probably do anything I wanted. *Except* get married. That was something which did *not* depend upon my own efforts and energy.

By the time I became fully aware of the long-term social hazards of being the sort of self I had chosen and shaped for myself, I was already so deeply into that kind of identity that I could not have changed. At that point I was forced to admit to myself that probably no man would enjoy or tolerate a woman like me. And yet I still yearned to be married, because our culture teaches you to want that. *That* part of the lesson I really had learned.

Mind and Will—in a Woman's Body

Then life played a funny trick on me. I found someone who, yes, really did like who I was. I then began a strange pilgrimage into other aspects of myself as a woman. It is here you may start to glimpse what my experiences may add to a more inclusive woman's definition and understanding of her self.

I had previously viewed myself almost exclusively as mind and will. That was simply who I was. Because I felt I was not attractive physically, I was spared that self-preoccupation and self-absorption which some see as peculiar to women. My selfhood until now had no real reference to my body. Instead, my body was merely what allowed me to act out my mind and will.

How do I tell you what I discovered about my selfhood in relation to this body of mine when I got pregnant? I was bed-ridden and nauseated for a two-month period. Within the limiting six surfaces of that one room where I was laid low, I discovered my world view was suddenly constricted by this new weakness of my body. I now realized mind and will were limited by body.

Or again, at thirty-nine I had a soul-searing brush with death, fearing I had breast cancer. You discover then that you really are mortal. This is not just a clearly held conviction at the surface of your mind but something you now know deeply in your gut. You know a loneliness and a fear that belong to being a woman with woman's breasts.

Still again, during pregnancy and in child-birth you find experiences which, if not soul-searing, are still soul-changing—because again your body is a *woman's body*—not a man's body.

In all of these experiences you discover that *all* of you is in that body. Your mind and your will and everything that there has ever been or ever will be of you is "in" that body. All of it is being expressed through that body. That body, that *woman's* body, is what is experiencing your life; that *soma,* as the Greeks called it, is your "self."

Gradually you realize that, even while you grow in love with your husband, no matter how "equal" to him you are and how *sympathique* he is with you, he still cannot go through and know these physical experiences that you do. He is different, a man. His is not only *another* body but it is a *different* body, a man's body.

I realized that what I was thinking was akin to H. Richard Niebuhr's reaction to his brother Reinhold's stroke. Richard Niebuhr saw his brother, so thoughtful and dynamic and creative, encased as it were and imprisoned by the limitations of his paralyzed flesh, and he reported finding here a new appreciation for the incarnated quality of the spirit. He saw in his brother's condition after a stroke how en-fleshed in a particular body the You that is yourself actually is. For Richard Niebuhr, to know this was to respond to God as "limiting" us. It was God reminding us of our mortal and created existence in which "all flesh is grass" (Isa 40:6–7) and transitory.

It was gradually dawning upon me that any self-concept I might have of myself was seriously deficient if it did not take sufficient account of my body. It had to take seriously my body's experiencing its own pleasure and pain and mortality. Whatever more I was than my body, I was also very much a woman in everything I thought and did. From now on, I would have to include my body when I was thinking of myself.

Doing and Being

There is still another dialectic I straddle, which my life-experiences have helped me see I cannot separate and push apart. I have come to know myself also as both Doing and Being.

From what I have told you of my growing up, you know that if you asked me who I was, I would have described myself almost entirely in functional terms. I was (and am) a doer, one who gets things done. I am active, accomplishing, an achiever, and so on.

But my destiny in a womanly body has catapulted me into experiences so different from these and so strange as to make me feel I had lost my former world, my entire life of doing things. Who was I now? I was one who had died, or who had been exiled into a strange and different and alien land, a land where doers did not achieve and where Being was totally dominant, because little that was done seemed to matter much. To be, not to do, was all. Like a balloon suddenly punctured by a sharp object, I felt a great collapse.

Who was I when, at three different times in my life so far, I have had to lie flat on my back for two months? Two months meant 9 weeks down, or nearly 60 days and nights. I was Being then, not Doing.

Who was I when I had so often to be in a rocking chair feeding my baby, no matter what the hour of the day or night? I was not Doing then. I was Being.

Or I was walking a small child endlessly down non-achieving streets where the house numbers I was passing were the only milestones marking my accomplishment. Who was I when I was suspended in time with a small child, with meals to prepare which were quickly consumed, cleanliness which was quickly dirtied, and my only accomplishment was that for another day I had kept my child from physical harm? Who then was I, in this strange land of Being without Doing?

I had lost any outlets for my achieving self, and in so doing I felt I had lost the only self I had ever known. And such doing as was left to me was the endless physical activity of a woman at home. I felt like a servant, not a self. This was not the Doing of initiative-taking, of potency. It was the doing of servility, the "doing" of a serving which I had had no self-concept for. It reminded me of my martyr-mother, and it was in this sense doubly distasteful to me.

As much as any heroin addict misses their drug, I missed the ego satisfactions and the ego nourishments of the achieving life. My withdrawal symptoms were excruciatingly painful. There was no one at home to tell you what a great job you were doing scrubbing that floor. And if you are used to doing a great job and being told it, you really miss this recognition and feed-back.

As an aside, I would also note that these withdrawal symptoms I was experiencing are, I think, what a man experiences daily when he comes home and tries to "be" with his wife and children. He tries to find this way of "being" satisfying and involving after his exhilarating if exhausting day of "doing" out in the "real world." Again, I can imagine how these same withdrawal symptoms can also go with retirement. The man typically does not understand, as I did not understand, why the reality of Being is so difficult for him to enjoy actively. The only time he can enjoy really settling into "being" is when he is exhausted or sick. Only then does he want to collapse for a time into simply Being without Doing.

I look back now with horror upon the psychic stress of that period in my life. It was my own choice to stay at home. It was not something I did as my role. In conversations with my by-then-clinical-psychologist brother I had come to the conclusion that children need from us not just care but active mothering. But actually doing that mothering was no less painful for me because I was doing it by my own choice.

Finally I must also add that the period of pregnancy and young-motherhood, had a further and special dimension of difficulty for me. I felt that in my marrying and mothering I had lost my real calling. My religious vocation which I loved, and had grown in and been so good at, was gone. It had given a special meaning and significance to my life and what I was doing with it. But where was it now?

Being

It took me years, lots of years, gradually to edge myself into an appreciation of Being as a mode of living. I finally came to see Being as simply a mode of living less familiar to me than Doing. Like changing to brushing your teeth with your left hand, Being was not easy or natural for me at first. Like a butterfly in a maze, I was struggling to find my way.

ELIZABETH DODSON GRAY

What is this mode of living I call Being? If Doing can be said to be psychologically "loud," as a Beethoven symphony in full flight toward a coda is loud, then Being can be said to be "soft." Being is soft as a tree is soft against the sky, as the opening of a bud is soft, or as a stream is soft, rippling in bright sunlight or in reflected moonlight.

Being is non-competitive. It does not measure your performance. Nor does it give marks or cast you against another in striving.

So Being can be seen as not intersecting your ego. Being does nothing at all either *to* or *for* the ego. You are neither congratulated nor condemned. Instead, Being feeds another kind of hunger inside you. As a food, it is bland yet nourishing, whereas ego rewards would be hot and spicy. The ego rewards which can be gained from Doing are head trips without the heroin. They give you a "kick." But, again like heroin, ego rewards wear off quickly. You soon need another dose to get you high again.

Being also is relational. You not only are, but you are-*with*. You are *with* people. Or *with* nature. You are *"with"* in a non-competitive way. Barbara Borack in her book *Grandpa*[1] tells how "Grandpa sits by the radio and listens and stares. I listen too. We don't say anything to each other and it's all right." That can be "being-with." Some people have this sense of being present with the wind and the waves of the ocean, some have the sense of "being in tune" when they are in the mountains or in the woods.

Being, more than Doing, is non-cognitive. It is feeling-oriented. It is not focused in your thoughts or conscious fantasies but in your senses and in the inner reaches of the heart in tune with itself or its circumstances.

Being points the self toward the joy and exultation of the self just existing, just being alive. When I was facing that cancer biopsy, the feelings that "this cannot be happening to me" were followed by feelings that "I will never experience these ordinary things again." Suddenly you know it is not important to have money or to have done things, even great things. It is suddenly not important if people do not think you are great for all you have done. You know it is not even important to be loved. For you know now that what really is important, and always has been important, *is to be alive.* It is important simply to be and to exist, and to experience and feel what it is at this instant to be one part of this fantastically mixed glorious-and-painful world.

It is Being, not Doing, then, that lifts the curtains from the eyes of the soul. It is Being, not Doing, which restores to us the world of wonder which our adult goal-oriented living has made us too busy to wait for. "To Be" is to come into the world of intimacy and tenderness where the generations learn together to treasure one another not for what we can "do" for each other (which gets to be less and less), but to value one another for what we "mean" to one another (which can become more and more).

ELIZABETH DODSON GRAY

Wonder

In her book for children *One Step, Two. . .*[2] Charlotte Zolotow expresses magnificently the way children can open up the eyes of adults to wonder.

One spring morning the mother and her little girl came down the steps to their house—one step, two steps, three steps—and they were down. They started to walk to the corner.

"See that!" said the little girl.

"What?" asked the mother. And then she saw—a little crocus shining in the grass.

One step, two steps, three steps, four—and the little girl stopped again. "See *that!*" she said, and pointed to a bluebird floating down to earth with its white-tipped wings spread wide.

One step, two, three, four, five, six, seven steps.
"See!" said the little girl.
And her mother saw the dresses and pants and towels dancing on the line.

One, two, three, four, five, six, seven, eight, nine steps.
"Clip clip clippety clop, clop clop clippety clip."
"Hear that!" said the little girl.
It was the milkman's horse passing on the other side of the street.

One, two, three, four, five, six, seven, eight, nine, ten, eleven. . . Suddenly the bells of the church burst into music like a flock of birds in the sky. The little girl took her mother's hand and stood still and listened until they stopped ringing.

Then they turned back and headed for home. When they got to their house,

Her mother gathered her up and hugged her close.
"What a lovely walk, and what a lot of things we saw.
Thank you little girl for showing me—
The yellow daffodils,
The clothes drying in the sun,
The milkman's horse clopping by,
The blue jay flying in the sky,
The little crocus,
The prowling cat,
The small white pebble like a moon,
The lovely bells that rang at noon."

But the little girl didn't hear. She was fast asleep.

This sort of opening up of the eyes of the soul is very relational. You share with another their joy in discovering new being. I shall never forget a summer's evening when our then-two-and-a-half-year-old daughter first rode on a merry-go-round. For more than an hour we bought ticket after ticket as she refused to get down, wanting to ride on and on in some inwardly intoxicating fantasy of her own. Her face and eyes glowed with an excitement that awed and amazed us.

Only finally, when she climbed down, did we have a clue to the meaning of that experience for her. She said to us simply, "I'm 'National Velvet'!" Her mental context for riding that merry-go-round was the 1944 movie we had recently watched together on television, about a young girl (Elizabeth Taylor) who rode and trained her horse to race in the Grand National Steeplechase.

Or again. I remember when our son was two-and-a-half and he staggered up to our house from what had been for him a mind-blowing experience with his father flying a kite on our beach. He had just held a kite all by himself for the first time. He gasped out his excitement and triumph to me, each gasp bigger than the last: "Me fly kite. ME—BIG—BOY!"

In these situations we the adults are given the literally priceless experience of rejoicing in the pure bursting-into-being of the selfhood of another.

When We Look at Things Together

In tender and deep moments of reading to children, as you contemplate reality together, you discover in still a different way what you can mean, and be, for one another. It is like looking through a telescope together, or standing side by side on a mountain top. You are sharing what you are seeing, focusing on what is important or real in life.

Jonathan,[3] by Eleanor Graham Vance, suggests the wonder of a small child looking at the world. "Jonathan was four and the world was full of wonder. There were sunshine and rain, there were lighting and thunder, there were autos on the avenue and squirrels in the park. There were stars in the sky in the soft, lovely dark. Jonathan was four, and the questions that he knew got deeper and deeper each day that he grew. 'Where does the fire go when it goes out?' 'What makes the rain come down the rain spout?' 'How do little boys grow into men?' 'When is my birthday coming again?' 'Who lights the stars in the deep evening sky?' 'Why does it thunder? Why? Why? Why?'"

I find extraordinary the way in which books like *Jonathan* and this next book, *Now I Lay Me Down to Wonder,*[4] by Bernice Hogan, suggest a child's creative questioning of the reality he or she contemplates.

How did you think of a bubble, God?
How did you dream it so?
With colors so white that sparkle so pink,
How did you make it grow?
Did you ever carry a bubble, God?
Then tell me, how did you know
That children could lift such fairy balls
And that children would love them so?

Sometimes books help us think with our children about what it is to be a man. Eugene Fern's story of *The King Who Was Too Busy*[5] tells of a king's struggle to be kingly, a process in which he nearly lost sight of what was most precious to him. Looking back later, the king thought,

> What a fool I was. In trying to become a great king and having all the things a great king should have, I have almost lost the most important treasures of all—the trust of my people, the affection of my friends, and the love of my daughter. . . . It's not great crowns that make great kings, nor rooms of gold, nor diamond rings. More important, more by far, than what we own, is what we are!

Ultimately the realm of Being is like a gift. You do not reach out and seize Being with the greedy hands of your desire. Nor do you mold Being with the manipulation of your own doing. Instead, Being comes to you like a gift from beyond yourself, like a butterfly that to your surprise alights on your shoulder. Being is akin to grace, like a surprise gift of flowers, like sunrise and sunset, like rain given equally to the just and to the unjust.

Co-Sustainers with God

Where does all this leave me in my pursuit of a more adequate concept of myself as a woman? The human self, at least as I have known it, is again and again described in terms which are dialectical, or profoundly both-and. I am *both mind and body*. I am also *both Doing and Being*. Perhaps I am both masculine and feminine, although my sense of "being" is not what most people mean by feminine. "Being" as I have described it is human, not just feminine. Being for me, as for Tillich, has roots in ontology and creation, roots which transcend our sexual stereotypes.

I do not view even the supposedly "feminine" virtue of "being supportive" as a "feminine" mode of being. When I am supportive to my children and husband, I do not feel like a woman or mother. Instead, I find myself modeling my understanding upon my theology of God as Sustainer (as well as Creator and Redeemer). One of my favorite hymns sums it up: "New every morning is the love our waking and up-rising prove." God brings us into being and is not some absent watchmaker who, having made us, then abandoned us. God is sustaining us *in being* each moment, each up-rising day. Without such sustaining, we would "fall out of being."

So day by day when my husband and I sustain the being of our children, we are not being feminine. We are both being co-sustainers with God, just as we are co-creators with God. We are sharing with God a work which is too high or deep (as you prefer) for the limiting labels of our culture's sex-stereotyping.

We are co-sustainers with God of an adolescent daughter, who wants and needs to be aware of our parental support mixed with large doses of affirmation. She needs this sustaining of her being so that she can project herself all day long into a world of doing where waves of challenge and anxiety constantly wash the beach of her identity, constantly defining it but threatening also to wash it bare and clean. Here is a child, trying to grow up into a woman.

Our son's is a robust selfhood, but still fragile too. He is defined in motion and by a boy's dreams of glory, while she is more defined in her struggles to relate to and yet resist her peers. He is creative in music and sculpture, still interested in collecting things but loving his cats even more. She struggles to grow and affirm herself as the person and woman she is becoming; he struggles in another way to grow up as a different person who will one day become a man. Both need very much to be sustained by our love.

A woman's self, then, is a human soul created by God to be capable of a variety of Being and Doing which bedazzles us. Being and Doing—I want them *both*. And I can have them both. No one can now define for me a selfhood that takes either one away, now that I can feel equally comfortable in either mode. And I want my daughter to have a self-concept which will enable her to feel comfortable both doing and also being.

The One Who Is Many
"Who am I?—I am the one who is really many." My life experience is that I exist in a complex web of relationships. I am daughter, wife, mother, sister, teacher, student, friend. I am defined in all these relationships, defined and enriched. Because of this I resist those who suggest I should tear myself away from all such relationships except to "sisters." I resist those who suggest these other relationships are a trap, a spider's web which becomes a prison.

I do not deny that these relationships can become prisons. As Valerie Saiving has said, "A woman can give too much of herself, so that nothing remains of her own uniqueness. She can become an emptiness and be dependent on others for her self-definition."[6] A friend of mine married very young, and she asked as her children were leaving home, "Who am I when I am not being a wife and a mother?"

Anne Morrow Lindbergh places these varying roles in what I think is a proper place. "To be a woman," she says, "is to have interests and duties raying out in all directions from the central mother-core, like spokes from the hub of a wheel. The pattern of our lives [as women] is essentially circular. We must be open to all points of the compass—husband, children, friends, home, community—stretched out, exposed, sensitive like a spider's web to each breeze that blows, to each call that comes."[7]

I think most women know that they are truly alive when they are in these many relationships. But how also do you not get lost in such roles? We do not wish to give them up, for they are such a deep part of who we are. Yet their demands upon us continue to be a problem for us.

For Lindbergh the problem is "how to remain whole in the midst of the distractions of your life."[8] She suggests the answer lies in women's "coming of age" and learning to stand alone. "Woman," she says, "must find her true center alone. She must become whole." I take this to mean that just as a woman must freely choose the complexity of primal relationships in which she lives, so too she must also find and come to terms with her own alone-self and center. I think another friend of mine did this when, in the precious hour each day her toddler slept, she read poetry for her soul's health, leaving herself and her family rejoicing, even as they picked their way through an unstraightened-up house.

The Courage To Be
Paul Tillich's book *The Courage To Be* pushes us toward a better understanding of how each of us finds and comes to terms with her own alone-self and center. Each of us has been given in creation a precious and unique selfhood. Each of us in our aloneness learns to drink deeply here and find courage to assert that selfhood.

I discovered in my times of illness that, if you can *only* affirm and assert yourself when you are *doing,* what is there to affirm and assert when you can *do nothing?*

Tillich's sermon, "You Are Accepted,"[9] opened up to me another perspective on myself. So did the discovery that my family continued to love me even when I could do nothing for them, or (even worse) when I was in a foul humor and needed them to do for me. My little daughter once said, explaining it to me as one does to a little child, "Mommie, I still love you even when you're witchy." As Tillich said, *"The courage to be involves accepting oneself as accepted, in spite of being unacceptable."[10]*

There is the paradox again: the stark affirmation of the solitary self (which we need if we are to survive our aloneness) comes to us through other people and through God—and thus is very relational.

I have found very helpful H. Richard Niebuhr's suggestion that we grasp reality in symbolic forms rather than in words. Our mental processes really need symbolic forms, he says, for their proper functioning, symbolic forms which are adequate to the external reality we are trying to comprehend. The amoeba has been for me such a symbolic form. It has helped me have a mental model of my woman's selfhood.

The amoeba has a nucleus or central mass, which I liken to my most inmost sense of self, my most focused sense of the primitive life-force I sense in my Me-ness. Its central property is what Tillich calls the dynamic "self-affirmation of life."[11] But the amoeba also has many protrusions, some long, some short, and these are forever changing. These are my relational involvements as a self, and these color and move and, yes, define my nuclear self. Yet these relationships are dependent upon that strong nucleus. Otherwise the whole cell collapses.

The Self in Time

The self of a woman exists not only in her body and in her many modes of relationships, but finally also it endures, it exists *through time.* An adequate understanding of the self must factor time in as a crucial variable. When women agonize between career and marriage, I want to cry out that there is time, and that no choice is forever. Nothing you choose lasts for a lifetime. For everything and every difficulty there is its season, its time. Then time moves on.

Have you ever thought about the fantastic psychic flexibility required for the life span of most women? You must find an identity in adolescence—alone. Then if you marry or partner, you must adjust to another person. Then if you have children, you become the hub of the wheel. Then you adjust to the spokes dropping off like starfish appendages (except that unlike the starfish you cannot now grow replacements). And finally you are back to life with your partner alone, before having to adjust to the widowhood that statistically you can expect before your own death. Lindbergh's *Gift from the Sea* is a powerful and suggestive treatment of these stages to a woman's life.

A Kaleidoscope of Changes

As a woman, I must have a selfhood which can guide me through these changing circumstances—yes, even unto my own death. At some times in your life as a woman, your "doing" appendages are long and fully developed (as when you are in college or in your career). Then every feeler is out to learn and to become, to aspire and achieve, to exult in being yourself and expressing yourself fully. But there are other times when that way of existing has shrunk to a mini-appendage of your selfhood, and the being-with and doing-for-others appendages are long. You are then up to your neck in meals and small children and the etcetera of being at home. For a time your self-expression through "doing" is down to the choice my friend made between reading poetry or taking a nap while her child slept.

But your woman's life and selfhood does not get stuck at this stage either. It too quickly passes on, as do your children. And today's woman faces the possibility (if not always the necessity) of another new burst of self-expression through doing in her forties and fifties and after. My friend of the "Who am I when I'm not being wife and mother" has gone back to finish college and prepare for a career. She is now totally free to soar on the wings of her own selfhood for the next 30 to 40 years. In her case, she is free even from the necessity to pay the bills, because her husband does that quite nicely for them both. She is discovering she loves her life now, "after children." To see her open and blossom is like watching a springtime miracle in July.

My friend's problem of "Who am I" was not really in her actual living of those "after-children years." It was instead in the fact that our culture gave her no self-concept or self-expectation which was sufficiently spacious to encompass both these years and her former years. She was unprepared to become "her own self" (or, as Lindbergh puts it, to "find her true center, alone—and become whole"). She did not know yet that she would *not* be able to find a life-long identity for herself in who she was for other people. Previously our culture did not tell women that. Thank God the women's movement now does.

Aging and Self-Concept

It is not only the "role periods" in a woman's life which change. One's self-concept must also be many-faceted enough and flexible enough to allow for the crucial time-factor of aging. Many of our friends (and especially the men) are now caught up in the throes of trying painfully to adjust to the dawning realization of aging—and that they are now middle-aged.

It is not enough to know and affirm that you are an incarnated spirit and self, and that you are experiencing life in a certain body, and are experienced by others as being in that body. You must also factor in the reality that *this body you are in, ages.* It is also my observation that men and women who have been especially beautiful and handsome as young people later experience additional difficulties as they age.

Many of our male friends had self-concepts that assumed they were always going to be clothed in an eternally young and vigorous and sexually potent male body. It has been a shock, not only to the body but to the self within, for them to find in mid-life that a hard game of tennis can now immobilize them for days. Or that their young students look at them with undisguised horror, saying "*You* are thirty-five!"

Somehow in our youth we assumed we stepped off the escalator of time and aging when we reached twenty-one. We knew everyone else was growing up or growing old. But then one day, to our horror, we discover a nasty trick has been played upon *us,* and that we too have been aging all this time. Suddenly we realize that our teachers and parents and trusted older mentors are no longer forty or fifty but are passing into old age or are already dead. Our children are now no longer growing but grown.

Almost overnight, it seems, we have been betrayed by the older generation and we now fill their places. We bear their responsibilities. And we know we too shall go as they have gone. Too often men (and women too) flee from this realization, this adjustment. We flee in ways that are grotesque imitations of by-gone youthfulness.[12]

When you think of it, it was silly of us not to have known all along that we are growing older and, yes, we too will age. How ridiculous of a man or a woman to have an image of themselves that does not take seriously the aging and mortality built into our lives by their being lived in these mortal bodies. Like our environmental problems, our middle-age aberrations related to our aging reveal the absence in our culture of any real sense that life is lived within limits.

New Life in the Middle Years

The British psychoanalyst Harry Guntrip points the way to an enlarged self-concept which incorporates our aging, understands it, and even enjoys it. Guntrip suggests that the first half of [men's] lives is given over to achieving. He would include here a woman's achieving in running a home and raising children, and puts this alongside a man's achieving through establishing himself economically in his work and in a household. But Guntrip suggests that for both women and men the latter part of a life span is for wisdom and not for achieving. It is a time for turning inward, for a spiritual pilgrimage and for a whole new burst of selfhood and inner life undreamt of in earlier years.

Examples come swiftly to mind. I think of the vibrant woman of fifty I met one fall at Harvard. Her children were grown, she was widowed. After several years teaching in public schools she was doing graduate study, not to make a name for herself but to do her thing and be able to do it better. It was she who said to me "Wisdom *begins* at fifty!" I think too of my husband's college classmate who, after some years as second in command at Yale, resigned as provost to start his training as a Jungian psychoanalyst. "I feel," he said, "I want to spend the rest of my time improving our *inner* life."

If the major task of these later years involves this inner life of Being, then women are given some important clues from our life-experiences as women. Most men are so caught up, as I was, in the ego addiction of achieving, that the quieter, subtler realms of Being seem like the far side of a distant moon. So these men are restive and unable to "be" when at the end of the day they return home or on weekends or when they get sick or when they retire. To say that such men do not understand the emerging task of their later years is a gross understatement.

The Self and Vocational Success

Viewed in this perspective, what can we make of those who advocate women staying on the professional ladders of career advancement rather than stepping off to raise their children?

Many women *want* to rear their own children. We want to do it because we understand that doing it right is going to be important to our children as well as to us. We are also often drawn to those "being" depths within the mothering relationship which I have talked about. Furthermore, choosing *only* the ladder of vocational success is too simplistic a view of the total life span. It does not take sufficient cognizance of the later years. It is in these years that many men lift their heads from their work and say to themselves and their wives, "I really don't want any longer to do this for the rest of my life." Despite the intensity of their preoccupation with achieving on their professional ladder, these men have been changing and maturing through their living. Many would choose their work differently today if they were choosing it now rather than in their college years. Yet many are chained to those jobs and professions by economic necessity, chains of gold.

Unless, like Yale's provost, they can afford to begin again at the bottom of another professional ladder. Or unless like tens of thousands of men in middle-aged revolt, they leave emotionally the wives of their youth to have affairs. Or they leave them legally, divorcing in order to marry some more youthful reminder of their bygone vigor. And some simply leave one evening, never coming home again, disappearing into the night to start a new life elsewhere, alone and anew.

The Freedom of the Middle-Aged Woman

Even within traditional role definitions, a woman has a distinct advantage over the man who has stayed on the achieving professional ladder. After your children are reared, you as a woman are free to start a new life in a way that most men are not. And if she stays married, a woman does not necessarily have to worry about supporting herself or her home as she does this. Many middle-aged men envy her that freedom.

Yet tragically this freedom is of no use to a woman unless she has the self-strength and self-concept to use it. If you have seen and defined yourself *only* as wife and mother, then you are in bad shape, because now your children are gone and your husband often has little time or need of you, for he is either in a peak-producing period in his life or a peak-anxiety period.

But if in those earlier relationally demanding years, you as a woman have nourished and protected your fledgling inner self-identity—by continuously understanding and asserting that you are most basically *yourself,* as well as being wife and mother—then at forty or whenever you are like a freed bird. That selfhood which has been sustained and mellowed through those deeply relational experiences of mothering and being a wife, can now fly. Studying, writing, teaching, leadership, accomplishing of all sorts—fantastic flights of both achieving and being can open up now. All this does not depend upon the physical vigor of youth as much as it depends upon your having lived long and deeply and well. You now have the steadiness and tenderness and flexibility to serve and lead in a multitude of ways.

ELIZABETH DODSON GRAY

I think of Eleanor Roosevelt in her seventy-fifth year writing: "When you cease to make a contribution you begin to die. Therefore, I think it a necessity to be doing something which you feel is helpful in order to grow old gracefully and contentedly." To reporters on her seventy-seventh birthday, she said, "Life was meant to be lived. Curiosity must be kept alive. The fatal thing is the rejection. One must never, for whatever reason, turn [your] back on life."[13]

Dying
Yet the self does move on toward death. We move from flight to homing. Guntrip seems to me right in positing a spiritual arc to the later years of life, because one of our tasks in these years is to prepare the self for death.

To live is not only to be born, to be created. It is not only to live and to dream and to create, to love and to despair and to age. To have been alive means finally also to die. We really are like the flowers of the field cited in the Bible, which flourish in their beauty, and then wither and die. Only God the Creator, who was and is, THE GREAT I AM, is going on forever to "be."

As I write this, I am not yet wrestling with old age. But I wrestle with the angel of middle age, seeking a blessing here. And I can see ahead an inseparable connection and continuity between becoming whole as a self now, and coming ultimately to the grace to lay this life down finally and die. I want to close with two poems I find enormously perceptive and suggestive of that whole aloneness of self I sense one experiences, either gracefully or grotesquely, in old age and dying. The first poem is "Ascent," by Anne Morrow Lindbergh.[14]

> Plunge deep
> Into the sky
> O wing
> Of the soul.
>
> Reach
> Past the last pinnacle
> Of speech
> Into the vast
> Inarticulate face
> Of silence. . . .
>
> Up, up beyond
> The giddy peaks of fear,
> The glacial fields of doubt,
> The sheer
> Cliffs of despair. . . .

ELIZABETH DODSON GRAY

There,
Where the wing
Has ceased to beat
For its own
Victory or defeat,

Find,
Far behind
The pale cloud-pastures
Of the mind,
The unbroken blind
Brightness of sheer
Atmosphere.

Here, crystalline,
Deep, full, serene,
Here flows
The still, unfathomed river
Of repose.

Here out of sight,
Unseen but known,
Here glides the stream
Of compassion.
Here alone
May rest
The strangled breast
Of long-impassioned flight.

Here soar
With more than wing
Above earth's floor;
Here ride
Limitless on a tide
No hawk has ever tried.

Here turn
In marble-firm
Security;
Here learn
To pivot on a needle-point—
Eternity.

ELIZABETH DODSON GRAY

Here whole
At last, above
The halting flight
That blindly rose
To gain a hidden height,

Wing of the soul
Repose,
Serene
In the stream
of Love.

The other poem is also by Anne Morrow Lindbergh, "Bare Tree."[15]

Already I have shed the leaves of youth,
Stripped by the wind of time down to the truth
Of winter branches. Linear and alone
I stand, a lens for lives beyond my own,
A frame through which another's fire may glow,
A harp on which another's passion, blow.

The pattern of my boughs, an open chart
Spread on the sky, to others may impart
Its leafless mysteries that once I prized,
Before bare roots and branches equalized;
Tendrils that tap the rain or twigs the sun
Are all the same; shadow and substance one.
Now that my vulnerable leaves are cast aside,
There's nothing left to shield, nothing to hide.

Blow through me, Life, pared down at last to bone,
So fragile and so fearless have I grown!

In closing, I return to the theological question with which I began: "Who am I?"—Who am I, really? And who am I becoming?" You know now much of what I see it means to say, "I am a woman." Yes—a woman's definition of her self, and her knowledge of herself as a woman, must be at least this complex.

NOTES

1. Barbara Borack, *Grandpa* (New York: Harper & Row, 1967).

2. Charlotte Zolotow, *One Step, Two . . .* (New York: Lothrop, Lee & Shepard, 1955, rev. 1981).

3. Eleanor Graham Vance, *Jonathan* (Chicago: Follett, 1966).

4. Bernice Hogan, *Now I Lay Me Down to Wonder. . .* (New York: Abingdon, 1961).

5. Fern, *The King Who Was Too Busy* (New York: Ariel, 1966)

6.Valerie Saiving [Goldstein], "The Human Situation: A Feminine View," *Journal of Religion* 40 (April 1960): 100–112. Reprinted in *Womanspirit Rising: A Feminist Reader in Religion,* ed. Carol P. Christ and Judith Plaskow (New York: Harper & Row, 1979), pp. 25–42.

7.Anne Morrow Lindbergh, *Gift from the Sea* (New York: Pantheon, 1955), p. 28.

8.Lindbergh, p. 29.

9.Paul Tillich, "You Are Accepted," in *The Shaking of the Foundations* (New York: Scribner's, 1948), pp. 153–163.

10.Tillich, *The Courage To Be* (New Haven: Yale, 1952), p. 164.

11.Tillich, *Love, Power and Justice* (New York: Oxford, 1954) p. 36f.

12. See Edmund Burgler, *The Revolt of the Middle-Aged Man* (New York: Grossett & Dunlap, 1954); Leslie J. Tizard and Harry Guntrip, *Middle-Age* (Great Neck, NY: Channel, 1959); Pauline B. Bart, "Depression in Middle-Aged Women" in *Women in Sexist Society,* ed. Vivian Gornick and Barbara K. Moran (New York: Signet, New American Library, 1972), pp. 163–186.

13. Joseph P. Lash, *Eleanor: The Years Alone* (New York: W.W.Norton, 1972), pp. 302-3.

14. Lindbergh, "Ascent," in *The Unicorn, and Other Poems* (NewYork: Pantheon, 1956), pp. 66–69.

15. Lindbergh, "Bare Tree," in *Unicorn,* p. 86.

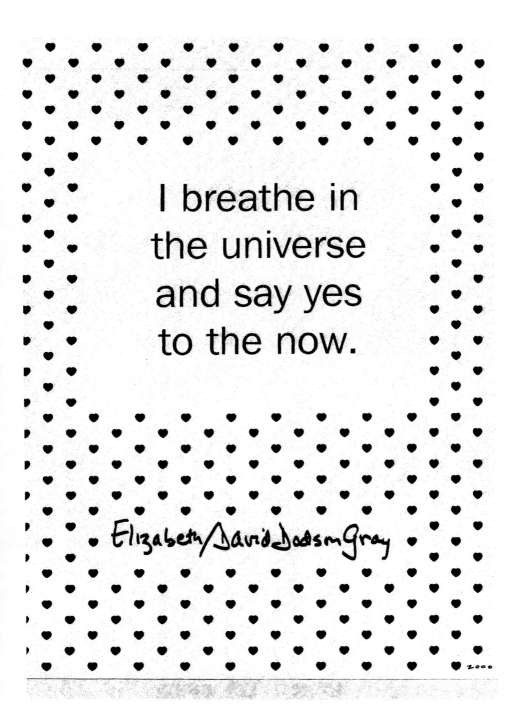

I breathe in
the universe
and say yes
to the now.

Elizabeth/David Dodson Gray

40.

A Memorial Meditation

Reunion Class of 1951

Saturday, May 27, 2006

Smith College, Northampton, Masssachusetts

40.

A Memorial Meditation
Reunion Class of 1951

Smith College, Northampton, Massachusetts

Saturday, May 27, 2006

We stand here today before the mysterious randomness of life, in which some of us die early and others die later. We want to allow ourselves to feel the sadness of the loss of each of those long-ago classmates who have died.

But we also want to celebrate the richness and diversity of those women's lives with whom we shared our Smith years. And we want to remind ourselves of the uniqueness of each of these women, and the way their unique talents and perspectives helped create the magnificent multi-colored tapestry we still share in—which *is* the complex fabric of women's lives.

1.

I light this first candle *to celebrate our bright college years—years of hope and promise.*

We believed we were invincible. We believed we could do anything. Special friendships with women very like us, and very different from us—women from the next state and women from around the world.

Bicycles and Bermuda shorts, Rally Day and Rahars's—all we remember, all we have forgotten.

Smith nurtured us, encouraged our potential, and rewarded us with the solid foundation of a superb education.

"Roots hold me close, . . .wings set me free." After four years we were freed to fly.

2.

I light this candle *to celebrate our great migration.* We took off like birds, in all directions.

Some to graduate schools—law, medicine, social work, divinity—off into the professions.

Some married, supported their husbands, and started families.

Some were off to city life in New York City, Washington, DC, San Francisco, Los Angeles, Chicago, Denver—for the bottom-rung jobs in publishing, advertising, journalism, government, entertainment, climbing the ladders to success.

Some to travel.

All to aspire, to hope, to dream of full lives of happiness and achievement.

3.

I light this candle *to celebrate the mothers many of us became through the years.*

By day we walked the children when they were healthy. By night we walked them when they were sick.

We were trustworthy in feeding and nurturing them so that they could learn to trust the world into which they had come.

We devoted our whole time to childrearing—we juggled children with WORK, and we never felt okay about either choice.

We were the center of the wheel of our family's life, and within the wheels of so many other wheels—PTA, League of Women Voters, political parties, choirs, churches and synagogues—"saving the world."

But when Betty Friedan wrote about "the problem which has no name," we recognized ourselves.

4.

I light this candle *to celebrate those of us who did not mother.* Those who want to be mothers but could not be. Those who could be mothers but *chose* not to be.

Those who took that love and nurturing and expressed it in a million ways—in social work, in counseling, in nursing, in teaching—whose children numbered *in the hundreds,* whose passion to change the world made a difference to generations of children—who served on boards of institutions whose existence and momentum brought stability *and* change to countless areas of life—whose roles as aunts and sister, daughters and nieces, brought tenderness and inspiration to others.

5.

I light this candle *to celebrate those of us who became single mothers,* who struggled so hard to keep it all together, who balanced work and family because there was no other way, who coped so bravely with the absence of a partner both in living and in childrearing, who were sustained by the friendship networks we created around us—all those whose "grace under pressure" year in and year out produced amazing children.

6.

I light a candle *to celebrate the artists*—those who painted, sculpted, played or sang, musicians and composers, weavers and knitters, and all kinds of handcrafts—who wrote books, acted in the theater—who created gardens which sustained our spirits.

All of these saw visions of loveliness and, with their art, helped us to see their visions too. They brought the grace and blessing of beauty to us—and left us with the reality that "a thing of beauty is a joy forever."

7.

I light this candle *for all the communities who experienced the love and energy of these women*—the town planning committees, the PTAs, the Leagues of Women Voters—all the boards they served on, all the churches and synagogues they sustained, all the organizations already-formed to which they gave their energy, all the *new* organizations which they brought into being to do good things for their town, their city, their state or country—good things never known before.

The communities were suffused with the light of their energy and their spiritual adventures. The radiance of their accomplishments will not soon be forgotten.

8.

I light this candle *for all the dark days in these women's lives*—days of grief over losing a child or a parent or a close sibling, a spouse or a life partner—days of sadness and mourning—days when a marriage crumbles, days when a single mother thinks she can barely make it through the day—the day when we hear the diagnosis of a terminal disease—dark days of chemo and radiation, days at the hospital saying goodbye to friends and family—all the dark days.

9.

I light this final candle *for memories*—memories of these women by friends and family—wonderful memories of golden times spent together—of Thanksgiving and Christmas—big delicious dinners cooked by these women, in houses cleaned by these women—birthdays, anniversaries—golden vacation days—sunlight on the water, swimming, boating, families together—skiing, sledding, skating—times inside by the fire, talking or reading—special, unforgettable memories of the good times.

WE WANT TO CELEBRATE the richness of the unique personhood of each of these women—and the blessing they were to those who knew and loved them, and the blessing they were to the world.

We are
enveloped
in the
generosity
of time.

— Elizabeth/David Dodson Gray

1992

41.

The Season
Is Turning

Autumn 1991

41.

The Season Is Turning

Autumn 1991

Glimmer As Symbol

As I write these words by the seashore, the glimmer is on the water. What I call glimmer is when strong sunlight strikes the rippling waves in such a way that a million tiny diamonds sparkle on the water and a silvery burnished sheen lights up the entire ocean surface from beach to horizon. It is a dazzling and glorious sight.

Why do I love this glimmer so? Why is it for me not just a beautiful sight but a sacred space and a symbol of the deep meaning of our lives?

I think it is because the magic of these diamond sparkles is created out of ordinary elements, out of sun and wind and moving water. That is a parable to me. It tells me that here is a transcendent dimension—a potential magic—in all of the ordinary in life. Often we miss that dimension, depth, magic. Instead we experience only the sun, the wind, the water in separation, in isolation, in their ordinary dimensions. So we search for meaning elsewhere—in our projects accomplished, in busyness itself, in other people, in our addictions.

Meanwhile the real meaning in our experience dwells with us undiscovered, latent, possible, but not yet manifest, potential but not yet harvested within every element of experience. *Life is luminous with meaning*—if we can but open the eyes of our soul to perceive it.

So glimmer on water speaks to me of this transcendent dimension in life which is possible but hidden. It speaks to me of the presence of God in every moment, that mystery which lights up the ordinary and makes it the doorway into a deeper universe of awe and wonder and magic.

Today

I sit on the deck after our week's absence, refocusing again on the glimmer which is at mid-passage across our water from left to right. In the morning it begins past the rocks to our left, and slowly it advances with its thousands of sparkling diamonds until at mid-day it covers the water with its silvery sheen from beach to far horizon, from left to center.

But then slowly the water on the left loses its dancing sparkles, while the water to the right of center slowly takes them on. When that happens we know that the day is half-spent and is slowly turning to mid-afternoon. By then the center sweep of silver from beach to horizon has faded away and we know we are beginning the late afternoon.

Finally only the far-right water has any sparkles left—and you know the heavenly/oceanly glimmer is about to end its splendor for this day. It is like our own private sun dial which marks the passage of the sun and the pathway of the day.

The Passing Also of the Season

I sit here today aware not only of the passage of the day but the passing of the season. This past week September turned into October.

When we drove home at the end of last week-end, only a few gold-leafed or orange-leafed trees dotted the highway. That was late September, with a hint of autumn in the air and in the trees.

But today when we drove to the ocean, it was a different season. Autumn had rolled out upon the trees its magnificent colors of gold and orange and fiery red. It was a feast for the eyes.

But I was not yet ready for autumn.

I was still in late September, still desiring the warm sun-filled days on the deck, still craving the glory of the glimmer so I can meditate upon it.

"Stop the days!"—I feel like crying. Stop the inexorable turning of the seasons, the passing of the days, the movement of glimmer from the "promise" of morning to the sadness of late afternoon. "Stop the world's turning!"—I pray. I want to stay right here and enjoy forever this experience, and never experience the winding-down into dusk, into night, into old age.

For I am knowing in my heart that, at sixty-two, I am past the center sheen of my life's glimmer. I am heading into the right side of these dancing particles. Never will the promise of the morning's glimmer be mine again.

I Am Greedy for Life Itself

I know this is natural. I know it is inevitable. I know it is something given, which comes with the gift of my body and this life. But I am saddened by this moment because I am greedy. I love this glimmer. I love the promise of the morning. I love the sheen of mid-day. I love the sparkling gift of life itself which comes to me every day. I am greedy for life itself.

I love the sun, the air, the water, the flowers, the trees, the seasons, the wonder of nature that greets me every morning. I love my husband, my children, my friends, the rich relationships which are the context of my being. I do not want the gift of life, that wonder and all this richness, to wind down, to flow through or flow beyond me.

So I am pleased that today is only one o'clock, and that I do not have to yield up just yet the mid-day sheen. But the sweep of the glimmer to the right is unmistakable. Rippling underneath the sheen, the tidal currents are flowing strongly to the right, like a river moving to the sea. Life, it seems, is determined to push me in the direction I must go.

But now, for this precious moment, I will not go.

I will clutch the precious glimmer to my meditating soul. I will feast my eyes upon its wondrous beauty. I will nourish my spirit with its sacred light and presence.

If day after day I can fill myself up with its mysterious energy and power, perhaps then I can be satiated sometime, somewhere, and be at peace with my own turning of the seasons of my life.

Ten thousand flowers in
spring,
the moon in autumn,
a cool breeze in summer,
snow in winter:

if your mind is not clouded
by unnecessary things,
this is
the best season of your life.

Wu-mei (1183–1260)

Liz / David Dodson Gray

2002